The Other Victoria

ANDREW SINCLAIR

THE OTHER VICTORIA

*The Princess Royal and
the Great Game of Europe*

WEIDENFELD AND NICOLSON
London

To Ladislas

The author and publishers are grateful for permission to reproduce copyright material. Paintings from the Royal Collection are reproduced by gracious permission of Her Majesty The Queen: 1, 2, 3, 4, 6, 13, 14, 16 (and Courtauld Institute), 26 (and Courtauld Institute), 32, 33. Photographs from the Royal Archives, Windsor Castle, are also reproduced by gracious permission of Her Majesty The Queen: 5, 7, 8, 9, 10, 11, 12, 15, 17, 18, 19, 20, 22, 23, 24, 25, 27, 28, 29, 30, 31, 34, 35, 37, 38, 39, 40, 41, 42, 43. Bildarchiv Preussicher Kulturbesitz, Berlin, 21. BBC Hulton Picture Library, 36.

First published in Great Britain by
George Weidenfeld & Nicolson Ltd
91 Clapham High Street, London SW4 7TA
1981

ISBN 0 297 77987 7

Printed in Great Britain by
Butler & Tanner Limited
Frome and London

Contents

Illustrations

Acknowledgements

By gracious permission of Her Majesty the Queen, I have been able to research in the Royal Archives at Windsor Castle and to use the letters and documents which make up the main part of this book. Her Majesty, as the owner of the copyright in Queen Victoria's letters, has also given Her gracious permission for their use in this work.

During the time which I have spent in Windsor Castle, I have been given selfless and illuminating guidance by the Queen's Librarian, Sir Robin Mackworth-Young. With his help and that of Miss Langton, I have been able to complete this work. Their wise advice has prevented me from making many errors of fact and judgment. Those which remain are my own.

I am also indebted to Wolfgang, Prince of Hesse, who is the owner of Queen Victoria's letters to the Empress Frederick, and of many other royal and imperial letters and papers at Friedrichshof, Kronberg. He has graciously granted me permission to use part of them in this book.

For their assistance in aiding me to secure and select the illustrations, I am grateful to Sir Oliver Millar, the Keeper of the Queen's Pictures, and to Miss Frances Dimond, Curator of the Photograph Collection at the Royal Archives.

For permission to quote from the Salisbury papers, I am indebted to the Marquess of Salisbury. Extracts from the Ponsonby papers, the Malet papers, the Lascelles papers and the Lansdowne papers in the Public Record Office appear by permission of the Controller of H.M. Stationery Office. Mr. J. M. Armstrong of the Institute of Historical Research at the University of London has helped me untiringly in the examination of these collections and at the Public Records Office.

As always, the London Library has provided the background of my work. Its staff and facilities are beyond praise.

I am also in the debt of Lord Fulford, who is completing his edition of the private correspondence of Queen Victoria and the Crown Princess of Prussia. He has published four volumes of the correspondence, *Dearest Child*, *Dearest Mama*, *Your Dear Letter*, and *Darling Child*: these cover the years from 1858 to 1878. Although I have consulted the original letters as much as possible, his help in deciphering the handwriting and his notes on the text have been invaluable. I have followed his practice of eliminating much of the underlining in the letters, a habit beloved by Queen Victoria and her children.

Finally, I must acknowledge with grief and infinite regret the death of my collaborator, Ladislas Farago. Without his inspiration and enthusiasm and hard work this book would not have been written. I hope that it may serve in some measure as a fitting tribute to the originality and energy of this exceptional man.

ANDREW SINCLAIR

Foreword

BY

WOLFGANG PRINCE OF HESSE

This book is largely based on two collections of correspondence: one consisting of letters written by Queen Victoria and the Prince Consort to my grandmother, the Empress Frederick, which are in the keeping of our family foundation at Kronberg, and the other of the counterpart letters from the Empress Frederick to her parents, which are in the Royal Archives at Windsor.

It is only through informed discussion of the problems raised by Dr Sinclair that justice to the Empress's memory will be done in the long run, and no such discussion is possible without access to these papers. In furtherance of this aim I have not only released them to Dr Sinclair, but also take this opportunity, with the author's kind consent, of joining in the debate, the more so as the interpretation which the book places upon the record of the Empress Frederick's aims and activities is in some respects far from my own.

It is not so much with the details of this book as with its general thesis that I take issue. The marriage of Queen Victoria's eldest daughter to the future King of Prussia is presented as an extraordinary event whose main purpose was to place a political agent and spy at the heart of the Prussian court. However the Princess Royal's situation in Germany can not be seen as the result of some deep-laid conspiracy to subvert the independence of a foreign state.

The life of a sovereign's daughter who married a future foreign sovereign was never easy. Of course there were conflicting loyalties, but the line of duty was clear. Loyalty belonged first to the country of adoption. Everyone familiar with the life of the Empress Frederick would agree that she was a person of exceptionally high principles, and it would have been out of the question for her to have taken any action which conflicted with her duty to her adopted country. The Empress's correspondence with her mother may have been exceptionally voluminous, but nowhere can it be shown that anything in this correspondence actually led to consequences adverse to Prussia or Germany. We must also not overlook the fact that the emphasis in it was on domestic and social matters rather than on politics. The moral integrity of the Empress is reflected in a letter written by her in 1888 shortly after the Emperor Frederick's death, outlining what was in reality the philosophy on which her political beliefs were based:

Our patriotism wanted to see the greatness of the Fatherland linked with the noble sense for right, morality, for freedom and culture, for independence of the individual, uplifting of the single person as human being and as German, European and Citizen of the World. Improvement, progress, ennoblement were our motto. To this belongs peace, tolerance and charity; those things, man's most precious possessions on earth, we saw trodden under foot.... One day there must and will come a reaction – they will praise the heroic deeds of the German Army, the ability, the readiness to sacrifice, the capacity for work and the health of the German people, also the cleverness, the sagacity, the genius, the luck of the great German statesmen of this time. But they will revolt against the poisonous spirit which is now spreading so widely.... Of course long before I shall rest next to Emperor Frederick in my grave and one will hardly know what we wanted, and how much we loved our Fatherland for which we were permitted to do so little.... And yet our tragic fate belongs to German history.

(Ludwig Bamberger: *Bismarcks großes Spiel*, 1932)

Friedrichshof, Kronberg
August 1981

Princess Victoria's Family Tree

VICTORIA   m. Albert of Saxe-Coburg-Gotha
(r. 1837-1901) | (1819-61)

Victoria,
Princess
Royal
(1840-
1901)
m. Frederick III,
German Emperor
(1831-88)

EDWARD VII
(r.1901-10)
m. Alexandra of
Denmark
(1844-1925)

Alice
(1843-78)
m. Louis IV,
Grand Duke of
Hesse-Darmstadt
(1837-92)

Albert
Victor,
Duke of
Clarence
(1864-92)

GEORGE V
(r.1910-36)
m. Mary
of
Teck
(1867-1953)

Louise
(1867-1931)
m. Alexander
Duff, Duke
of Fife
(1849-1912)

Victoria
(1868-1935)

Maud
(1869-1938)
m. Haakon VII,
King of
Norway
(1872-1957)

GREAT BRITAIN

NORWAY

Victoria
(1863-1950)
m. Louis
of
Battenburg
(1854-1921)

Elizabeth
(1864-1918)
m. Serge,
Grand Duke
of Russia
(1857-1905)

Irene
(1866-1953)
m. Henry
of Prussia
(1862-
1929)

Ernest,
Grand
Duke of
Hesse
(1868-1937)
m. Victoria
Melita of
Edinburgh
(1876-1936)
(div. 1901)

Alix
(1872-1918)
m. Nicholas II,
Tsar of
Russia
(1868-1918)

Mary Victoria
(1874-8)

RUSSIA

William II,
German
Emperor
(1859-1941)
m. Augusta
of
Schleswig-
Holstein-
Augustenburg
(1858-1921)

Charlotte
(1860-1919)
m.
Bernard
of Saxe-
Meiningen
(1851-1928)

Henry
(1862-
1929)
m.
Irene
of Hesse
(1866-
1953)

Sigismund
(1864-6)

Victoria
(1866-
1929)
m.
Adolphus
of
Schaumburg-
Lippe
(1859-1916)

Waldemar
(1868-79)

Sophie
(1870-1932)
m. Constantine,
King of
Greece
(1868-1923)

Margaret
(1872-1954)
m. Frederick
Charles of
Hesse
(1868-1940)

GREECE

GERMANY

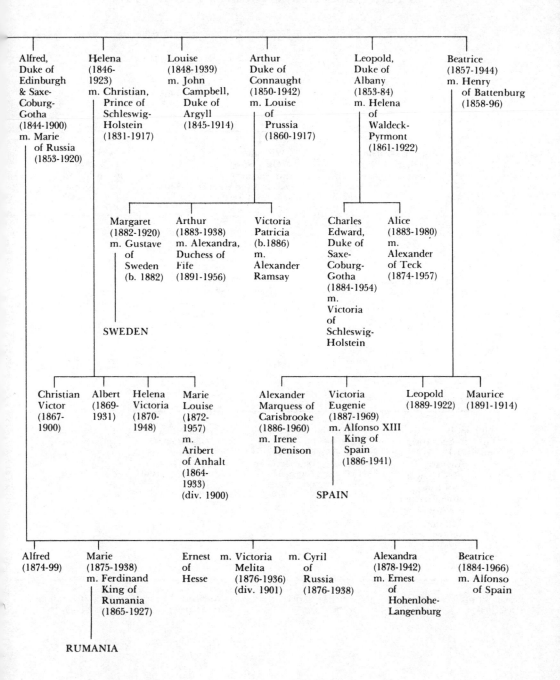

Alfred,
Duke of
Edinburgh
& Saxe-
Coburg-
Gotha
(1844-1900)
m. Marie
   of Russia
   (1853-1920)

Helena
(1846-
1923)
m. Christian,
   Prince of
   Schleswig-
   Holstein
   (1831-1917)

Louise
(1848-1939)
m. John
   Campbell,
   Duke of
   Argyll
   (1845-1914)

Arthur
Duke of
Connaught
(1850-1942)
m. Louise
   of
   Prussia
   (1860-1917)

Leopold,
Duke of
Albany
(1853-84)
m. Helena
   of
   Waldeck-
   Pyrmont
   (1861-1922)

Beatrice
(1857-1944)
m. Henry
   of Battenburg
   (1858-96)

Margaret
(1882-1920)
m. Gustave
   of
   Sweden
   (b. 1882)

SWEDEN

Arthur
(1883-1938)
m. Alexandra,
   Duchess of
   Fife
   (1891-1956)

Victoria
Patricia
(b.1886)
m.
Alexander
Ramsay

Charles
Edward,
Duke of
Saxe-
Coburg-
Gotha
(1884-1954)
m.
Victoria
of
Schleswig-
Holstein

Alice
(1883-1980)
m.
Alexander
of Teck
(1874-1957)

Christian
Victor
(1867-
1900)

Albert
(1869-
1931)

Helena
Victoria
(1870-
1948)

Marie
Louise
(1872-
1957)
m.
Aribert
of Anhalt
(1864-
1933)
(div. 1900)

Alexander
Marquess of
Carisbrooke
(1886-1960)
m. Irene
   Denison

Victoria
Eugenie
(1887-1969)
m. Alfonso XIII
   King of
   Spain
   (1886-1941)

SPAIN

Leopold
(1889-1922)

Maurice
(1891-1914)

Alfred
(1874-99)

Marie
(1875-1938)
m. Ferdinand
   King of
   Rumania
   (1865-1927)

RUMANIA

Ernest
of
Hesse

m. Victoria
   Melita
   (1876-1936)
   (div. 1901)

m. Cyril
   of
   Russia
   (1876-1938)

Alexandra
(1878-1942)
m. Ernest
   of
   Hohenlohe-
   Langenburg

Beatrice
(1884-1966)
m. Alfonso
   of Spain

Prince Frederick William's Family Tree

Frederick William III
(1770-1840)
m. Louise of
Mecklenburg-Strelitz
(1776-1810)

Frederick William IV
(1795-1861)

William I
(1797-1888)
m. Augusta
of Saxe-Weimar
(1811-1890)

Charlotte
(1798-1860)
m. Nicholas I
of Russia
(1796-1855)

Victoria   m. Frederick III
(1840-1901)   (1831-1888)

Louise
(1828-1923)
m. Frederick
of Baden
(1826-1907)

William II
German Emperor
(1859-1941)
m. (1) Augusta
of Schleswig-
Holstein-
Augustenburg
(1858-1921)
(2) Hermine
of Reuss
(1887-1947)

Charlotte
(1860-1919)
m. Bernard
of Saxe-Meiningen
(1851-1928)

Henry
(1862-1929)
m. Irene
of Hesse
(1866-1953)

Sigismund
(1864-6)

Crown Prince William
(1882-1951)

Eitel Frederick
(1883-1942)

Adalbert
(1884-1948)

Augustus William
(1887-1949)

3 sons 3 daughters

Alexander II
(1818-1881)
m. Marie
 of Hesse-Darmstadt
(1824-1880)

Victoria
(1866-1929)
m. Adolphus
 of Schaumburg-
 Lippe
(1859-1916)

Waldemar
(1868-79)

Sophie
(1870-1932)
m. Constantine,
 King of Greece
(1868-1923)

Margaret
(1872-1954)
m. Frederick Charles
 of Hesse
(1868-1940)

Alexander III
(1845-1894)
m. Dagmar
 of Denmark
(1847-1928)

Nicholas II
(1868-1918)
m. Alexandra
 of Hesse-Darmstadt
(1872-1918)

Oscar
(1888-1958)

Joachim
(1890-1920)

Victoria Louise
(b. 1892)

Introduction

'WHY', ASKED *The Times* during the Crimean War, 'should we place a daughter of England in a situation in which devotion to her husband must be treason to her country?' The editor had heard that the young Princess Royal was to be engaged to Prince Frederick William of Prussia, the heir to a throne that was linked with England's enemy, Russia. The match was not at all to the liking of the editor of *The Times*, but he did not ask the true question: would not an English princess's devotion to her own family and her homeland make her seem treasonable to the chief minister of her husband's country?

This was what Bismarck asked himself as he worked to make Prussia powerful enough to become the German Empire. He was endeavouring to create a modern nation state complete with media manipulation and mass armies, secret Intelligence systems and devious diplomacy. Paradoxically, his long-lasting period of power depended upon the whim of an aged King of Prussia, whom he made into an Emperor – and his fall, on the decision of a young Kaiser, who himself was to fall together with the Germany that Bismarck had created. Although Bismarck came from the Junker aristocracy and served the Crown, he resented royal and feudal constraints on his policies. Even worse to him was the rival diplomacy carried on through princely marriages and international kinship. These foreign contacts repudiated Prussian patriotism and the new nation.

Above all, he feared the Princess Royal of England once she had married Prince Frederick William of Prussia. She would for many decades be the wife of the heir to the throne and would become the German

Empress. To Bismarck, she would always be *die Engländerin*, the alien agent at court. He suspected the marriage had been arranged by Queen Victoria and Prince Albert, to place their daughter close to the chief source of power in Germany, so that a liberal and constitutional state might arise there on the English model. The Princess Royal seemed to be the cat's-paw of an international conspiracy, a pawn in the great game of Europe. Bismarck meant to scotch that.

He succeeded. This is the story of that tragedy. Behind the lovers, 'Vicky' and her 'Fritz', the exponents of two rival systems struggled for war or peace. Opposed to Bismarck and his *realpolitik* stood Queen Victoria with her widespread sources of information through marriages and relations. The diplomacy of iron and blood was opposed by the diplomacy of gold band and blood royal. The creation of the new nations of the nineteenth century was still being achieved in the ancient way by kings and battles. Even Bismarck's making of Germany would have broken apart without Prince Frederick William's leadership at König-grätz, at Wörth and Sedan. Both Germany and Italy were united by aggressive monarchies, while the crucial Franco-Prussian War of 1870 was actually a traditional war of succession – its issue, the placing of a Hohenzollern candidate on the Spanish throne.

Bismarck and Queen Victoria would have been surprised to have been considered as mere vehicles of social forces beyond their control. They thought that their decisions mattered. They believed that what they advised and did changed their countries and, as they believed, so they acted – Queen Victoria was certain that France had fallen into republicanism and revolution only because of the failure of the people at the top. She did not intend to fail. As for Bismarck, he certainly provoked the three wars he needed to unify Germany. The Franco-Prussian War, particularly, was inevitable only when he arranged it. As Lord Granville pointed out, it was inconceivable that hundreds of thousands of men should be hurled at each other on a point limited to a matter of etiquette.

No one who reads the correspondence between Queen Victoria and her eldest daughter can doubt the real influence of the Queen on the policy of her various governments, and her direct power, when she chose to intervene, with the crowned heads of Europe. She was kept admirably informed by her daughters and royal cousins and through aristocratic sources. After Prince Albert had defined the policy lines and had put in order the diplomatic files, her incessant letter-writing throughout fifty years provided her with better Intelligence than her changing foreign ministers ever had. Without doubt, she prevented or postponed the outbreak of major wars on several occasions, and once Bismarck had fought his three necessary wars, she and he were the respectful adversaries who kept the map of Europe largely unchanged until the end of the century.

The price her eldest daughter paid was the accusation in Prussia of disloyalty. As a child, she had been brought up to yield total obedience to her mother and father. Her 4,161 letters to her mother, often full of details of confidential German state affairs, end: 'Your most dutiful and devoted daughter, who kisses her mother's hand.' It was inconceivable that the Princess Royal of England would not be her mother's ambassadress, sent to report from abroad. With nearly all the thrones of Europe held within the blood group of one Germanic family, kinship transcended frontiers. The extended royal family was greater than the national state.

This was the secret behind the long peaces and short wars which kept the great powers of Europe roughly in equilibrium between the fall of Napoleon and the outbreak of the First World War. When ministers brought rival countries to the brink of war over national interests, royal diplomacy would often inspire a compromise or a truce because of mutual understanding. A quarrel in the family rarely leads to bloodshed; a quarrel between nations often does.

Queen Victoria, herself, knew nearly all the royalty and aristocracy concerned with politics, who ran the affairs of the great powers during her long reign. A few hundred people with common backgrounds and assumptions ruled throughout the century. When an intruder of genius such as Disraeli joined their ranks, he was soon ennobled and assimilated. This common understanding at the top meant that individuals and their influence were thought of great consequence, while movements were discounted. This was the legacy of the past, which the new nation states inherited and destroyed in the massacres of the First World War. Then the aristocrats were decimated, thrones were toppled, and those who contacted their kinsfolk abroad might be interned or assassinated.

In this twilight of the old system, the Princess Royal and the Crown Prince played out their tragedy. It was what might have been. If the King of Prussia had abdicated without finding his Bismarck ... If Dr Nobiling had severed the artery in the German ruler's arm instead of nicking it ... If the King turned Emperor had not lived almost as long as Queen Victoria and disappointed his son as she endlessly disappointed Edward,

Prince of Wales ... If the Crown Prince had not been dying of throat cancer when he became Emperor at last ... If his son had not been crippled at birth and had not believed with Bismarck that his mother was an English agent ...

But history is not about what might have been. Speculation is unnecessary in this story of Queen Victoria and her eldest daughter, of the King of Prussia and his only son and his crippled grandson, the last Kaiser; and of Bismarck, the minister of genius, who proved that the *realpolitik* of the nation state must triumph over the old manners, ceremonies and decencies of court and European diplomacy. Based on thousands of letters exchanged between Queen Victoria and her daughter, the book examines fully the English Queen's sources of information and importance in international affairs – an importance exercised also by King Edward the Seventh, but which died with him.

The book also furnishes a peep-hole on the unwritten history of the rise of Bismarck's Germany, brought about by modern undercover methods of Intelligence-gathering and press manipulation, distortions, intimidation and surveillance. It is, finally, the tale of a royal love which became a divided loyalty – of a princess who adored her father and her husband and who was forced to split her devotion between her homeland and her adopted country.

CHAPTER ONE

Minuet Before a Wedding

'OH, MADAM,' THE doctor in attendance said, 'it is a princess.' 'Never mind,' Queen Victoria replied, 'the next will be a prince.'[1]

She had been in labour for twelve long hours before giving birth to the Princess Royal on 21 November 1840. Her husband, Prince Albert, had been as gentle as a woman during the time of trial. He had hardly left the bedroom in Buckingham Palace, only retiring behind a screen with the Queen's mother, the Duchess of Kent, during the actual birth. When the infant was brought to him, he was secretly delighted, but, in the way of royal husbands, he had to complain to his elder brother, Ernest of Saxe-Coburg-Gotha, 'Albert, father of a daughter, you will laugh at me.'

Because of the baby's sex and birth, her marriage and the waste of her qualities were, in a way, already on the cards. She was born a princess who, unlike her mother, would have brothers. Her father was a product of the great industry of the thirty-eight small German courts, which hoped to finance themselves by marrying their many offspring into the reigning houses of Europe. To be born a German prince or princess was the surest way of marrying a throne or of being offered one by a new nation needing a king.

Prince Albert, himself, had been groomed by the chief adviser to the Coburgs, the wise and stealthy Baron Stockmar. There were too many candidates for too few thrones, but Prince Albert was successful. He was presented twice to his young cousin Victoria; once when he was fat and awkward at the age of sixteen, and again when he was handsome and blooming at nineteen, an angel with a glossy moustache and piercing blue eyes. 'Albert's beauty is most striking,' Queen Victoria had confessed to her Coburg uncle Leopold, King of the Belgians, 'and he is so amiable and unaffected – in short, very fascinating.'[2] Within three days of their second meeting, the cousins had become engaged. Married at the age of twenty, they had their first child after nine months together.

Holding the little princess in his arms, Prince Albert knew that he held a golden counter in the great game of royal marriages and European diplomacy. His own position was also changed. He was no longer the foreign husband of the youthful English Queen, but the father of the heiress to the throne. As if to confirm his new position, he had to leave the Queen's bedroom to attend a meeting of the Privy Council in her place. This was the first time he had done so, and it marked the importance of the first child. His name was now included in the Liturgy; the nation would pray for him as well as for the new princess.

Queen Victoria was too young and high-spirited and busy with affairs of state to devote herself to the baby. She refused to feed the infant herself, believing that royal mothers should not be milch cows. A wet-nurse was engaged, and the sister-in-law of the poet Southey became Superintendent of the Nursery. The Queen called her baby 'Pussy' and saw her twice a day. The young parents found the infant 'quite a little toy', but the Queen could not allow the having of children to dominate her life. This she called the shadow-side of marriage. The changes made to her body during pregnancy offended her feeling for her person. A queen should not need to endure the natural processes of birth.

Before the Princess Royal had been christened Victoria Adelaide Mary Louise, her mother was pregnant again. She was angry about it, but there was nothing she could do. She had told her uncle, King Leopold, that he could not wish her to become the mamma of a large family. 'Men never think, at least seldom think,' she wrote, 'what a hard task it is for us women to go through this very often.'[3] But she did have to go through it again in the following November, when she suffered the most severe of all her labours, to bear a son, the future Prince of Wales.

His birth started the first steps in the marriage minuet around his elder sister, not yet one year old. After much anxious discussion, the Queen and Prince Albert chose the King of Prussia as a sponsor at the christening of the Prince of Wales. Frederick William IV, who was known to be eccentric and romantic, supported an alliance with Russia, which was becoming the chief opponent of the British Empire. It would be politic to draw the Prussian king closer to England. When he appeared at Windsor Castle, his fatness, his squeaky voice and his small head put off most of the court except for the Princess Royal, who sat on his knee and played with the gold watch-chain spread over his stomach.

The King had no children. The heir to the Prussian throne was his brother William, the Prince of Prussia who, two years later, was chosen to act as a sponsor for Queen Victoria's second son, Alfred. Unlike his brother, Prince William was a handsome soldier of a man, who growled beneath the flowing locks and whiskers of a Teutonic Knight. He had little to say for himself, but listened politely as Prince Albert expounded a plan for Prussia to unite the many smaller states of Germany under its leadership. This was Baron Stockmar's plan and Prince Albert had become its chief apostle.

This 'Coburg' plan had many variations, but one central theme. In essence, Prussia would become a constitutional monarchy like England, in place of the semi-feudal military state which had been thrust into prominence by Frederick the Great. It would serve as England's Protestant ally in Europe against France and despotic Russia. Its example and policy would cause the lesser Protestant states of North Germany to confederate with their powerful neighbour and protector. Eventually, the Catholic states of South Germany would see that the unity of a German nation was more important than the support of the Austrian Empire, which shared with Prussia a dominating role in the weak German Confederation set up after the defeat of Napoleon. Above all, Prussia should resist the temptation to unite Germany by conquest and by war with Austria. It already dominated the German economy through the *Zollverein*, the Customs Union. Now it should develop financially and liberalize its institutions, and it should respect the smaller states of Germany such as Hanover and Saxe-Coburg, which were so closely tied to the English royal family. Gold, not iron; trade, not blood; example, not force, should create the new German nation with Prussia at its head. Finally, Prussia should merge into Germany; Germany should not be forced to join Prussia.

Prince Albert took every opportunity to put variations of the 'Coburg' plan to the King and the Prince of Prussia. He lectured them when they visited England and wrote them memoranda and position papers when they returned home. His ally was Augusta, Princess of Prussia, who came from Saxe-Weimar, the first German state to grant a modern constitution to its subjects. There, Goethe had once been the royal tutor, and his liberal views were enshrined in various state policies. Augusta, herself, was as set as Prince Albert on an alliance with England and on the 'Coburg' plan. She even employed the plan's originator, Baron Stockmar, as an educational adviser to her only son. What he had done for Prince Albert, he might do for Prince Frederick William of Prussia. So the old baron was given the chance to influence the future of the heirs to the Prussian and English thrones.

Princess Augusta believed that a marriage between her son and the Princess Royal of England would support her hopes for the future of her country. She had thought of the Princess Royal as a most suitable daughter-in-law ever since the child's birth.[4] Although she was a difficult woman, often vain and demanding, she took care to strike up a close friendship with Queen Victoria, and came to England in 1846 to further her plans.

Queen Victoria was much taken with the Princess of Prussia's show of respect and devotion. 'There are whispers of her being false,' she wrote to King Leopold, 'but ... I cannot and will not believe it. Her position is a very difficult one; she is too enlightened and liberal for the Prussian Court not to have enemies; but I believe that she is a friend to us and our family, and I do believe that I have a friend in her, who may be most useful to us.[5]

Queen Victoria was right. Princess Augusta was suffering from the problems that any future English daughter-in-law would encounter at the Prussian Court. While princely life in Weimar had been progressive, palace life in Prussia was formal and frugal, narrow and censured. There, a free spirit was confined within a corset of etiquette. To talk of change was to seem disloyal, and to try to oppose the King's will was to seem treasonable. In a country that was still dominated by Junkers ruling peasants on their large estates, in a small power threatened with being crushed between the greater armies of France and Russia, liberal views could be taken for a betrayal of the monarchy and of national security.

Princess Augusta had other difficulties. She had little influence over her soldier husband, who had followed tradition and become a lieutenant in the Prussian Guards at the age of ten. His wife had not been of his choice. As a young man, he had fallen helplessly in love with his second cousin, Elise Radziwill, a beautiful Polish princess, whose family was associated with the Prussian Court. Unfortunately for him, the Radziwills were considered minor nobility whose blood was not worthy to mix with that of the Hohenzollerns. Marriage into the family would have offended the Romanovs, who had blood ties with the Hohenzollerns, and who would have resented a relationship with the nobility of a country subject to Russia. The King of Prussia had forbidden his son to marry his love. The son had accepted his father's royal will, writing to him:

With feelings of deepest reverence for you, but also with a broken heart, I reply to you, beloved Father. You have decided my fate in a way which I feared you would do, but tried nevertheless not to believe possible, so long as I saw a ray of hope on the horizon! But you have always found me an obedient son. This, I will continue to be in this decisive hour of my life![6]

His arranged marriage to Princess Augusta was loveless. Elise Radziwill did not marry, and died of tuberculosis soon afterwards. Augusta, after giving birth to her son 'Fritz' and her daughter 'Wiwy', refused to have any more children. As if to keep the wound bleeding in William's heart, she had insisted on surrounding herself with the Radziwill family. He could never forget his love, and became something of a tyrant to his son, who paid the price of his father's terrible obedience.

Prince Frederick William was born under a bright star. A frank and open child, with a natural generosity, his early frailty was fortified by military training, when he too became a Guards officer at the age of ten. His father had ridden by his grandfather's side during the defeats of Napoleon in Germany, and the boy wanted to ride out and defeat the French in his turn. In contrast, his mother was careful to see that he had a liberal education. He was encouraged by her to admire England and its example of freedom, but he was also taught to carry out all the orders of the King and of his father, now a Prussian general. His duty was to do his duty without question. That was the mark of a Prussian prince.

Only a nature as generous and uncomplicated as Prince Frederick William's could have avoided being warped by the conflict of values between his father and his mother. On one side, he was taught absolute obedience to a godlike figure, usually resplendent in uniform, only fulfilled in war. On the other, a dominant mother taught him to probe at the old traditions, to think more freely, to look outside the confines of Prussia, to oppose the rigid system of the army and the Junkers. To get him to become what she wanted him to be, she had to set him against his father, but as a Prussian prince, he had to bow to his father's will. The contradictions remained dormant in the young man; not until later would they affect him psychologically.

There was no conflict between Queen Victoria and Prince Albert about the education of their children. The Prince had a great gift for management. Finding chaos and extravagance at Buckingham Palace and Windsor Castle, he soon instituted method and order. While the Queen looked after necessary affairs of state, he took control of his homes and his children. Stockmar was asked for advice on running the royal nursery; it gave him more trouble – he complained – than the government of a kingdom would have done.[7] He produced nursery regulations which provided for the constant care of the Princess Royal. Whenever the child left the room, somebody had to go with her, she was never to be left alone.[8]

The Princess Royal was inquisitive and talkative by nature, and she developed under her special supervision. Stockmar helped to choose her governess, Sarah Lady Lyttelton, who was firm, kind and devoted, and who sacrificed herself to the lives of the royal children. She had her hands full with the Princess, whose fierce independence by the age of four, had convinced her mother that she was disobedient and not kind enough to her brother and sister.[9] This did not last. As the Princess Royal grew, she became close to Prince Edward and Princess Alice. The three elder children were to be particularly devoted to each other all their lives.

There was a fear that bad heredity might affect the Princess Royal, the Prince of Wales, Princess Alice and Prince Alfred, and the five brothers and sisters born after them. It was thought their natures might become warped if they were not constantly watched. Stockmar ignored the questionable history of Prince Albert's own mother, who had run away because of her husband's infidelity, leaving her son when he was only five. Stockmar merely damned Queen Victoria's predecessors and the English royal dukes who had either been ill-educated or exposed to the wrong influences, often abroad. In Stockmar's opinion, the bad behaviour of the royal dukes had seriously weakened the influence of the Crown, but they had been tolerated because their faults were considered English faults. The lesson was plain: 'The Education of the royal Infants ought to be from its earliest beginnings a truly moral and a truly English one.'[10]

So it was done. Queen Victoria and Prince Albert issued their own rules as to how the children were to be taught. Before they were five, they must be started on the two principal foreign languages, French and German, as well as speaking, reading and counting. After the age of five, they must learn about religion; the Queen herself taught the Bible to the

Princess Royal. Arithmetic, geography, history and grammar must now find their place in the child's day. The morning began for the Princess Royal with a writing lesson at breakfast at eight o'clock.[11] Truthfulness at all times was an absolute rule. When the child told one of her rare lies, she was seriously admonished and locked in a room with her hands tied. This, Lady Lyttelton trusted, made her aware of her fault in the right way.[12]

This careful preparation was not so formal as it might seem. Queen Victoria believed in fresh air more than the Germans did. On weekdays, the children were taken out to play in the royal gardens for two hours in the morning and one in the afternoon. Sundays were to be 'happy Play Days', when the children were allowed to jump and run about with their dogs – an essential thing, in the Queen's opinion.[13] Prince Albert was also fond of romping with his children before they went to bed. The passionate and tempestuous Princess Royal was his particular favourite. She insisted on being called 'Vicky', and would burst into tears of rage if she could not get her own way. While the Prince of Wales often seemed slow and dull, Vicky was the child of her father's heart, and she doted on him in return. Prince Albert would sometimes dress his 'Vicky' in a sailor suit to watch her swagger about like a principal boy in a pantomime.

The royal children loved the seaside. It was no longer considered certain death from exposure, after George IV had made Brighton fashionable and had built the fantastic Royal Pavilion there. At first, the children spent their summer holidays with Lady Lyttelton beneath Nash's curious domes and minarets. Whenever they went to the beach they were mobbed, but when the pier was closed for their use for an hour, the public complained. The Princess Royal's first letter to her mother was written in Brighton: 'I wish you very soon to come back,' the child wrote to the Queen, 'and I will give you a very good love. I have been munching very well.'[14]

Wanting privacy for her family and a seaside estate for her husband, Queen Victoria purchased several hundred acres in the Isle of Wight. Here Prince Albert designed Osborne House, in the Italian style, with a pavilion and two differing towers, and a chalet was brought from Switzerland and erected in the grounds for the children. 'The greatest maxim of all is –,' the Queen wrote, 'that the Children should be brought up as simply and in as domestic a way as possible; that (not interfering with their lessons) they should be as much as possible with their Parents, share and place their greatest confidence in them in all things.'[15]

The Queen and Prince Albert began to spend their summers at Osborne, though public duties often called them away. Lady Lyttelton kept a diary to report on the royal children in her care. On one occasion the Princess Royal was angry because her mother was coming back two days later than promised, so she said she would not do one good lesson and would be naughty during the whole remaining time. Happily she did not carry out her threat.

On one Queen's Birthday, a military band played on the lawns in the afternoon, while all the royal children listened and ran about. But then the Princess Royal had one of her tantrums. 'The evening of a festival is almost always disastrous,' Lady Lyttelton wrote, 'people grow naughty after much excitement – and accordingly the Princess Royal fell into a transport of rage on perceiving that the day was nearly over; and shrieked and roared in the open carriage, for no other reason. Luckily in a lonely part of the road ...'[16]

Because of her ever-increasing family, and a husband who had what she thought to be a wonderful turn for architecture, Queen Victoria decided to extend Buckingham Palace. The sale of the Brighton Pavilion provided funds for a new east wing, to house numerous small suites and rooms for the children and foreign guests. What began as a matter of convenience became a style and a scale of rule. Although Queen Victoria was small in stature, she did not think, unlike Napoleon, that vast halls compensated for lack of inches. If she could not make people look up to her, she would make it hard for them to reach her. Even her children remembered having to proceed along endless corridors and through room after room, becoming more and more awestruck, until they were finally admitted to their royal mother.

Queen Victoria protected the mystery of her majesty by antechambers and anticipations. She reigned from the heart of a maze, where she read the state papers of British diplomacy and weighed their contents against the Intelligence she received from her European relations and advisers, whose letters told her of their fear of revolution and the threat of war.

'Old things are falling,' wrote Baron Stockmar in 1847, 'times are changing and a new life will come from the ruins.'[17] His prophecy was only too true. The Holy Alliance of reactionary powers, which had tried to keep the peace of Europe since Napoleon's defeat, was crumbling internally. In 1848, revolutions overwhelmed most of the major cities of

Europe. In Brussels, Marx and Engels had written *The Communist Manifesto*. In Milan and in Venice, in Vienna and in Paris, governments were suddenly toppled. Everywhere, monarchs and institutions were under attack from radicals and republicans. King Louis-Philippe was forced to renounce the throne of France and flee with his queen to England, escaping in a humiliating disguise, wearing huge goggles and wrapped in a coarse overcoat. Queen Victoria gave the royal refugees house-room on their son-in-law King Leopold's estate at Claremont. Yet she had to be careful not to mix her sympathy with the policy of her government which would have to recognize a new French republic. 'The public good and the peace of Europe go before one's feelings,' the Queen wrote. 'God knows what one feels towards the French.... All our poor relations have gone through is worthy only of a dreadful romance.'[18]

To the Princess Royal, the arrival of these royal exiles in disguise seemed very exciting. Their stories of mobs and flights, threat of death and loss of thrones were indeed worthy of a 'dreadful romance'. Such a catastrophe might even happen to her. She had been forbidden to leave Buckingham Palace during the Chartist riots. There had been more than one attempt to assassinate her mother. Clearly, to be born royal was to live dangerously.

Soon an even more significant refugee arrived; the Prince of Prussia himself. Hated for his military manners and his association with the army and the reactionary Junkers, he had been forced to flee by a revolution in Berlin. He had to ask his shamed son Frederick William to bring scissors to cut off his beard. Without his imposing whiskers, he could run away undetected to England. His son had to watch his father escape, shaven and disgraced.

This was the most humiliating period in the Prince of Prussia's life. No longer a commanding military figure, he had to beg asylum from the Coburg princeling who had married the Queen of England. In his opinion, the Berlin revolution might never have happened, had the Queen responded to his brother's appeal in February for a joint declaration by the sovereigns of Europe against the spreading principles of revolution.[19] As it was, the King of Prussia lost his nerve. He ordered his army to withdraw from Berlin rather than fight the citizens at the barricades. He rode out in the streets under the national colours of black, red and gold. He even agreed that the Kingdom of Prussia should merge with a united Germany under an elected national assembly at Frankfurt – a solution in line with the 'Coburg' plan. Prince Albert sent him another paper, advocating the revival of the Holy Roman Empire, but in a constitutional manner. The King refused to take on the imperial role offered by the representatives of the German nation; he would rather be a certain monarch of Prussia by God's will than an uncertain German Emperor by the people's grant.

He soon recovered power in his own capital. The middle classes became frightened at the demands of the workers and radicals, and the ranks of the revolutionaries split. A secret group of Junkers advised the King to declare martial law and adjourn the new democratic national assembly. A royal decree gave limited powers to a reactionary government headed by the King's uncle, Count Brandenburg and, later, by the arch-conservative Otto von Manteuffel. In fact, the Crown still ruled, and the electorate was weighted in favour of those who owned property; as the reactionary leader Stahl said, 'Authority, not majority.'

While the revolution in Germany took its course, the Prince of Prussia stayed at Windsor Castle, endeavouring to regain his self-esteem. He saw the Princess Royal and the Prince of Wales every day and spoke German with them. He became fond of the children and was grateful for the kindness of the royal family. Prince Albert continued to hold up the virtues of the British Constitution as a model for Germany. The Prince of Prussia seemed to listen, but Prince Albert mistook his silence for assent.

After spending three months in England, the royal refugee was able to return to Berlin. He wrote to thank Queen Victoria for her tact and understanding during his time of humiliation. The support of England had helped to have him recalled to Prussia, where he was soon placed at the head of the reactionary forces. In 1849, he commanded the troops of the German Confederation against the revolutionary forces from Baden. He avenged his exile by hanging most of the radical army's officers after their last stand at the fortress of Rastadt.

The Prince of Prussia would never forgive or forget the revolution. He had been forced to flee by a conspiracy of radicals in Berlin, and his pride had been wounded before a foreign court. Becoming as determined, as had King Charles II, never to set out on his travels again, he accepted his brother's restoration of a reactionary government and his refusal to look beyond the borders of Prussia. It was not only his duty to obey, it was also to his taste, even if his wife and son disapproved.

A single event caused all the neighbouring countries of France to look towards an alliance with England. A Napoleon was elected in Paris.

Prince Louis Napoleon became President and, soon afterwards, Emperor. The memory of French armies sweeping through Europe was enough to make even the Prussian reactionaries who hated England look to her for support against the French. The Princess Royal's hand seemed a good insurance against revolution at home and an attack by France. A royal marriage would involve England on the Continent, even if her politicians tried to keep her free from entangling alliances. A joining of blood royal would compromise the policy of splendid isolation.

Prince Albert and Baron Stockmar were anxious that the Princess Royal be fit for her future role in European diplomacy, and the intensity of her education was increased. A brilliant teacher, Miss Hildyard, used the child's natural curiosity to stimulate interest in science and literature, Latin and history. Her father encouraged her to begin thinking about politics and foreign affairs. Her brother, the Prince of Wales, needed more pushing. He, unfortunately, was lazy as well as intelligent, stubborn as well as tenacious, quick of temper but slow of speech. His father had a low opinion of his capacities, and this view was sometimes shared by his mother. In fact, the Prince's faults often stemmed from a natural reaction to his parent's overwhelming expectations of him.

'Other children are not always good,' the Prince once complained to his German tutor. 'Why should I always be good? Nobody is always good.'[20]

He was straightforward, affectionate and loyal, especially to his elder sister. Although she outshone him and was close to their father, he was close to her. She knew that he would displace her and become the King of England; he would often tell her so in their children's arguments about who was the better, but she did not seem to resent it. It was she who basked in her parents' approval, although the Queen would sometimes scold her for her temper and willfulness.

Prince Albert was gradually emerging from his role as controller of the royal household. He was engaged in his first great contribution to his adopted country: the planning of the Great Exhibition of 1851. Under his persistent and inspiring leadership, Paxton's extraordinary design for a Crystal Palace in iron and glass was chosen and set up in Hyde Park. The glittering exhibition hall, which extended for nearly a third of a mile and covered eighteen acres, was constructed in less than nine months. When the site was being cleared, a number of immemorial elms were not cut down, but left enclosed beneath the curved transept; they became known as 'John Bull's Trees of Liberty'. Prince Albert was the business manager of the whole vast project, which was paid for by public subscription, and which seemed to rise as quickly as a mirage. Like a sudden Xanadu in the park, it was an instant marvel. Even the scoffing *Times* had to praise it as a splendid phantasm, and Thackeray wrote of it:

> . . . By a wizard's rod
> A blazing arch of lucid glass
> Leaps like a fountain from the grass
> To meet the sun!

The wizard's rod had been waved by the Prince Consort, and the opening of the Great Exhibition was his supreme hour. The immense display of manufacturing power, housed in a triumph of new technology, proved that British craftsmanship only needed an organizing genius to dazzle the eyes of the world. Queen Victoria was filled with devotion when she saw the gleaming edifice risen from her husband's imagination and thoroughness.

'This is one of the greatest and most glorious days of our lives,' she wrote in her private journal. 'The Park presented a wonderful spectacle, crowds streaming through it, - carriages and troops passing, quite like the Coronation, and for me, the same anxiety. The day was bright and all bustle and excitement. At half-past two the whole procession in nine State carriages was set in motion. Vicky and Bertie were in our carriage (the other children and Wiwy did not go). The Green Park and Hyde Park were one mass of densely crowded human beings, in the highest good humour and most enthusiastic. . . . The tremendous cheering, the joy expressed in every face, the vastness of the building, with all its decorations and exhibits, the sound of the organ (with 200 instruments and 600 voices, which seemed nothing) and my beloved husband, the creator of this peace festival "uniting the industry and art of all nations of the earth", all this was indeed moving, and a day to live for ever.'[21]

This was a far cry from 1848, and the crowds which then took to the streets and manned the barricades. All the crowned heads of Europe had been invited to the Great Exhibition. Few had accepted, either because of jealousy or for fear of losing their thrones during their absence. It was the only fly in the honey of Queen Victoria's joy. As she scathingly observed to Stockmar, 'We regret for their own sakes that so few Princes have come, here again dividing themselves from their people. Deeply will they repent it when it is too late.'²²

The Prince of Prussia and his family did come. At first, the King of Prussia had been deterred by Queen Victoria's uncle, the King of Hanover, from allowing his brother to attend this 'rubbishy' event. He had written to Prince Albert that he had heard that the Crystal Palace might collapse and, even worse, that the Prince of Prussia might be assassinated, while the international crowds would cause another outbreak of the Black Death. Prince Albert had tartly reminded the King how glad he had been in 1848 to have his brother safe in England. If the refugee prince did not return to visit the Exhibition, it would be taken as an insult by the British people.

So the Prince of Prussia arrived with his family and an entourage of twenty-nine. The visitors stayed for four weeks, spending the last few days at the seaside house of Osborne. While Prince Albert and Princess Augusta agreed on their private plans for a liberal and united Germany, her husband said little about his brother's reactionary government in Prussia. He might be impressed by the power of British technology, but he was not convinced by Prince Albert's claims that British institutions would work on the Continent.

Disappointed, Prince Albert turned his attentions to Augusta's son, Prince Frederick William. The young man of twenty was handsome and fair-haired, impressionable and looking for a sympathetic father-figure to help him form his opinions. He was already awed by the display of British power, surprised by the ease of manner and open affections of the royal family, and flattered by the attentions of Queen Victoria's husband. He was persuaded to look upon Albert as an intellectual father and adviser, while his own father remained a distant military tutor who demanded total obedience. The struggle for the young man's mind had begun.

The Princess Royal was only ten, but she was deputed to show Prince Frederick William round the Great Exhibition. Her German was excellent; his English was imperfect. She had been thoroughly briefed by her father on the technicalities of many of the innumerable exhibits, so that she could tell the Prussian prince about things he had hardly dreamed of. She already had an old head on her child's shoulders; she knew who she was and who she was meant to be.

Prince Frederick William was impressed by her. He had never been allowed to go abroad before. His meeting with such an educated and loving royal family, so free from the rigidity and narrowness of the Prussian Court, was both a shock and an inspiration. He could see that his mother's liberal views, far from being eccentric, were being applied successfully in the most powerful industrial country in the world. By adopting them, he could assert himself against his father. And there was the Princess Royal, who was being steered towards him by her father and his mother. Allied to her, he might go his own way.

These visions of the future were no more substantial than the Crystal Palace itself. At the end of that enchanted summer of peace and display, it was to be dismantled. There was only a slight possibility that it might be re-erected; Tennyson's 'Temple Made of Glass' seemed a season's wonder; the dreams of its visitors appeared to be doomed to a cold awakening. In answer to Princess Augusta's letter of thanks for the visit, Queen Victoria warned her of the difficulties that lay ahead for her son because of the differences between his parents. She begged Augusta to have more confidence in him so that he, in turn, would have more confidence in himself. She was afraid for the young man. She could see him torn apart if his father strongly recommended something and his mother warned him against it.[23]

Two years later, the Prince of Prussia and his wife and daughter visited England again without their son. The ambitions of Louis Napoleon were causing concern to the British and to the Germans. Army manœuvres impressed the Prince of Prussia, while the Princess Royal impressed his wife. The twelve-year-old already wore her hair up like an adult, and talked about art in mature terms. Yet any progress towards a royal marriage between the two houses had to be delayed. The British government's relations with Prussia were worsening, though they were improving with France.

By the end of the year, Prince Albert was so unpopular for opposing war with Russia that a crowd gathered outside Buckingham Palace, expecting to see the Coburg pacifist taken to the Tower of London on a charge of treason. In fact, Prince Albert had been urging military reforms for years, and had even persuaded his brother Ernest to smuggle a specimen of the new Prussian needle rifle to London for examination. Parliament exonerated the Prince from the absurd charge of treason, but Her Majesty's Government, in alliance with Louis Napoleon, decided on war with Russia. In the last resort, England was not like Prussia; the Crown could advise, but not insist, on peace.

The reasons for the Crimean War were not convincing. Ostensibly,

France and Britain were sending their fleets and expeditionary forces to the Black Sea in order to prevent the collapse of Turkey. In reality, the British were defending their empire against its chief threat, while Louis Napoleon was avenging his predecessor's retreat from Moscow. The war proved the most prodigal of all European conflicts, from Waterloo until the First World War. A single fortress at Sevastopol was taken, at the cost of half a million men. The Prince Consort had not been wrong.

The King of Prussia was terrified by the new alliance between England and France, for he feared that it might lead to another Napoleonic assault on his country. Wooed by Austria to join the other western powers in the attack on Russia, he chose neutrality. Revolution was his bugbear, not Russia. His family was linked to the Romanov dynasty by marriage, so he kept Prussia out of the war.

His brother, the Prince of Prussia, favoured an alliance with England and France. He was stung by Queen Victoria's sending her declaration of war to his wife and adding, 'For us it is extremely painful to see Prussia irresolute when we had hoped to proceed hand in hand.'[24] He forced a political crisis on his brother and was exiled to Coblenz. His partial banishment was a forewarning of what would happen to his own son and heir, if he were ever provoked to support an English alliance against the wishes of his father.

The Prince of Prussia's fall from grace was largely brought about by the rise of a new Intelligence system created by Wilhelm Stieber, an extraordinary spymaster, who had first ingratiated himself with the King of Prussia in 1848. A criminal lawyer, with many contacts among the radicals and the underworld, he was also an *agent provocateur* for the Berlin police. As spokesman for a group of rioters, on a deputation to the King, he revealed to His Majesty that he was a police agent who would protect the King from the rioters. The King was impressed by such artfulness, and Stieber continued to play both sides of the law, advising his clients how to outwit it, and telling the authorities how to entrap them.

In 1850, Stieber was appointed Commissioner of Police. The court was moved for safety to Potsdam, and Stieber was charged to report on radical activity in Berlin and to put an end to it. The following year, he attended the Great Exhibition, and went to Paris to investigate German socialists and revolutionaries in exile, who included Marx and Engels. Stieber won the confidence of some of the exile groups and returned to Berlin with lists of sympathizers still in Germany. Dozens of radicals were seized and hundreds were forced to flee abroad as had once the Prince of Prussia. By the end of the Crimean War, Stieber had become the indispensable tool of Prussian Security, a dangerous and ruthless schemer devoted to the Crown.

Outside France, Prussia and Austria, secret Intelligence systems had not yet been developed. Most Intelligence came through diplomatic sources, particularly from military attachés, whose position was known and agreed. Although they were expected to report to their governments on the armed forces of foreign powers, the report was considered more as a deterrent than a betrayal. A code of military honour bound the attaché. His job was to observe and inform; spying meant dishonour and instant dismissal.[25] In Prussia particularly, the British Military Attaché was often close to the Crown and was used as a direct channel of communication with Queen Victoria, who was constitutionally the head of her country's armed forces.

There were, in fact, five major sources of foreign Intelligence. The first was through the secret services. The second was through the normal channels of diplomacy, the information sent home by resident ambassadors or envoys. The third was through the special attachés at the legations, or the foreign correspondents of important newspapers such as *The Times*. The fourth was through the reports of nationals who had travelled abroad and had been briefed for a particular purpose. And the fifth came from the proliferation of royal and aristocratic correspondence, which transcended national frontiers, and so seemed an international threat to Stieber and other agents of the state.

During Victorian times, the emergent nation states were beginning to dominate European diplomacy. Although the Austrian Empire was still in existence and prevented the unification of Italy and Germany, it was ailing like Turkey. Even in the Balkans, smaller nationalities were demanding their freedom. As each nation rose to demand the control of its own destiny, it also demanded patriotism from its citizens, and formed a new secret service answerable only to the state. These national loyalties conflicted with the wider loyalties of the aristocrats and the royal families, who still ruled in Britain, Austria, Russia, Prussia and Spain.

The alliances of the well-born were formed through marriage. Cousins provided more certain information than spies; common blood was a surer source than secret service pay. The wide correspondence of European royalty and nobility made for an alternative diplomacy through connected families, and it was usually carried securely through diplomatic bag or private messenger. It relied on personal knowledge and shared values, not on the equivocal claims of double agents who must manufacture information to earn their pay. It was more accurate, and usually sought to keep the peace, not provoke a conflict.

The immensely extended families of Victorian royalty and nobility did not want war. To them, war meant a father fighting a daughter's husband, a cousin at odds with a nephew. National quarrels led to ruptures between kin; a lost war could mean a toppled throne and refugee princes. Whether or not the new systems of secret Intelligence might benefit republics and nations which practised diplomacy by the deteriorating standards of Louis Napoleon, they were ranged firmly against the old system of family diplomacy and international correspondence which depended upon common standards of accuracy and trust.

The decline in standards of international diplomacy after the Crimean War, and the rise of Stieber and the other spymasters of the nation states were to condemn the heirs of the old traditions. By being true to what she had been taught, the Princess Royal might seem disloyal to her second country.

Royalty follows the flag. Queen Victoria thought the French immoral, and loathed the very name of Napoleon, but, as allies, she had to invite the new Emperor and Empress of France to Windsor in April 1855. Unexpectedly, Napoleon III and his wife charmed Queen Victoria. Although the French Emperor was short and stout and wore long waxed moustaches, he had an air of mystery and dared to flirt with the Queen. The Empress Eugénie was elegant and wore the first crinoline ever seen in England. The Emperor had been threatening to go to the Crimea and lead the allied troops in person against Sevastopol. Queen Victoria had the courage to ask him not to go; she knew her troops would not follow a Bonaparte. At a Council of War the following day, he seemed to accept her plea, and invited her and her family to the Paris Exhibition in August. It would be the first time an English sovereign had set foot in the French capital since the Hundred Years War.

Queen Victoria did not lose the opportunity of pointing out to her friend, the Princess of Prussia, how successful the French Emperor's visit had been. The return visit to Paris was a further triumph and a warning signal to Berlin. Queen Victoria and her husband were accompanied by the Princess Royal and the Prince of Wales. The young people were delighted with their reception. They were treated as adults and were entertained as if their pleasure were more important than their duty. The Princess was almost fifteen and realized herself beautiful for the first time. In the Hall of Mirrors at Versailles, the French Emperor asked her to dance, and as she spun round, catching reflection upon reflection of herself, she saw a vision of what she would become. It was a heady experience for the young princess.

At Versailles, Queen Victoria and her daughter met the heir of a Junker family, Otto von Bismarck, whose sensitivity and political genius was masked by a reckless wit and demonic energy. The heir of Teutonic Knights, with estates on the Elbe at Schönhausen, Bismarck had grown up with a wild reputation. Over six feet tall, imposing and red-haired, he had fought twenty-five duels during his first nine months at Gottingen University. He enjoyed being provocative, but only to prove his passionate commitment to the future of Prussia. A traditional conservative and royalist, he had armed his peasants in support of the King during the troubles of 1848, but he had antagonized Princess Augusta by proposing a dangerous scheme for a Regency under her young son. He was thought too manic by the King who noted against his name: 'Red reactionary – smells of blood – to be used later.'[26]

His connections with the King's military advisers such as Albrecht von Roon, and his speeches against the Liberals in the Prussian Parliament made him known. His marriage to Johanna von Puttkamer, a Pomeranian, curbed his wilder side. He was duly sent to represent Prussia at the Federal Diet of the German Confederation at Frankfurt. There he developed his rough style of diplomacy, which he later said he had learned in the horse fairs of Pomerania. He resisted Austrian pressure to join in the Crimean War; with the King, he supported an understanding with the Tsar. For this, he was said to smell of Russian leather and to be a Berlin cossack. When presented to Prince Albert at Versailles, he thought the Coburg prince handsome and cool in his black uniform, but full of malevolent curiosity beneath a surface courtesy. Queen Victoria, herself, found Bismarck reactionary and enigmatic and a supporter of England's enemies. 'Paris is beautiful,' the Queen said to him. 'Even more beautiful than St Petersburg,' he replied, although he had not yet visited the Russian capital.

Bismarck's reports of the growing Anglo-French understanding caused panic in Prussia. The Allies seemed to be winning the war in the

Crimea, and Princess Augusta saw an end to her hopes for her son's match with the Princess Royal. He, himself, was in despair. Ever since his visit to England for the Great Exhibition, he had done everything to prepare himself for his marriage to the Princess. Having been sent to St Petersburg to attend a Russian imperial wedding, he criticized the barbaric luxury of the Tsar's court in his letters to Prince Albert. He studied English as much as he could. His tutor found him eager for any information about England, and made him compose imaginary letters to cabinet ministers and society leaders. He attended the Anglican church at Bonn, borrowing a prayer-book and joining in the liturgy for Queen Victoria. He was jealous of the Princess Royal's visit to Paris; there were imperial rivals there who might ask for her hand.

Prince Frederick William wanted to leave for England immediately to propose marriage to the Princess Royal. His parents encouraged him, agreeing for once about the English alliance. But their son could not leave Prussia without the consent of his uncle, the King. He went to the palace to beg the royal blessing for his wooing. The King was uneasy at the idea of an heir to the throne seeking a foreign princess. It was not traditional. There were enough princesses of good German blood to make dozens of royal marriages. But he was even more uneasy about the Anglo-French alliance. A marriage between the Hohenzollerns and the English royal house would at least provide a counterbalance. So the King of Prussia gave his blessing.

Prince Frederick William let it be known that he was taking a holiday, to bathe in the sea at Ostend. This ruse was necessary because the Queen of Prussia was lending a favourable ear to the pro-Russian group at court. Incognito, the Prince slipped across the Channel and took train to Scotland. Unluckily, he was seen at a station by the Duke of Cambridge, who told his mother that he had been astonished to see the young Prussian prince on his way to Queen Victoria's estate at Balmoral. Evidently, the marriage was to be arranged.[27]

This was more than Prince Frederick himself knew. He was nervous and uncertain by the time he arrived at Balmoral, where Prince Albert had just finished building a comfortable baronial *schloss*. Here, everything was kept deliberately informal. Both Queen Victoria and her husband loved playing at Scots lairds and ladies. Prince Albert would wear the kilt; the Queen draped herself, the furniture and the beds with Stuart tartan. They agreed with Lady Lyttelton, who thought that the life of a country gentleman and his family, which the royal couple condescended to imitate, was about the richest in materials for happiness.[28]

The Princess Royal did not know the reason for Prince Frederick William's sudden arrival, but her parents did. Even if Queen Victoria had exaggerated her attachment to imperial France, the effect had been gratifying. Within a month of her return from Paris, the young heir to the Prussian throne had arrived with royal consent to offer his hand to Princess Victoria. Her acceptance was now essential for the success of the 'Coburg' plan, whose elements Prince Albert was already beginning to instil in her. He did not reveal the part she might play in it by marrying the Prince of Prussia's son, because he wanted her to choose what her father had already chosen for her.

Prince Frederick William had come at a joyful time. Sevastopol had fallen on 9 September 1855; the ashes of the celebration bonfires were still hot on the heaths by the Dee. Princess Victoria was placed next to him at dinner, and hardly stopped talking to the silent and handsome young man, who looked down at her from large blue eyes above a sweeping blond moustache. Her own huge green eyes filled with pleasure at seeing the handsome Prince again, but he could not tell if she felt anything more for him. The next day, he was taken off to hunt stags by Prince Albert, but his aim was poor, his mind was on the Princess. He thought the Princess's gaiety was girlish mockery of his chances; after all, she was still a month away from her fifteenth birthday.

After four days at Balmoral, he was left alone with the Princess, who suddenly took his hand and squeezed it hard. It was her first contact with him, her innocent declaration. At last, he could sleep well. After breakfast the next morning, he spoke privately to the Queen and Prince Albert and told them that he wanted to belong to their family more than anything in the world. The Queen was full of emotion and clasped the young man's hand; he had her consent. But the Princess Royal was still too young; she must not be told until she had been confirmed, the Queen said. The prince could return in eighteen months' time to propose to her daughter.

Princess Victoria still seemed unconscious of the young man's desire. On their walks through the woods, she looked for some smoke-quartz to give him. 'Oh,' she said, 'I would love to give you every beautiful thing I find.' Yet he was still unsure of her. All he could report to his parents was that he was certain she liked him.

Prince Frederick William was too impatient to wait. On a morning of clear frost, he went out riding with the girlish Princess in a party making for Craig-na-Ban. She wore a large riding hat and a plaid over her long skirt. He made her lag behind the others until they were alone together. By the side of the path he dismounted and picked a sprig of white heather – for good luck – for life. He gave her the heather and lifted her down from her side-saddle and kissed her. Then he put her on her pony again and rode on beside her, telling her that he wanted her to stay in Prussia always, always. She blushed. He was afraid of having said something to annoy her, but she said, 'Oh, no.' She said she wanted to tell her parents. At Glen Girnoch, where the royal carriage was waiting, the prince gave Queen Victoria a look full of meaning. She knew the young man had declared himself. Her daughter would confide in her later.[29]

The Princess Royal was still half-child, half-woman, but she had a mind of her own and had been brought up to be wiser than her years. She told the Queen that she had always loved Prince Frederick William. She had not had the chance to love any other man, so to the pure young Prussian Prince was given all the passion of her calf-love, her first love. He was four years older than her own father had been when he had married her mother at the age of twenty. Yet he still seemed so young, and her father so wise.

Prince Frederick William was allowed to give the Princess Royal a bracelet to confirm their engagement, after which he had to leave for Prussia. The secret could not be kept for long. Queen Victoria had to tell her Coburg uncle, King Leopold, of the success of their long planning. She confided to him that their wishes for her daughter's marriage were coming to pass in the most gratifying and satisfactory manner.[30] The Foreign Secretary, Lord Clarendon, also had to be told, because the marriage might affect British diplomacy. He replied that he had heard of the admirable qualities of the young prince, also that the Princess of Prussia was set heart and soul on the marriage.[31]

Queen Victoria was glad of Clarendon's approval, especially as the Prime Minister, Lord Palmerston, was thought to favour France and dislike reactionary Prussia. Behind the love-match lay something more essential. Politically, the Queen wrote to the Foreign Secretary, the marriage alliance was of great importance and might lead to a very different state of things between England and Germany.[32]

The 'different state of things' worried the editor of *The Times* when he began to suspect a royal engagement. In an editorial, he claimed that there had been a secret understanding early in 1851 when the Princess

Royal was only ten. It was unfortunate for royalty that such private matters should have to be made public, but they did affect the future of Britain. To *The Times*, a royal marriage with the Hohenzollerns meant a step towards an alliance with the Romanovs and Russia. 'What is His Prussian Majesty to us, or we to him? We never seem to agree to do the same thing at the same time.' The marriage would divide the loyalties of the Princess Royal. Devotion to her husband must be treason to her country.[33]

This blast from *The Times* caused consternation at Balmoral and at the Foreign Office. Lord Clarendon wrote to the Queen that the worst enemy of his country was that newspaper, but there was no way of stopping the nuisance. The complaints about it were general, but nobody would give up reading it.[34] Unfortunately it was read in Berlin as well. There the nature of a free press was misunderstood because the Prussians did not have one. The King, himself, thought that the editorial was inspired by a Cabinet Minister in London, although the British Envoy assured him that the newspaper was merely a malignant, commercial speculation, without politics or principles.[35]

The engagement was not broken off. The King of Prussia admitted to a childish dream that a beautiful English princess would sit on the Prussian throne, and Princess Augusta praised him for standing alone at court in favour of her son's marriage.[36] The Princess Royal was unconscious of the political furore, although her confirmation, which would give a religious sanction to the engagement, was hurried ahead for fear that worsening relations might make the match impossible. The service took place on 20 March 1856, in the private chapel at Windsor. The Princess Royal was wearing a rich white silk glacé gown, with five pinked flounces, the bodice trimmed with white ribbons and Mecklin lace. The chapel was filled with the royal family and their German relations, including the Princess's godfather, King Leopold of the Belgians. She answered perfectly the religious questions put to her by the Archbishop of Canterbury, and her beauty and assurance made her seem ready to accept marriage as well as God.

This was Queen Victoria's point. The Lord Chancellor considered the Princess Royal too young to know her own mind about a husband. It was not the case, the Queen wrote to Lord Palmerston. The Lord Chancellor was probably unaware that the Princess's choice had come entirely from her own heart, even though her parents had approved: 'She is as solemnly engaged by her OWN free will and wish to Prince Frederick

William as any one can be.' She had pledged her word to him before God. She was old enough to know her own feelings, even if she was not yet old enough to leave her parents' roof, and consummate the marriage. It was only this that made the parents delay the wedding until after her seventeenth birthday.[37]

The Princess Royal had a great deal to learn. At Balmoral, she was enthralled to meet Florence Nightingale, whose accounts of the neglect of the wounded in the Crimea gave the princess a lifelong interest in the care of the sick. For two hours every evening, her father taught her Roman and recent European history. She had to produce essays for him, particularly on Prussian and German affairs. Prince Albert instructed her in the 'Coburg' plan and also wrote to her future husband about it. Prince Frederick William sent her his diary of the events of 1848, and came to see his betrothed in the May following her confirmation. He was now her 'Fritz' and she his 'Vicky'.

This visit gave Prince Albert – soon to be created Prince Consort by his wife – the opportunity to catechize his future son-in-law on the virtues of constitutional monarchy and the English example. The young man's mind was more concerned with the Princess. She was enjoying her first London Season and sometimes seemed almost frivolous with her new gowns and her dancing. One evening, a candle set her muslin dress on fire. She was quickly rolled in a rug to put out the flames, but her right arm was badly burned. In this moment of danger, the prince realized that he would be devoted to her for life. 'Through this accident,' he told her, 'you have really been given to me a second time.'[38]

At the end of the Season, Queen Victoria confided her worries about her eldest daughter to her notebook: her Dear Child did try her rather often with her wayward temper, her want of self-control and her sharp answers. She was contradictory and took criticism badly, but she had a very warm, affectionate and loving heart. Even though she was so clever and advanced for her age, she was still so simple, so childish, so inexperienced. She clung so passionately to her home and her father, her family and her country, that the Queen's heart bled to think of her daughter's future separation from her, and isolation abroad. No doubt her Prussian Prince adored her and had the kindest and best of hearts – and the purest of minds. Yet his character was inferior to hers. He would not be the support to her that he ought to be.

'It makes me very anxious!' the Queen concluded, 'Every thing for the last time – an infant taking leave, this is so dreadful for our poor dear Child!'[39]

Prince Frederick William made a more interesting impression on the Imperial Court in Paris, when he was ordered there on a visit. At a state ball, he thought that the Empress Eugénie looked like a true fairy queen in her tremendous crinoline and waterfalls of diamonds. She was intrigued by him and discovered hidden depths in his character. Although he looked like a Teuton straight from the pages of Tacitus, he was chivalrously polite and resembled Hamlet.[40]

In Berlin, a situation was developing which made him a Hamlet in reverse. His uncle, the King, was slipping into madness. His father was taking over state affairs as the King's Lieutenant. The Prince of Prussia had to tread warily and maintain the King's policies in case His Majesty recovered his wits. He was surrounded by reactionary courtiers and spies of the Queen of Prussia, but at least his new power helped his son's marriage plans. There was 'a state of fidget' in Berlin for a formal marriage treaty, but Prince Albert first wanted the question of his daughter's dowry settled. Parliament had granted the Princess Royal £40,000 outright and an income of £8,000 a year – enough, but not a fortune. Prince Albert insisted that she keep control of her dowry. His principle was that while the Prussians were giving nothing to the Princess Royal, they ought not to take anything from her.[41]

There were further quarrels between the two families over her household. The young bride would be surrounded by elderly women, who would report back to her husband's mother and to the Queen of Prussia. Prince Albert insisted that two young women join the household, Countess Marie zu Lynar and the brilliant Countess Walburga Hohenthal, who later became Lady Paget. He approved of the Count and Countess Perponcher to run the household with the Countess Blücher. Baron Stockmar's son Ernest must be appointed treasurer. Prince Albert warned his future son-in-law that ill-natured people would say that the young Stockmar was acting for England as a secret political agent, but in any event, such people wanted the marriage to fail.[42]

One last demand annoyed Queen Victoria. The Prussian Court wished the marriage to take place in Berlin. Through Lord Clarendon, the Queen flatly refused. There was no possibility of the Princess Royal being married abroad. 'The assumption of its being too much for a Prince Royal of Prussia to come over to marry the Princess Royal of England IN England is too absurd, to say the least,' the Queen declared.

'It is not every day that one marries the eldest daughter of the Queen of England. The question therefore must be considered as settled and closed.'[43]

Otto von Bismarck was gloomy about the prospects; they did not suit his view of Prussian politics. 'If our future Queen,' he wrote, 'remains even only partly English, I can see our court in danger of being surrounded by English influence.' Bismarck distrusted the Anglomania of sections of German society. Such servile admiration of a foreign country was unpatriotic.[44] He was already prepared to see the arrival of Queen Victoria's daughter as the intrusion of something alien and dangerous.

As the wedding-day approached, the Princess Royal grew more aware of everything she was about to lose. Her letters to her brother, the Prince of Wales, show how much she loved and depended on him. From Balmoral, she wrote to tell him that she was always thinking of him, and that she sometimes wished for a magic looking-glass to see what he was doing. And when her 'Fritz' left her for the last time before the marriage, she told her brother how sad she was to see him go – and yet she feared what was to happen. 'The next time he comes,' she wrote, 'we shall not have to part; but then it will be good-bye to everybody – it is too dreadful – but we are always between two evils in this world.'[45]

After her father and her future husband, her eldest brother would always remain the strongest influence on the Princess Royal. She did not share her parents' view of his defects. She knew that he had been driven and supervised more than she had because he was the heir to the throne. As his tutor admitted, the Prince of Wales had been forced early into life, and too much was expected of him. The result was that he rebelled from his intensive education and his parents' excessive sense of morality. Once, when he lied about smoking, he was punished by three days' solitary confinement, and had to write to his father, begging forgiveness formally for the sin he had committed.[46]

The first two of the royal children particularly bore their parents' hopes and disappointments on their shoulders; too much was desired for them, too much resistance was provoked in them. Queen Victoria could never see why her two elder children had given her the most trouble. She thought the fault lay in their characters, not in her treatment of them. 'A more insubordinate and unequal-tempered child and girl I think I never saw!' she wrote to her first child after her marriage. 'The trouble you gave us all – was indeed very great. Comparatively speaking, we have none whatever with the others. You and Bertie (in very different ways) were indeed great difficulties.'[47]

The difficulties were that they were Victorian adolescents and heirs of most demanding parents. After she was married, the Princess Royal told her eldest brother that she had been neither fish nor flesh when she was younger. She had always felt shy and out of her element. She may have thought like a grown-up person, but she knew she still had all the faults of childhood. Nevertheless, she had learned the lesson of creating harmony in the royal household. 'Try and do what dear Papa wishes,' she told her brother, 'and you will see all will go right and dear Mama will be pleased and satisfied.'[48]

She had done that herself. The Queen was pleased and satisfied at the marriage which Prince Albert had been so long making, but yet she could not accept the loss of her daughter. During the months before the wedding, her ambivalence became almost obsessive. Now that her daughter was an attractive young woman, the Queen was glad that this rival for her husband's love was leaving home, but she could not bear the thought that her child might be happy elsewhere.

For the Queen was sure that the Princess Royal loved her father even more than her future husband. The girl could not exist without Prince Albert. How different their two marriages would be! The Queen had married an angel of a husband and did not have to leave her home. Although the man of her daughter's choice was good, the Queen thought, he did not have the strength to control his wife's temper and laziness. No marriage could compare to the Queen's, no happiness could be like hers. That would be a sacrilege.[49]

When a young French cousin died in childbirth, the Queen became even more anxious. She remembered Princess Charlotte dying during her labour, forty years before – a death that had put her cousin Victoria on the throne. What then of 'Vicky', this beloved and difficult child? She might die herself, and never return from Prussia to see again the sweet sights of her childhood. On a last visit to Osborne, her daughter bade adieu to her pretty room, her favourite haunts, to her Swiss cottage and her garden. She would never again see them in the same way. The girl in her would have vanished and she would return only for a short time like a visitor. The thought filled the Queen with bitter sorrow.

Then the Queen checked her thoughts. She, herself, had had a very unhappy childhood, quite alone and full of difficulties and trials. She ought not to be bitter. 'Fritz' was only doing what he ought to do. He was good, straightforward and pure, and he adored 'Vicky'. So be it, even if he were not the man of character her daughter needed. 'None of our daughters will ever find such a Husband as Albert,' the Queen told herself. 'That is hopeless – and I know it.'[50]

A fortnight before the wedding, the Queen began to think about the physical aspect of marriage. The Princess Royal had been told nothing; the Queen would tell her nothing now. She must trust her husband and do what he said, however strange it might seem. Her thoughts so filled the Queen with pity and anxiety that she did not dare to dwell on the subject. It was awful to give up a child to a stranger – and a man, but the child did love him tenderly and he loved her.[51]

In fear and concern, in turmoil and emotion, Queen Victoria awaited the marriage of the Princess Royal of England to Prince Frederick William of Prussia. It was what she and her husband had always wanted. Political duty must stand above personal feelings. In this lay the essence of royalty.

CHAPTER TWO

Adieu to England

Deal kindly by her, noble man,
  She's but a child in years;
Cherish each hope, each new-found plan,
  And banish all her fears.

Deal kindly with her when afar
  From her sweet Island home;
Be thou to her a guiding star
  Through all her days to come....

Deal kindly for her Mother's sake,
  So womanly and true.
Let not a fear her heart awake
  When she bids her child adieu.

Deal kindly. She's her Country's Pride
  Who gives her for thine own.
And to thy keeping does confide
  A Jewel from her Crown.[1]

ON NEW YEAR'S EVE, 1857, the Princess Royal sent this poem from the magazine *John Bull* to her brother, the Prince of Wales. She was frightened at the prospect of leaving her home with a stranger, to live in a foreign country she had never seen. She loved her noble prince, or thought she did, but she knew little of what awaited her in Prussia. Her mother and father had arranged for the members of her household to come to Buckingham Palace during the weeks before the wedding so

32

that she could meet them. She was reassured by the competent Perponch-ers and found the Countess 'Wally' Hohenthal very good company.

To the countess, the Princess Royal seemed extraordinarily young. 'All the childish roundness still clung to her and made her look shorter than she really was. She was dressed in a fashion long disused on the Continent, in a plum-coloured silk dress fastened at the back. Her hair was drawn off her forehead. Her eyes were what struck me most; the iris was green like the sea on a sunny day, and the white had a peculiar shimmer which gave them the fascination that, together with a smile showing her small and beautiful teeth, bewitched those who approached her. The nose was unusually small and turned up slightly, and the complexion was ruddy, perhaps too much so for one thing, but it gave the idea of perfect health and strength.'

If there were any fault to be found in the Princess Royal's face, it was in the look of determination about the chin, but her very gentle and almost timid manner disguised her will-power. Her voice was very delightful. Never too high, it lent a peculiar charm to the slightly foreign accent with which the Princess spoke both English and German. Coun-tess Hohenthal also noticed the flaw which Queen Victoria knew well: the Princess Royal took violent fancies or dislikes to people, from intui-tion or because of their mannerisms. 'She was no judge of character, and never became one, because her own point of view was the only one she could see.'[2]

To the Princess Royal, the arrival of her Hohenzollern relatives was like an invasion. Everywhere, erect young princes with bristling mous-taches, scarred cheeks and heels clicking like castanets, bowed stiffly and spoke sarcastically of England. They were surprised by the warmth of the crowds which cheered the Queen and her daughter, but they despised the lack of formality and ceremony at court. There were dinners for a hundred guests almost nightly in Buckingham Palace. At a state ball for a thousand guests, the wedding presents were displayed on great tables covered with jewels and candelabra and lace – and most magnificent of all, the bridegroom's gift, a necklace of large matching pearls, perfect in their whiteness. Queen Victoria glittered with all the diamonds of India, worn against cornflowers and grasses on her silk and tulle costumes. Beside all the wealth, she had to show her love of a simple life.

Prince Frederick William arrived two days before the wedding. He had been preparing a home in the palace at Babelsberg, and trying to make it less alien and cheerless for his bride. He had also been organizing their state entry into Berlin, testing the coach which swayed like a ship and looked like a gilded monkey-cage. He was nervous because his father was behaving ominously. The Prince of Prussia was now the effective Regent in his brother's name. He had tried to refuse to attend the wedding in London because of state business, and had only given way under great pressure from Prince Albert, who wanted to confide his daughter personally to the protection of another father-figure in Berlin.

On the morning of 25 January 1858, the Princess Royal went to see her mother; both were still in their dressing-gowns. She was given a pretty book, *The Bridal Offering*, and dressed with the Queen. She wore white moiré silk trimmed with Honiton lace, and white roses on her bridal veil. Her mother wore a dress of lilac and silver, and a tiara. A daguerreotype was taken, because Prince Albert wanted a memento of this last intimate occasion together. Father and daughter were composed, but the Queen was trembling and her likeness was blurred.

The marriage took place in the Chapel Royal of St James's Palace. The Queen and her daughter drove in a carriage alone to the Royal Closet of the palace, then made their way to the Throne Room, where the Royal Procession was assembling. Headed by drums and trumpets, the Poursuivants of Arms, Rouge Croix, Blue Mantle and Portcullis, and the Heralds in their tabards, led the Queen with her two youngest sons in Highland dress, the Privy Counsellors, the royal dukes and the lords and ladies of the court to the chapel. When the Queen and the royal guests were settled in their places, the drummers and trumpeters returned to bring in the processions of the bridegroom and the bride. Eight bridesmaids bore her train; 'a cloud of maidens' who were all unmarried daughters of dukes or marquesses or earls. She stood by her Prince before the altar to make her vows, with her father behind her. The Archbishop of Canterbury conducted the service and bungled his words.

The Princess Royal made no mistakes. Her mother thought that everything went off admirably, beautifully and most solemnly. She could see her daughter looking lovely and innocent, serene and calm. The service was like a dream to the Queen, as if she herself were being married again to her Prince Albert. He seemed as if he were renewing his vows to his wife, not giving his child away.

After the ceremony was over and the register had been signed and the organ had played Mendelssohn's Wedding March, all the guests went to Buckingham Palace. Great crowds cheered the bride and groom when they appeared on the balcony. Soon it was time for the Princess to leave for a short honeymoon in the pretty rooms prepared for them in Windsor Castle. When she came to bid farewell to the Queen, in her white épinglé dress and mantilla and bonnet to match, trimmed with orange flowers and a white lace veil, she was in tears. The Queen told her not to be distressed; she was as safe and happy with dear Fritz as if she were with her mother. She must not be frightened, but should do whatever Fritz asked her. The Queen no longer felt any annoyance or alarm. After the holy scene of that day, all her fears seemed past.[3]

Yet the Queen knew her daughter was unprepared. Even the marriage sacrament made it no easier for her to surrender her child into the hands of a young man. She felt depressed and anxious until she received two letters from her daughter and her new husband, both telling of their happiness together. Reading them brought on a fit of crying, but her tears were of gratitude and joy. She had struggled against these emotions all the time, and the reaction was sure to come.

Once she had overcome her fears and her prudishness, the Queen felt closer to her daughter than ever before. The court moved to Windsor, and the Princess Royal came to tell her mother about her feelings for her husband. 'I am not shy,' she declared. 'Why should I be, if all is right?' The Queen was impressed. 'What purity and simplicity and excellence there is in those words!' she wrote in her notebook. 'How, just again, what I felt!' She praised her daughter's independence at last and was glad that the trying little rubs of the past few weeks were over.[4] All she dreaded was her daughter going away to Prussia and breaking up the family for the first time. She also feared the effect this might have on her husband. He was gloomy about losing his eldest child, he still thought her absolutely dependent on him.

The day of parting was overcast and gusty, with dark clouds threatening snow. At Buckingham Palace, the Princess Royal slept badly, and then wept in her mother's bedroom. She could hardly control herself while she said 'that dreadful word goodbye' to members of her family in the Audience Room. Nobody knew what she was suffering as she and her mother descended the staircase, with an aching head and a far more aching heart.[5]

Snow was falling on the way to the dock at Gravesend. The enthusiasm of the enormous crowds in the City of London was indescribable as they cheered the royal carriage. It was as if she were their own child.[6] Girls had scattered flowers before the gangway of the royal yacht *Victoria and*

Albert. Roses lay in the snow as the Princess Royal went aboard. The most dreadful goodbye was yet to come. She could bear parting from her two elder brothers, but in the ship's saloon she clung to her father and wept on his breast. His undemonstrative nature prevented him from showing the emotion he felt. He could only write to her saying that she could hardly know how dear she had always been to him, and what a void she had left behind in his heart and in his life.[7]

She did not hide her feelings from him. She wrote to him that she thought her heart would break when he shut the cabin door and was gone – that cruel moment she had been dreading for two and a half years. She was weighed down by grief. 'I miss you so dreadfully, dear Papa, more than I can say.' She declared she owed him most in the world. Both she and her husband still felt secure and happy that they could rely on his precious advice.[8] Prince Albert would not fail them with that.

Slowly, the tearful and grief-stricken bride of seventeen was carried across the Channel through a blizzard and into thick fog. The royal yacht reached Antwerp half a day late. In the thick dull evening, the assembled crowds could not even see the Princess, although they could hear a military band playing 'God Save the Queen' in the muffled dark.[9] This was her uncertain introduction to a shrouded continent, but that very evening, the Princess was universally admired at a State Ball given by her Coburg great-uncle, the King of the Belgians. He had always supported the policy behind her marriage.

The fog dispersed, and the triumphal progress by train to Potsdam began. In Belgium and in the smaller German states, crowds gathered at all the stations *en route*. The bride had to show herself at the compartment window, and smile through countless petty ceremonies, receiving bouquets from maidens in white, admiring garlanded arches and listening to the speeches of local dignitaries. At Cologne Cathedral the mob was so great that the ladies were nearly crushed, yet the feeling in the crowds was good. The British Envoy would have liked to have heard a good English cheer, but had to be content with the silent gasping of the Germans expressing satisfaction.[10] The tact and readiness of the Princess Royal was a tribute to her training. She seemed to have the right words and an enchanting smile for every one. She had, as her father said, a man's head and a child's heart.

If the journey had been exhaustingly ceremonious, with little privacy, the arrival in Prussia was even worse. This was an affair of state, and royal dignity was second only to respect for God. Although the old Field Marshal Wrangel inadvertently sat on a presentation meringue cake, and had to be cleaned up before the train arrived, the Prince of Prussia with his full retinue was waiting to meet his son and the bride. At this first great reception in Potsdam, the young Stockmar reported that every one praised the Princess Royal's kindness of manner. The affair was brilliant with decorations, illuminations, deputations, presents, music and enthusiastic crowds, hurrahing energetically.[11] The Princess was learning the first lesson of the Prussian Court: Anything which could be done on a larger scale always was.

Her ceremonial entry into Berlin the following day was more like a war than a celebration. Eight black horses with nodding plumes drew the gilt coach through the Brandenburg Gate. Massed cannons thundered, forests of flags waved and the Prussian Guard stood rank on rank in glittering helmets and cuirasses. Although the sun was shining, it was bitterly cold. The Princess Royal had to keep the coach windows open throughout the drive and the loyal speeches. 'It must have been perishing work for her,' Lady Churchill wrote to Queen Victoria. The Princess, herself, said that she felt like a bird perched in a gilt cage, petrified too. 'I am all one lump of ice,' she told the Queen of Prussia when they met. 'My heart alone keeps warm.'[12]

There was no respite for her. She must meet all the court and the German relations and the diplomatic corps. A huge *cercle* was held, where she must find something to say to each ambassador, and dance the polonaise with all the princes. This meant that she had to progress round the ballroom twenty-one times, making low bows all the way, without tripping over her long silver and pink train. Her style and grace were enough to win over the watching Prince and Princess of Prussia; she would obviously prove an asset at the innumerable formal occasions that made up court life. Her popularity with the German crowds proved that she was also a political asset. Her reception was far warmer than anyone could have expected, a spontaneous display of the true feelings of the nation.[13]

The personal triumph of the English princess disconcerted the reactionaries surrounding the Queen of Prussia. The country evidently approved of the new alliance. The eventual heir to the throne was happy in his choice of a bride. Even though she was forced to stay in the dank and primitive wing of the old *Schloss* until the palace at Babelsberg would be ready, the Princess Royal enjoyed her success and was unconscious of the snares being set for her. She surprised everyone by taking her ground so quickly and naturally.[14]

It could not last. Lady Churchill soon informed Queen Victoria that she could only write about small matters because all her letters to England were being opened.[15] Stieber and his state spies would not leave the foreign princess alone. She was warned, and apologized to her mother for sending her a letter by ordinary post. In future, she would always wait for the royal messenger who brought her mother's letters, or she would see that her messages home were put in the diplomatic bag. She could not be too careful in Prussia. Here the royal family was the subject of perpetual stories and criticisms. There was no respect for the princes – and there could not be. This hurt the Princess Royal deeply; things had been so different in England.

All the princes had spies in their households who freely related everything that was said or done. The place was a hotbed of gossip. The Princess Royal tried to be guarded when speaking to her cousins and aunts and uncles by marriage. She would not open her lips on two topics – her husband and her parents-in-law. In this way and with God's help and her mother's advice, she hoped to keep out of scrapes.[16]

The Princess Royal may have become disillusioned with the intrigues and atmosphere of the Prussian Court, but she could not have been happier in her relationship with her husband. In these early days he devoted himself to her. She boasted of her happiness to her mother, who was both pleased and annoyed. Queen Victoria did not like her daughter appearing to compare her marriage with her mother's. Prince Albert was obviously so superior to Prince Frederick William; he should remain a Holy Grail to his daughter. In one way only was the Princess Royal better off than the Queen of England: her husband held the power in the marriage, while the Queen was in the 'dreadful position of sovereign and wife!'[17]

Soon nets began to close round the Princess Royal. The Prince of Prussia ordered his son to undergo intensive military training, which took him away from his young wife. Lady Churchill had to return home to Queen Victoria. She had come to settle the Princess in her new country, and had stayed longer only because the Princess caught a bad cold from the changes between the overheated rooms at court and the chill air outside. During her last week in Berlin, she drove with the Princess and her husband to the Babelsberg. It was a pretty little palace, beautifully situated above the river, but still not ready for them.

The waiting was sinister. The Princess's bedroom in the old *Schloss* was next door to the death chamber of her husband's grandfather. This room had been left untouched for decades as a mark of respect for King Frederick William III. The Princess had to pass through this ghostly, musty room every day to her dressing-room and boudoir. She thought it was haunted; when a wind blew the door open, it seemed to bring in the chill of death.

There were not even any bathrooms in the old *Schloss*, but this did not worry her husband, who had always washed in cold water in the military way. The windows were hardly ever opened and were shrouded with thick curtains; draughts blew up and down the gloomy corridors. The Princess wanted light and air and hot water. These requests seemed a dreadful change to the Prussian Court; they showed a lack of respect for royal traditions and the mad King was in no mood to agree to such alterations. But the Princess was unwilling to wait, and this was her first false move. Her English influences seemed an affront to Prussian dignity. Her young love of life was in conflict with the state cult of death.

The English influences remained strong. Her mother wrote to her almost daily, her father once a week. In turn, they insisted on a flood of letters home, spelling out the details of her life and thoughts. They reminded her constantly of her duty to her parents as well as to her adopted country. Although most of the correspondence concerned social and domestic matters, it still reflected their hopes that the young couple might guide Prussian policy towards the English model and the ideals of the Coburg relations. By maintaining their influence they were inducing the conflict of loyalties to which their daughter was inevitably exposed. When the correspondence touched on political matters, she had to decide how far she could reveal confidential information learned from her husband. If she withheld it, her parents might feel that she was not open with them.

The Princess Royal tried to remain English and become Prussian. Such discretion was foreign to her nature; she was candid and open and attached to what she had been. What her father said about her position was so right – she wrote back to him: if she were to lose sight of her English title and dignity, she would do herself and her husband much harm. She was aware that there were those who would be only too happy if they could forget who she was. Her influence depended on being the Princess Royal of England, not just another Prussian princess. If she forgot her origins, she would lose the means for doing good in

Prussia. 'I must take up my ground in this large family and then remain there. It must be completely neutral, if one can say so, and my extreme youth makes this only natural.'[18]

After her parents, the Princess Royal took only her mother-in-law into her confidence. Although the Princess of Prussia seemed liberal, and was very friendly with Queen Victoria, she wanted her son's wife to be her subordinate. She had done much to form her son's mind; she was not going to lose that influence to the Princess Royal. The two women were very different in their tastes. Princess Augusta loved expensive dresses and grand occasions, the formality and the glitter and the intrigue of court life. Her daughter-in-law hated the entire show, wishing only for privacy and close friends, honesty and plain talk. As yet, she was too young to assert herself, but she was soon disillusioned about the standards of her new society. 'I cannot tell you, dear Papa,' she wrote, 'since I am married, how scales have fallen from my eyes on so many subjects.'[19]

The Princess Royal knew her opinions mattered to her husband. She was able to influence his judgement, but he was not to be led by the nose as Queen Victoria had thought. He was nine years older than his wife, who was still emotionally inexperienced and dependent on him, even if she were educated beyond her years. He cared about his military duties and excelled as a commander of men. Trained in obedience to his mother and father, he expected the same obedience from his wife. Although he frequently asked Prince Albert for advice, he rarely followed it. He was ever a Prussian first, and an Englishman only because of his admiration for his wife and her mother. His politeness and tact in public made him seem malleable, but in private, he was often stubborn and always held his ground. On one thing he was determined: he would replace his father-in-law as the leading man in his wife's eyes.

Prince Albert could not let well alone. He sensed that his good advice made the Prince of Prussia evasive and his son-in-law reserved. A refugee or a suitor would listen, while a ruler or a husband would not. So Prince Albert decided to travel to Coburg at Easter and summon his eldest daughter to meet him there. He could show off his birthplace and recapture his dominance of her.

An attack of influenza made him postpone his visit. His daughter became pregnant and was forbidden to travel by her doctor. She was angry, but her husband supported Dr Wegner's decision. There was a quarrel between the young couple; its underlying cause was Prince Frederick William's suppressed jealousy of Prince Albert. But all was made well by the move to the Babelsberg Palace, which took place before Prince Albert's arrival in early June.

When the two fathers met, they were as spectres at the wedding feast: the Prince of Prussia was gaunt and sallow while the Prince Consort was pale and puffy and nervous. Neither of them looked as if he would make old bones. The Prince of Prussia revealed that he would soon assume the official title of Regent; Prince Albert tried to advise him on his future policy, but was put off. There were to be no private conferences, no interference from England. The Prince of Prussia had not forgotten his humiliating months of exile. He distrusted the Coburg Prince's influence over his son who would soon become the direct heir to the throne.

Prince Albert's fears proved groundless. He found the relationship between his daughter and her husband good, and assured Queen Victoria that it was all that could be desired. He rehearsed them, together and singly, on the 'Coburg' plan for Germany, and a constitutional monarchy for Prussia. He did not seem to notice that the Prince of Prussia had been cold to the Princess Royal, when – at her father's prompting – she requested that her husband be given more training in government and less in military manœuvres.

Convinced that he was right, Prince Albert could not see that his political influence on his daughter and son-in-law appeared meddlesome to the Prince of Prussia, and malign to Otto von Manteuffel's reactionary government. Prince Albert's agent in the Babelsberg household, Ernest von Stockmar, thought that there was an official plot to get rid of him. Certainly, the sudden visit of the Prince Consort had alarmed the powerful groups who suspected that English diplomacy stood too close to the Prussian crown.

Their fears were increased by Queen Victoria's decision to come to Prussia herself in August. She wanted to reassure herself about her daughter's pregnancy and check up on her way of life. Although the Queen insisted that it was a private visit rather than a state occasion, she brought with her the Prince Consort and three of the most powerful men in England, Lord Clarendon, Lord Granville and Lord Malmesbury, the new Foreign Secretary.

This diplomatic mission was prompted by the unsettling policy of the French Emperor. He had insisted on entertaining the Queen and the

Prince Consort at Cherbourg before they went to Prussia. There, he showed off huge harbour fortifications and menacing new ironclads. The display was meant to deter, a warning to the English not to intervene in Napoleon III's plans for Italy. The sight made the Prince Consort's blood boil, and forced the Queen to write to Lord Derby, insisting that he take immediate action to prepare the British Navy.

These were the war clouds massing behind the Queen's visit to her daughter. She had to undergo the same interminable railway journey from Antwerp to Potsdam, but her daughter was waiting to greet her at the Wildpark station, a nosegay in her hand. They fell into each other's arms. 'So much to say, and to tell, and to ask,' the Queen wrote, 'yet so unaltered, looking well – quite the old Vicky still.'

The Queen liked the Babelsberg, calling it a Gothic *bijou*. It was overcrowded with furniture and creepers, and had irregular towers like Osborne. Its intimate atmosphere drew her very close to her daughter. She personally settled the pregnant girl on her day sofa and fed her with broth and good advice about the expected child.

The Princess Royal was open with her mother. She broke through the barriers between them, and was not ashamed to talk about anything and everything. The Queen was touched, and agonized about not being able to come back for the birth because she had to be in London for the opening of Parliament. Her daughter seemed so sensible about her pregnancy, and felt so comfortable with her that they were now like sisters. The only fly in the ointment was that Fritz had to be away so much; he had foolishly Prussian ideas of his military duties.

The Queen marvelled at this new ease with her daughter, whose marriage and delicate position in Prussia had given her a precocious maturity, even if she were still wilful and lost control at times. Much as she disliked and felt ensnared by her present state, the Princess Royal was sure that a child would be a great comfort to her. She hoped to educate the child differently from the previous princes and princesses of Prussia.[20] If she could not change her husband's country through him, she wanted to do it through their son.

Prince Albert was not taken with the Babelsberg. He found it too small, and cluttered with Princess Augusta's hothouse taste. His daughter drove him to see Frederick the Great's Neue Palais in Potsdam, an enormous pillared block, now neglected and crumbling, a mere rest-house for court pensioners. He suggested that she and her husband ask to move into it and decorate it in their own way. Their request was granted, and the Princess Royal was given a home, which would make court life in Prussia more tolerable.

Prince Albert was pleased that his daughter was breaking out of the limited and back-biting court circle. She was discovering liberal intellectual friends who could continue her education. Through two of her husband's old tutors, Professor Schellbach and Ernest Curtius, she met the historians Ranke and Droysen, the classical scholar Brandis and the philosopher Werder. For the first time in Prussia, a royal princess chose to surround herself with intellectuals; if it should cause scandal, at least she was learning from such good company.

Although the royal visit was primarily a private one, ceremony could not be kept at bay. The Prince of Prussia and his wife arranged formal dinners, military reviews and conducted tours of the royal palaces and tombs. The reactionaries who surrounded the Queen of Prussia did not hide their displeasure at this third invasion by English royalty within the year. Manteuffel, himself, was most unpleasant, cross and disagreeable to Queen Victoria. His anger had been excited by the Queen of England's unwise decision to invite her aged adviser, Christian von Stockmar, to the Babelsberg. The Baron was the bugbear of the Prussian conservatives, the plotter for a liberal and constitutional Germany. His presence in Potsdam made Queen Victoria's visit look even more like a conspiracy to influence state policy.

Old Stockmar caused less trouble between the visitors and their hosts than between mother and daughter. He thought that Queen Victoria was still trying to dominate her married child and make her feel inadequate. He complained to Lord Clarendon that the Princess Royal was becoming seriously ill because of her mother's incessant demands and rebukes. When Queen Victoria heard of his interference, she broke into a towering rage.[21] She thought she was doing the right thing in showing her love and concern for a daughter who, for diplomatic reasons, had been allowed to marry too young.

Stockmar, however, stuck to his guns, stressing the political consequences of such excessive mother love. In his opinion, the Prussian marriage was being wrongly treated by the Prince Consort and Queen Victoria and by England. They were proceeding much too actively, from over there. They were too much inclined to seek to arrange Prussian affairs in accordance with their own opinions and feelings. They were meddling far too much in trivialities. He advised rather more consideration, moderation, calm and passivity.[22]

He was absolutely right about the feelings of the Prussian Court. The Prince of Prussia became Regent in October, and King in all but name. This made his son the direct heir to the throne. His son's wife might shortly be crowned beside her husband. She had now to put her second country before her homeland, to obey Prussian customs and traditions, and not accept contradictory advice from her parents.

The new Regent began by dismissing Manteuffel's government and installing a Liberal Government under Prince Karl Anton of Hohenzollern-Sigmaringen. The electorate returned a strong Liberal majority to the Prussian Lower House. Without pressure from England, the new regime in Prussia seemed to be reforming from within. It did not need the Prince Consort to send his congratulations a hundred times over. The Prince of Hohenzollern-Sigmaringen was friendly with Queen Victoria and praised the Princess Royal, saying that she saw through everything and understood things better than many people in Berlin. She was kind to those crushed by the court and protected them.[23] She seemed, he thought, to attract outcasts and dissidents.

Even more significantly, the Regent dismissed Stieber, Berlin's Chief of Police. He had suffered from the spymaster's attentions during his banishment to Coblenz, when he had prematurely backed the alliance with England. Now he could retaliate by removing Stieber from office and having him put on trial for his many secret crimes. While indictments were being prepared, Stieber occupied himself by advising the Tsar's government in the organization of a secret service. His talents were appreciated abroad, if not at home, but he was devious enough to pass information back to Manteuffel and the reactionaries, in case they should return to power. Old spies never go away, they simply wait for a change.

Yet another visit from the English Court strengthened the Regent's resolve to form a new alliance against the French; the Prince of Wales came to see the Princess Royal. Queen Victoria hoped that exposure to the social world of the Prussian Court would improve his manners. His three weeks in Potsdam were a great success. He impressed every one with his charm and ability to dance; as his father admitted, he had remarkable social talent. He renewed his close relationship with his elder sister, but she could not make him join in her intellectual activities; he preferred to conceal his powers of thought. 'Usually his intellect is of no more use,' his father wrote, 'than a pistol packed at the bottom of a trunk if one were attacked in the robber-infested Apennines.'[24] His brother-in-law, however, became friendly with him, recognizing the considerable intelligence and tact which underlay the surface laziness and boisterousness.

The Regent took particular care to invest the Prince of Wales with the Order of the Black Eagle and to make him an honorary colonel in the Prussian Guards. In Prussia, the awards of decorations and rank were more than symbols, they were a form of diplomacy – in this case against Napoleon III's threats of war. When the Prince of Wales returned to England, he brought with him not only better manners, but reports of Prussian fears of attack by France. Even the Prince Consort was impressed and said of his son, 'The best school for him is the external stress of life.'[25]

This was certainly the best school for the Princess Royal. Although six months' pregnant, she appeared on horseback at the Prussian Army's deterrent manœuvres near the Rhine in November. Her mother might hope that her husband would be shocked at her sufferings, 'for those very selfish men would not bear for a minute what we poor slaves have to endure'.[26] But the Princess concealed her condition, and was a success with the soldiers, who were already devoted to her husband because of his concern for their welfare.

Her husband's absence with his regiment made her heart grow passionate. She found life in the castle intolerable without him. She missed him even more than she missed her father, so used had she become to his being near. She began to write him love-letters, declaring that they were one; the coming of the infant would bind them together. Once the child was born, Frederick William would displace her father as the natural source of love and authority.

With the New Year, Queen Victoria became very worried about her daughter's imminent confinement. She did not trust German medical training, so the royal physician, Sir James Clark, was sent to Potsdam with her own midwife, Mrs Innocent. When the Princess Royal began her labour a week sooner than expected, Dr Wegner diagnosed a breech birth. Clark slowly administered two-thirds of a bottle of chloroform. The labour lasted for four hours until half-past three in the morning, and she suffered greatly. 'In truth I could not go through such another,' Clark wrote to Queen Victoria. 'My close relation to the Princess from her birth, and my affection for her made it more like the case of my own child.'[27]

Two other Berlin doctors had been called in to help in the difficult birth. One of them, Professor Edouard Martin, shed tears to see the Princess's pain. As the more experienced of them, he assisted the birth manually. This was a dangerous thing to do. Long ago, old Stockmar had refused to help at the labour of the English Princess Charlotte, the heir to the throne, in case she died during her difficult childbirth. He had known that the blame for her death would be laid on him as the only foreign doctor present. When Wegner handed over responsibility to Martin and Clark, he was already despairing of the Princess's life, let alone a live birth. Martin's skilled hands brought out a boy, who took a long time to shake into life. He had saved both mother and child, but he and Clark would be blamed for wrenching the baby's left arm and neck during the birth. Wegner's incompetence would be ignored because he was a Prussian. The saviours, Martin and Clark, would be accused of ignorance and carelessness and of harming the child. They were foreigners.

Throughout the long labour, Prince Frederick William rarely left his post by the Princess's side. The Countesses Perponcher and Blücher and Mrs Innocent were always busy in the room; the Princess was surrounded by care and devotion. The birth of a son was the best thing she could have done for her husband and for herself. There was general rejoicing, a state of perfect excitement. Queen Victoria observed that the Son was an immense event for Prussia and would cause ecstasy. She and the Prince Consort had become grandparents at the age of thirty-nine.[28]

The birth of the boy lessened the Queen's obsessive efforts to run her daughter's life from England. It was as if the Princess Royal, by becoming a mother, could now really begin to take the place of a younger sister, as in the days of the Queen's visit to the Babelsberg. The Queen could now concentrate her attentions on her unmarried daughters at home, which was a blessing, and was politicially wise.

She had already made a New Year's resolution to let her eldest daughter go her own way. 'Have I improved as much as I ought?' she had asked herself in her journal. 'I fear not ... A married daughter! And here – self is still far too prominent! I must crush it – must try and bear patiently the utter change of position between Parents and a married daughter! Several times all has been right – but there have been relapses when I was wrong, and I must and shall struggle against these feelings and many strange prejudices and odd sensations I have.'[29]

The Queen did, however, still warn her daughter against baby-worship and spending too much time in the nursery. She herself had never

Queen Victoria, Prince Albert and their children, (*left to right*) Prince Alfred, Prince Edward, Princess Alice, Princess Helena and the Princess Royal. Winterhalter, 1846

The Princess Royal at two years old. Winterhalter, 1842.

Princess Victoria in Turkish costume. Ross, 1850.

The opening of the Great Exhibition in 1851. Roberts.

The Princess Royal and Prince Arthur as Summer in 'Tableaux of the Seasons', Windsor Castle, February 1854.

The Prince of Prussia, later
the German Emperor
William I. After von
Angeli.

Prince Frederick William
of Prussia, September 1855.

(*Left to right*) The Princess Royal, Princess Alice, Queen Victoria and the Prince of Wales at Windsor Castle, February 1857.

The Princess Royal (*right*) with her parents on her wedding day, 25 January 1858. Queen Victoria's image is blurred because she was trembling.

Prince and Princess Frederick William of Prussia at Windsor on 29 January 1858.

The Neue Palais, Potsdam, the home of Prince and Princess Frederick William.

Princess Frederick William (*left*) and Princess Alexandrine of Prussia in Berlin, 1859.

The Crown Princess by
Graefle, 1863.

Crown Prince Frederick by
Graefle, 1863.

liked babies much and had often found the company of her children tedious. The Princess Royal, her mother knew, doted on babies; indeed, she had to be stopped by her mother-in-law from breast-feeding her infant. This was not done by a Prussian princess, nor by the Queen of England. So a wet-nurse had to be found, whose milk immediately irritated the baby's bowels.

By Prussian custom, the christening of the child had to take place several weeks after its birth. The royal family filled the private chapel of the Crown Prince's palace. The gold vessels for the baptism were covered by a silver-brocade cloth on which the emblem of the Black Eagle was embossed. Above the altar hung a jewelled, purple canopy embroidered with the golden crowns of Prussia. The infant was swathed in lace to hide his deformed arm. At the ceremony, he was christened Frederick William Victor Albert. Fascinated by the Regent's decorations and Orders, he hardly cried, while the proud grandfather held him in his arms for the holy rite.

Most of the forty sponsors were there, but not Queen Victoria or the Prince Consort. They had hoped to come, but public duties kept them in England. The British Envoy's wife wrote to the Queen, giving details of the grand occasion, but adding that the Princess Royal was still very tired and weak, and in need of great care. Even the joy at christening another heir to the throne could not dispel the ominous gloom in Berlin. It was as if a great black thick cloud were hanging which might burst at any moment.[30]

The day after the baptism, the Regent appointed Otto von Bismarck as the Prussian Ambassador to St Petersburg. There Bismarck would get to know of the advantages of the Russian alliance and stay clear of the Regent's experiments in liberalism. As for the royal infant, there would be time to win him from the influence of his mother, *die Engländerin*.

So the year of 1859 began with a royal birth and a foreboding of war in Europe. If the succession to the Prussian throne were more secure, the future of the country was more at risk. The Princess Royal had grown closer to her husband, and had reached a new understanding of her mother. She was, as she wrote to Queen Victoria, so happy when she looked at her son, and remembered that he was not a girl and could not suffer what she had suffered.

'I think if I had a daughter I could never bear the thought of her having to suffer so much! How much I can understand what a poor Mother must feel when her daughter is going to be married; it must be a near torture to know all that she will have to go through, and not to be able to go with her and help her and be with her. It must be really a very hard trial; I can understand so well what you must have felt at my marriage now, but I could not then.'[31]

CHAPTER THREE

Divided Loyalty

'YOU AND YOUR child must look like two babies together,' Queen Victoria wrote to her daughter, 'as you have such a child's face still.'[1] The Princess Royal doted on her son, and took three months to recover from his birth. When she was able to return to court circles, she found her father turning to her for Intelligence during an international crisis. The King of Sardinia and his minister Cavour were intriguing with Emperor Napoleon III to drive the Austrians out of northern Italy. Prussia was undecided whether to join Austria against the hated French or to stand off, like England, and try to profit from the affair.

In a way, Austria was the obstacle to a united Germany as well as to a united Italy, and the French goal of making a new nation by expelling Austria was an example to Prussia in the future. Until the outbreak of war, the Prince Consort was like a terrier of personal diplomacy. At times he seemed to be trying to keep the peace almost single-handed from England. Queen Victoria complained that he worked too hard and wore himself out by all he did. His attempts to preserve the peace tried his nerves, while the endless contradictory telegrams arriving every hour raised and dashed his hopes continually.[2]

Some of the disturbing news was coming from the Princess Royal. Although her letters home dealt mainly with her baby son and household arrangements, she was an accurate mirror of Prussian attitudes, reflecting them almost artlessly. She was also beginning to engage in her own sort of diplomacy, telling her mother that the Prussian situation was a very critical one. If Prussia stayed neutral and the Austrians won a war, it would damage the reputation of the country and its army. If Austria

49

lost, the French could fall on Prussia alone. The Princess Royal suggested that an alliance be formed between Prussia and England. It would help the security of both nations, deter the French and stop Berlin from continually sniping at London for doing nothing to curb French ambitions.[3]

Such minor royal diplomacy could not deter Napoleon III from taking the field in Italy. The Princess Royal regarded the outbreak of war as a personal attack on her happiness; foreseeing the moment when her husband would be called to join his regiment. She complained to her mother that it was all very fine for the men to talk of defending their country, of a soldier's life being the only one for a man, and of wanting death on the field of battle. Yet they did not think of their poor unhappy wives, taken from their homes and left behind alone.[4]

The fact that her husband was privy to the plans of the Prussian general staff placed the Princess in an delicate situation. She had been accustomed to telling her father and mother everything she thought was important. Her husband sometimes told her of the movements of the Prussian forces. There was no reason that he should conceal such information from his wife, and she was still too young and inexperienced to know when she should be silent. Her errors of judgement were still the faults of youth.

French victories in Italy scared the Prussian Court. It was feared that Napoleon III might destroy Austria and turn his armies on Prussia as his predecessor had done. Partial mobilization was ordered; the Princess Royal informed her parents immediately. 'There is general consternation here!' she wrote to Queen Victoria on 16 June 1859. 'All is preparing for war.' The mobilization of six army corps had been ordered, she wrote – and her husband had been given command of a Guards division. She herself was swept away by war fever. She hoped that the Prussian forces would soon cross the Rhine and make their country the leader of Germany by force of arms. For once, she wished she were a man, and that her son was a man, so that they might fight the French. She could not help feeling savage.[5]

Such bloody sentiments provoked her mother's worst rebuke. Her daughter was obviously suffering from enthusiasm, and the Queen feared that they would diverge more and more. To feel that her daughter's interests were so different was a sad trial.[6] Already the Queen could see that her married daughter would have to choose to follow her husband's sentiments in time of war. In a conflict of interest, Prussia must come before England. A daughter had been lost, no influence gained.

The Princess Royal guilelessly continued to reveal military plans. Two days after having written to her mother, she was writing to her father: she supposed he would have heard of all that was happening in Berlin; in case he had not, she told him, eight army corps were not being called to the colours, military organization had fallen apart, full mobilization was proving impossible, although that was what was needed. 'Please keep this to yourself, dearest Papa,' the Princess added uneasily, 'because I know this only from Fritz.'[7]

Her father's reply showed that his daughter was sending him better Intelligence than was the Foreign Office in London. He had known nothing of the partial mobilization. This confession startled his daughter. She wrote back that she found it strange he had not heard of the mobilization sooner. She was becoming more discreet – or else the Prussian Government was beginning to withold delicate information from her husband, and so from her and her parents. 'We know as little as you do,' she wrote on 2 July, 'and I think that they have no intention of keeping anything from you.'[8]

The Prussian Government almost certainly did have that intention. Together with his advisers, the Regent was suspicious of England's neutrality. They knew of the regular secret communications carried by royal messengers between Prince Frederick William's household and Windsor. Unfortunately, the Prince Consort now chose to intervene, using the information sent by his daughter and suggesting its source. He wrote directly to the Regent in Berlin, counselling against military preparedness in face of the French.

The Regent did not mention nor show this letter to his son, and this omission provoked the Princess Royal into a disingenuous comment on the relationship between her husband and his father, who very rarely showed his son anything of importance. His daughter-in-law was convinced that this stemmed from nothing but forgetfulness. She would question the Regent about a great many things, and he would tell her and her husband about everything – but, then, they could not always be asking.

She continued to reveal matters which might help her father keep the peace. She wrote home about the Austrian Empress coming to Berlin with the Prince of Windisch-Grätz, who had said, 'If we did not help them now, they would never forgive us – and not help us if they made peace now and we were attacked.' Prussia was still trying to prepare against a French assault. Two army corps had been moved towards the

Rhine, while another corps was being kept back to defend Berlin. The rest of the reserves were still disorganized.[9] The Prussians were simply not ready to fight. Their army badly needed reform.

The military information which the Princess Royal was sending back to her father was secret, but she had been brought up to consider her father as a keeper of international peace, and he could not help to prevent conflict between other nations without accurate Intelligence. As his daughter, she would have wished to keep him informed, while trying to make England side with Prussia in the probable war against France. As it was, she was under heavy pressure in Berlin because of the British Government's policy of strict neutrality. Her husband was also under attack because of her: 'Fritz says his peace of mind is gone.'[10]

News of the sudden armistice between France and Austria after the Battle of Solferino came as a thunderbolt in Berlin. Prussia was now isolated and vulnerable. It had lost credit in Germany and was exposed to France. Every one was on the alert. 'War is always thought of and talked of,' the Princess Royal reported. 'God avert this calamity from us, I say.'[11]

The calamity was averted because the French chose to digest their gains in Savoy and Nice and to defer their attack. The international crisis had proved that the Princess Royal's loyalty to her father had endured despite her marriage; she could reconcile her duty as a daughter with her devotion to her husband. She hoped to combine the conflicting policies of her two countries through the two men she most loved. She was being disloyal only to the Regent's anti-English advisers, not to the policy which her father and her husband desired for Prussia and Germany. It was not she who was at fault, but the ministers; the future, alone, could judge her.

The Prince Consort aimed to influence European politics through his royal relations, and English diplomacy through his wife's right to advise on messages sent to foreign governments. Increasingly, he taught Queen Victoria to rewrite the dispatches and letters destined for other great powers. Her blue pencil became the terror of, and caused delay in dozens of British administrative departments. On the subject of Germany, the Queen and the Prince Consort knew far more, and had far more influential contacts, than their foreign secretaries, who came and went with the fall of governments. The most recent, Lord John Russell, was not in favour of an alliance with Prussia against France, but he had to anticipate a threat from the Emperor Napoleon. He was thankful that the Prince

Consort showed him his private correspondence with the Prince of Prussia. No prime minister, be he as independent as Lord Palmerston, could ignore the power of the royal influence across Europe. Often enough, a private letter from Queen Victoria to a royal cousin was the last trump; playing it would prevent the outbreak of a war.

In March 1860, Russell asked the Prince Consort for a paper on the state of Germany, and for advice on future policy there. Prince Albert's influence was at its height. In his reply, he used information culled from his daughter in Berlin. The Regent of Prussia was very low and irritable; there were grave difficulties concerning increased taxation to pay for the army's reform, which recent events had shown to be necessary. In general, the Prince Consort declared, the Italian and the German questions had remained the same since the time of Charlemagne. Through the old Holy Roman Empire, the Habsburgs of Austria had held possessions in both Germany and Italy, thus preventing the unification of either nation.

The German situation was further complicated because so many princes, such as the Elector of Hanover, had become rulers of England, Denmark, Belgium or Poland. German politics had become international politics; England, for instance, was still interested in Hanover, not to mention Saxe-Coburg. Many foreign countries felt the right to interfere in German affairs. Austria's recent defeat had left her severely weakened. If Prussia adopted a policy like that of the Kingdom of Sardinia, it could unite Germany. The Prussian royal family, however, was too timid to play so bold a game, too honourable to play so false a one.[12]

Prince Albert's brilliant diagnosis ignored the one factor which could unite Germany. If the Prussian royal family could not be ruthless enough, its Minister President could. Already, the Prince of Hohenzollern-Sigmaringen's Liberal Government had proved weak and indecisive. As a replacement, one man was being mentioned to the Regent – the present Ambassador to St Petersburg. Otto von Bismarck had already been noted by British diplomats as a man of action, who wanted a war against Austria in order to unite Germany. 'You have no notion how we hate them,' he told one British Ambassador. The Prussian Army looked on the Austrians as enemies.[13] Bismarck foresaw a major war, with England standing at the sidelines. Apart from the forces in India, the British Army was too small to intervene, given the masses of men that Bismarck's war would deploy. The face of Europe could be changed without the British Navy being able to do much about it.[14]

The Regent hesitated about sending for Bismarck, even though the state of the army was driving him into depression and anger. His policies were contradictory. At times, he listened to the army leaders, who wanted a return to the military State, which would mean an alliance with Russia against France, and the stifling of reform. At other times, he seemed to favour liberal changes, and the English alliance championed by his wife and daughter-in-law. He was so sick of power that he often talked of abdicating in favour of his son, who was becoming daily more proud of being the commander of a regiment of Prussian Guards. Hopes were running high in the rococo Neue Palais, where the Princess Royal and her husband were now installed.

The prospect of coming to the throne may have made the Neue Palais seem more attractive to the Princess Royal. This building of Frederick the Great's reminded Queen Victoria of Hampton Court. Its grandeur was opposed to everything that the Princess had assimilated from her mother. Most of its two hundred rooms were enormous. At first, only a few were used, but as the court pensioners died one by one, the Princess took over more and more until the whole palace was hers. As a reminder of childhood intimacy, one small room was decorated in the style of the Blue Closet at Windsor.

The work of renewal was endless and daunting; the tapestries were rotting, the carpets eaten by mice, the chimneys full of bats. The silvered furniture was black with age, the painted ceilings covered with grime. As usual, there were no bathrooms, only an outside pump for water. Yet the fluted columns and carved mantles, the classical proportions and the sense of space and light were worth all the efforts of restoration. After all, The Three Graces supported the Crown above the main entrance. With the Princess Royal in residence, they might return inside the palace.

There were also overgrown gardens which could be rescued from neglect; nurture would recreate the careful nature beloved by Victorian ladies. Short of an entire state to remodel, the Neue Palais would do. This, and the business of having more children, would pass the time while her husband was about his military duties.

Her second pregnancy did not prevent her from visiting England with her husband, but they had to leave the baby behind, because he was too young. Their visit was all nostalgia and sentiment, as the Princess Royal visited the places of her childhood. Prince Albert was happy to be able to advise his daughter and son-in-law in privacy; by now, even royal messengers and the diplomatic bag were not entirely secure. One of his letters to the Regent of Prussia had fallen into the hands of Napoleon III. His reaction was masterly: 'If people have spies to open and read letters,' he said, 'they must expect to see what they may not like.'[15]

He and Queen Victoria agreed to pay a return visit to Coburg to see their grandson. In the meantime, the Princess Royal had an easy labour to give birth to her first daughter, Victoria Augusta Charlotte. It turned her even more from politics towards her home and her nursery, which was supervised by Mrs Hobbs, a traditional English nanny. Her household did not run smoothly, however; royal households rarely did. The opportunities for intrigue and petty theft were too princely. The English princess was surrounded by the jealousies and judgements of German ladies. She disliked her husband's Chamberlain, and was suspicious of his military friends and advisers. They encouraged in him the warlike obstinacy that had led to their first quarrel. Although her husband was being allowed to attend Councils of State, he was not allowed to comment. If he wanted to give orders, he could do so on the parade-ground or at home. A war seemed his only way to distinguish himself.

Despite the disapproval of *The Times*, Queen Victoria and the Prince Consort visited Coburg in September. There was a diplomatic reason behind their trip: the monarchs of Prussia, Austria and Russia were to meet. It was possible that they would try to form a new Holy Alliance against nationalism and the French. Britain might be left without influence in Europe. So Lord John Russell accompanied the royal party in the usual mixture of royal family visits and foreign relations. The Foreign Secretary even went on a wild boar hunt with Prince Frederick William and the Prince Consort, who had survived a bad carriage accident. The Prince Consort bagged at least three boars and his guests one each; the wounded beasts were finished off with spears.

Queen Victoria was enchanted by the sight of her first grandson. He was always to keep a special place in her heart. He came walking up to his grandmother holding his nurse's hand, 'in a little white dress with black bows, and was so good. He is a fine, fat child, with a beautiful white soft skin, very fine shoulders and limbs, and a very dear face ... He has Fritz's eyes and Vicky's mouth, and very fair curly hair. We felt so happy to see him at last.'[16] In her description, Queen Victoria chose to ignore the damage done to the child's neck and left arm. Her daughter confessed to feeling guilty about tripping over a chair during her pregnancy and falling heavily on her back, perhaps damaging the infant within her. Her mother reassured her, saying that the little boy would grow out of it or respond to treatment.

More important than the trip to Coburg was the royal rendezvous at Coblenz. There the Prince Regent and the Princess of Prussia went out of their way to welcome Queen Victoria and the Prince Consort. Their meeting formed the high-water mark of Anglo-Prussian friendship and of the 'Coburg' plan. Never again would the long-term policy behind the Princess Royal's marriage appear so convincing. Fear of a Russo-French entente had thrown the two Protestant powers together at a time when the Regent was still experimenting with a liberal government at home. The royal families shared their pleasure in their grandchildren and their heirs; diplomacy and kinship walked hand in hand.

The Regent was so swayed towards the English alliance that he chose to stalemate the meeting with the Austrian and Russian Emperors at Warsaw; more earth was piled on the grave of the Holy Alliance. Prussia could not support Austria when they were rivals in Germany, while Russia always feared an Austrian attack in the Balkans supported by Turkey and Britain. For the time being, the Regent of Prussia preferred to trust in the known commitment of the British royal family. This was soon strengthened by the engagement of Queen Victoria's second daughter Alice to Prince Louis of Hesse. Once more, the British Crown seemed to be the treasure-house of German princes; its heartland lay across the Rhine.

Prince Frederick William was heir to the throne and was behaving as heirs to the throne normally behave. Feeling that the father was not ruling so well as could the son, he set up two groups of advisers, in opposition to the reactionary court group which increasingly found favour with his father.

One group consisted of five military men who in time would rise to become generals: Mischke, Winterfeldt, Blumenthal, Stosch and Winterfeld. The first two had great loyalty to the Prince and a loathing of any one with 'a court bend in his back'. Blumenthal was a clever strategist who rose to be Chief of Staff, while Stosch became chief of the Admiralty for a decade. He was an intimate enemy of Bismarck, who distrusted his influence with the Crown Princess and suspected him of wanting to become Chief Minister.[17] Winterfeld was to prove the Judas among them.

The other group of liberals and counsellors was led by Prince Frederick William's brother-in-law, Grand Duke Frederick of Baden. His chief minister and adviser was Baron Roggenbach, the patron of Strasbourg University. A great raconteur, he was trusted by the Empress Augusta, and was a friend of Queen Victoria and the Crown Princess. The lawyer, Heinrich von Friedberg, was an intimate of the household, together with Professor Heinrich Geffcken, who had been a fellow-student of Prince Frederick William's, and who was now Professor of Political Science at Strasbourg University. Baron George von Bunsen, the historian and politician Max Duncker, and Count Usedom completed the group. On the fringes were Baron Walter von Loë and the novelist and poet, Gustav Freytag, whose words were bolder than his character.

A fat Englishman, who was to become Bismarck's *bête noire*, was their courier. Robert Morier was an elephantine, wily, brilliant and self-important man, who understood German affairs as thoroughly as the Prince Consort. When serving as a paid attaché at Berlin, his reports were among the few valued by Prince Albert. He ingratiated himself with the Princess Royal and helped her in her endeavours to influence Prussian policy through her husband's advisers.

From the outside, these military and civilian consultants to the heir to the throne looked like an opposition group, and could be represented as a conspiracy by spymasters such as Stieber. Fortunately, he had offended the Prince Regent by spying on him during his own period of opposition to the King, his brother. When Stieber had found himself on trial for misusing his police powers, Morier had written a long and foreboding memorandum on the trial. Stieber's organization and methods had not come to an end with their master's accusal. The Prince Regent's new Government had announced that it would not break violently with the past, but would improve on the previous system. Unless there were to be a house-cleaning, the past bureaucracy would prove too strong for the present Government. The new wine would not burst the old bottles, but the old bottles would infallibly taint the new wine.

The Minister of Justice, the President of Police and his hated underlings had been kept on, more from weakness than from generosity. Stieber had been merely the scapegoat for the sins of the Prussian police state, the press remained gagged, individual liberties uncertain, and the doings of the political police shrouded in mystery. Even at Stieber's trial, a decent veil had been drawn over the illegal acts of Manteuffel's government, including the theft of secret papers from the King's private secretary. Stieber himself was only accused of a minor offence, though Morier called him 'the life and soul' of the police spy system.[18]

Stieber had pleaded that all the illegal acts committed by him were on the orders of ministers still in the Cabinet; he had had royal authority for his work. If he fell, many powerful people would fall with him. His threat of further revelations had secured his acquittal, for to convict him would be to convict Prussian aristocrats, perhaps even point a finger too near the person of the mad and dying King.

Although Stieber was temporarily out to grass, and was busy advising the Tsar, his men were still working for the reactionary circles around the Prince Regent who was waiting to become King. The Regent, as Lord Clarendon discovered later, was surrounded by reactionary relations and advisers and enmeshed by the villainous police.[19] With or without Stieber, nothing had changed overmuch in the police state of Prussia. Daily the Regent had more poison poured into his ear than ever had Hamlet's father. As the Princess Royal reported, spies and secret informers inflamed his fears of another Berlin revolution like that of 1848, and pushed him into the hands of the reactionaries. He thought that he had the best police in the world and that he was better informed than his ministers. And so he became suspicious, irritable and nervous; convinced that the truth was to be heard only from those who played upon his fears.[20]

After 1861, nothing would be the same again. It had been a year of significant deaths. The first was that of the King of Prussia, who died in Potsdam on New Year's Day. His passing brought out the excessive melancholia of Prussian royal obsequies. The Princess Royal and her husband were wakened in the middle of the night to witness his death throes. The Queen of Prussia sat at the bedside supporting his head, while wiping the sweat from his forehead. The Princess Royal described the scene to her mother:

'You might have heard a pin drop – no sound was heard, but the crackling of the fire and the death rattle – that dreadful sound which goes to one's heart and which tells plainly that life is ebbing. This rattling in the throat lasted about an hour longer and then the King lay motionless. The Doctors bent their heads low to hear whether he still breathed and we stood, not even daring to sit down, watching the death struggle, every now and then the King breathed very fast and loud, but never unclosed his eyes – he was very red in the face, and the cold perspiration

pouring from his forehead. I never spent such an awful time, and to see
the poor Queen sitting there quite rent my heart – 3, 4, 5, 6, 7 struck and
we were still standing there – one member of the Royal Family came in
after the other and remained motionless in the room, sobs only breaking
the stillness. Oh it is dreadful to see a person die!'[21]

When morning came, all the watchers went to the next room. The
Princess Royal fell asleep on a sofa while the others walked up and
down. She was sent home by her husband, only to be called again at one
o'clock in the morning; the King had died at last. She had to pay homage
to the new King and Queen before visiting the deathbed. To her, the
dead man seemed to be sleeping; she expected to see him move or breathe
at any moment. She kissed both his hands for the last time; they were
quite cold by then. At the formal filing past the corpse, the dead King's
sister, the Grand Duchess of Mecklenburg-Schwerin, pushed the Princess
Royal close up to the pillow, so that her cheek almost touched the face
of the dead man. It made her shudder.[22]

At the lying in state, the obsessive cult of the dead continued. The
body was laid out in the black-draped room where Frederick the Great
had died. The coffin, covered by a mantle of violet velvet and ermine,
was set in a niche beneath the same canopy that had overshadowed the
christening of the Princess Royal's children. Born to inherit; born to die.
The King was dead; long live his heirs. The embroidered Crowns of
Prussia topped all.

The funeral was held in a freezing Berlin, where the temperature had
fallen to seventeen degrees below zero. By contrast, the royal guests and
diplomats found the atmosphere inside the palace like that of a Turkish
bath. The crown, orb and sceptre were carried into the royal chapel; the
coffin was borne on the shoulders of eight generals; a Field Marshal,
carrying the royal standard, brought up the rear. The new King and the
Queen Dowager sat at the foot of the coffin, the Prussian princes and
foreign mourners stood nearby. The service was chanted, the Address
was short.[23] The King, already sixty-four years old, seemed frail and
ready to follow his brother.

The ceremonies continued beyond the grave. Every evening, there was
a reception for all the German princes who had gathered to pay their
respects and meet one another. To the Princess Royal, a room full of
them was humiliating, but funny, rather like the collection of Scottish
earls she had met with her mother four years before. Death in the family
had mobilized a vast assembly of pomp, power and tedium. 'Half Europe

was together,' the Princess informed her father, 'and I had the pleasure of doing the honours all alone for all these Princes every evening here!' She found that the Prince of Bavaria looked like a telegraphist; another prince was an Ostrogoth.[24]

Prince Frederick William was now the Crown Prince and his wife Victoria the Crown Princess of Prussia, a title superior even to Princess Royal of England. She might now hope to sit beside her husband on a throne; her brothers would always keep her from that in her homeland. His new position involved the Crown Prince increasingly in state affairs. He was rarely in the Neue Palais and, in fact, now slept at the other end of the vast building – so far away from his wife that she complained she might just as well not be married at all. Yet she was delighted at his new responsibilities and their effect on his character. As she told her mother, he was so good and courageous, and so useful to the ministers and the Queen that it made up for her hardly ever seeing him.[25]

A gift from England pleased the new King; Queen Victoria sent him the Order of the Garter. This honour mattered to a military monarch who prized decorations and orders and court ceremonial as the emblems of a rightly ordered country. He resented, however, the flood of good advice from the Prince Consort, who treated him still as a refugee from Berlin rather than a ruler there. He put the letters from the Crown Princess's father on the fire, and scolded her when she approached him on some liberal errand at Prince Albert's or Queen Augusta's dictate. She was always burning her fingers for the Queen of Prussia, who used her as a cat's-paw to tell the King things she did not wish to tell him herself. Unfortunately, Queen Augusta usually spoilt the whole thing by throwing out hints in advance, so the King was always interrupting his daughter-in-law to say: 'I am sure Mama told you that.'[26]

The friction between the King and Queen was exacerbated by the blocking of the badly-needed reform of the army by the liberal majority in the Prussian Lower House. The King saw this refusal to increase his country's military strength as a deliberate plot against the nation's security. He began to listen more and more to the reactionaries. A swing to the right seemed inevitable as early as March 1861. 'Heaven knows what is to become of us, if the Old Régime is to begin again,' the Crown Princess told her father by letter. She would have liked to pour out her heart and her fears of a repressive future, but that would have to wait until they met again.[27]

The meeting was to be unexpectedly soon. There was a second significant death that year on 11 March, when Queen Victoria's mother, the Duchess of Kent, died of erysipelas. Although her childhood had been unhappy, Queen Victoria collapsed. Her own motherhood was sacred to her, so her mother's death seemed the violation of a holy state, an intimation of her own mortality. 'You, my darling, have seen a death bed,' she wrote to the Crown Princess, ' – I never.'[28] The strain of a death watch prolonged throughout a night and a morning prostrated the Queen. False rumours circulated in Berlin that she had gone mad, and was confined in a padded room in the Round Tower at Windsor Castle. 'To lose a beloved mother is always terrible,' she confided to Queen Augusta, 'and the blank can never be filled, that you know.'[29]

The Crown Princess hurried to England to console her. In June, she came again, this time with her husband and children. She wanted to relive the happiness of her childhood at Osborne, and watch her little boy and girl playing as once she had. The King of Prussia had been reluctant to let them leave Germany. His objections were given a brutal point, when a radical student tried to assassinate him while he was out riding at Baden. The bullet grazed his neck just below the ear. The Crown Prince rushed back to Germany and found the King so shocked by the affair that he was willing to entertain any protective measures proposed. Bismarck profited from the occasion to send a memorandum advising the use of repression and force, and the creation of a national assembly. His time was approaching.

The Prince of Wales needed to marry. The Crown Princess and her mother had reviewed all the possibilities. The next Queen of England must be a princess and a Protestant. The best, and the most beautiful, seemed to be the Danish princess Alexandra, whose father was heir to the throne. The Crown Princess artlessly arranged for the two to meet, when they were both sightseeing in the gothic cathedral at Speyer. She left them alone together while she went off with the Bishop to admire the frescoes. 'May God bless this budding romance,' she wrote to her parents, 'as He has done in our case.'

Her brother had told her that he had never seen a young lady who pleased him so much. Although Princess Alexandra was only sixteen, the Crown Princess thought her forward for her age, not shy at all. Yet there was no fault in the way she behaved. She was simple and unaffected and quite unaware of her charms. She was bound to grow upon the

Prince of Wales, even though he would not commit himself to his sister 'in his own funny, undemonstrative way'.[30]

The Crown Princess could not have performed a more reckless action. In trying to find a wife for her brother, she had angered the King of Prussia. The Danes were at daggers drawn with Prussia and the German Confederation, over the border provinces of Schleswig and Holstein, where a majority of German subjects was controlled by Denmark. If the Prince of Wales married Alexandra, it would suggest an alliance of England and Denmark against Germany. By arranging the rendezvous, the Crown Princess had seemed deliberately to flout the interests of her new country. Her active concern for her brother's happiness had betrayed her into committing a diplomatic error.

The rift between England and Prussia grew, with the approach of the King's coronation. Reacting against the English model, he would not be crowned, as his son had suggested, at a popular ceremony in Berlin. He would go to the ancient capital of Königsberg, where the old Prussian kings had exercised their divine right. There, on 18 October 1861, in full regalia, he insisted on placing the crowns on his own and on the Queen's head. His speech stressed that he was crowned by the grace of God, not by the Church or by men. He held up his sword and sceptre to demonstrate his earthly powers. His declaration was made in the presence of half of the sovereigns of Europe, who looked like a happy family shut up in a cage.

The Crown Princess's description of the ceremony was kinder; she found it a touching and magnificent spectacle. The diamonds of the ladies glittered in the sunlight as they proceeded to the royal chapel through the massed ranks of the Prussian Guards whose five bands played 'God Save the King'. The royal chapel was bedecked with red velvet and gold. The Knights of the Black Eagle wore red velvet cloaks, the Queen's four young ladies wore white and gold; the *Oberhofmeister* was in gold and white brocade with green velvet. The Crown Princess, herself, wore gold with ermine and white satin; one of her two ladies wore blue, the other red velvet. The sun poured in through the high windows and blended the colours magically. The music was very fine and the chorales were sung loudly and strongly. The King and Queen – and even the Crown Princess – were cheered loudly wherever they appeared.[31]

Amid pomp and rejoicing, the new King was crowned by his own hand. He now dissolved the liberal parliament that had opposed the army measures put forward by his Minister of War, Albrecht von Roon. The King felt that any reforms proposed by the liberals threatened the lawful powers of the throne. In the Crown Princess's opinion, the government was insecure and would not last. She and her husband were fully aware of the dangers that surrounded them. There seemed to be an impasse, which must lead to the King's abdication or to a social upheaval.[32]

In November, two Coburg cousins, the King of Portugal and his younger brother, died of typhoid, and their passing heralded the most significant death of that fatal year. The news depressed the Prince Consort, who was already sickening for typhoid himself, probably as a consequence of the insanitary drains in Windsor Castle. Agitated by the news that the Prince of Wales had been having a brief affair with an actress while stationed at the Curragh camp in Ireland, he hastened to Cambridge to reprimand his son for causing terrible pain and sorrow to his parents. On his return to Windsor, he fell ill, lingering for a fortnight at the mercy of doctors who, Lord Clarendon thought, were not fit to attend a sick cat. On 14 December he died 'from want of what they call pluck'.[33] He seemed to have had little will to live, no strength to fight off the fever. His last political act had been to tone down a bellicose dispatch which might have involved England in the American Civil War. He had exhausted himself by caring too much and working too hard for a country that was never quite his own.

Widowed at forty-two, with eight unmarried children, Queen Victoria was overcome by grief. Her eldest daughter was pregnant again, and ill. Her doctor forbade her to travel to England, but the Crown Prince came in her place. Irrationally, the Queen at first blamed the Prince of Wales, as though his wild oats rather than bad plumbing had caused his father's death. She had so worshipped her husband that his loss seemed too much to bear, both for herself and for the elaborate network of influence he had built up for the Crown.

'What is to become of us all?' she asked her eldest daughter. 'Of the unhappy country, of Europe, of all? For you all, the loss of such a father is totally irreparable! I will do all I can to follow out all his wishes – to live for you all and for my duties. But how I, who leant on him for all and everything – without whom I did nothing, moved not a finger, arranged not a print or photograph, didn't put on a gown or bonnet if he didn't approve it shall be able to go on, to live, to move, to help myself in difficult moments? How shall I long to ask his advice! Oh, it is too, too weary! The day – the night (above all the night) is too sad and weary.'[34]

The Crown Princess was afflicted almost as much as her mother. She had depended on her father for advice. Now she was left alone, totally dependent on a Prussian prince and husband. Earlier that year, she had written back to her mother that there was not a thing that she heard or saw or did, which did not make her consider what her dear Papa would say – what he would think. Now he could not say or think anything, only leave his ideas and his 'Coburg' plan behind him. She also abandoned herself to grief. 'He was too great,' she wrote to her mother, 'too perfect for Earth, that adored father whom I ever worshipped with more than a daughter's affection.'[35]

CHAPTER FOUR

Besieged by Bismarck

'HERE DO I SEE crumble before my eyes,' wrote old Baron Stockmar, 'that edifice which I have devoted twenty years to construct, prompted by a desire to accomplish something great and good.'[1] He had trained Prince Albert to implement the 'Coburg' plan. Now, Albert was dead. His heirs and pupils, the Queen of England and his eldest daughter Princess Victoria, had withdrawn from public affairs. Their inspiration and guide was gone; their will to act seemed buried with him.

For two months, Queen Victoria shut herself up at Osborne. Her ministers hardly dared approach her over Christmas, but with the new year, her sense of duty revived. Devoted to her dead husband's plans and to her family, she began to exercise her influence from her seclusion. She knew how the projected marriages of her children might affect her country's diplomacy; the royal family already had too many relations with duchies across the Rhine. If Princess Alice married Prince Louis of Hesse, there would be yet another English connection with minor German states such as Saxe-Coburg and Hanover that Prussia would have to sweep away in order to unify Germany. And if the Prince of Wales married Princess Alexandra, the Danish Crown would be strengthened in its efforts to hang on to the disputed Duchies of Schleswig and Holstein.

So the Queen went back to her match-making, anxious to prevent the quarrels between the nations from embroiling her family. She needed to occupy her weary days and nights. Within a month of her husband's death, she was tartly reminding Lord John Russell that no letters should be sent to foreign ambassadors until she had seen the last draft. As final revisions made by the dying Prince Consort had led to the peaceful outcome of the quarrel with America, she wished to continue his peace-making by his example and with her eldest daughter's help. She was encouraged in this duty by her uncle, King Leopold of the Belgians, who would not give up the 'Coburg' plan just because Albert was dead.

'There is but one CONNECTED with your DEAR ANGEL,' he wrote to the widowed Queen, 'to follow up his plans, his wishes, to give to him, who I trust is not cut off in the spirit from this earth, the satisfaction that the good he wished, the plans for every thing good and useful which he had so much at heart, are followed up as much as our diminished means permit; that in that way you will MORE THAN ever be WORTHY OF HIS AFFECTION. When once united, he will tell you how much he was pleased with your devoted effort.'[2]

This devoted effort was continued by the two women who had most loved him. On the thorny subject of Schleswig and Holstein, the Queen of England asked her daughter's opinion as to what would satisfy Prussia. She assured her own ministers that Prussia did not contemplate a war against Denmark. She could not tolerate the thought that her beloved Prussian son-in-law might be fighting against the family of her future Danish daughter-in-law. She sent on to Lord John Russell her daughter's pacific proposals which, the Crown Prince thought, might be acceptable to the Prussian Foreign Office. Prussia might well be prepared to recognize the Kingdom of Italy, which Lord Palmerston's Government desired, if the British would support the partition of Schleswig between Prussia and Denmark. This partition, Queen Victoria added, had also been an idea of the Prince Consort's.

Palmerston rejected the deal. He claimed that only three men understood the thorny problem. He was one of them and had forgotten about it; as for the other two, one was mad and the Prince Consort was dead. The trouble was that too many Germans lived in the Danish part of Schleswig and too many Danes in the German part. Anyway, the Danes did not want to give up Holstein, although it was mainly German-speaking. Palmerston resisted the efforts of the Queen and her eldest daughter to influence the Government. He told Lord John Russell that Prussia had no shadow of a right to demand such an agreement.[3] That was the end of this piece of royal diplomacy.

The rejection of the Crown Princess as a go-between, confirmed the King of Prussia's belief that his family alliance with the British Crown had no effect on policy. That was the trouble with a constitutional monarchy. Autocracy was better. The wearing of the Prussian Crown seemed to have changed his nature; weak and vacillating as Regent, he now appeared stubborn and overbearing as Monarch. He had that unfortunate quality which had proved the ruin of others – the British Ambassador reported to Lord John Russell – he never yielded until it was too late. Born and bred a soldier, he was always leaning on his sword.[4]

As his Minister President, the King replaced the ineffectual Prince of Hohenzollern-Sigmaringen by Prince Adolf of Hohenlohe-Ingelfingen. He was not much better. The Crown Princess thought that he was frightened of his own shadow. Reactionary and pliant ministers were also placed in the Cabinet, which was responsible only to the King, not to the newly-elected Prussian Parliament – which was soon to be dissolved again because the deputies refused to agree to a larger military budget. As early as April 1862, there was talk of recalling Bismarck to head the government, but instead, he was transferred from St Petersburg to Paris. The King wanted him nearer at hand in case he was needed to advise or to take over the administration and change its policies.

The crisis was making things impossible for the Crown Prince and Princess. They could not oppose the King without seeming disobedient, they could not support him without denying their principles and their friends and supporters. Government in Prussia was in such a mess that it made the Crown Princess ashamed, angry and depressed by turns. She began to speak her mind to both the King and Queen of Prussia, which only increased their displeasure with her. Except for her mother and her husband, she confessed that there was no one she now cared to please.[5]

She was no longer passing information to Queen Victoria about Prussian military planning. These secrets were being reported to the Queen by Major-General Hamilton, who relied on the military attaché in Berlin and on observers at the Prussian annual manœuvres. Queen Victoria had specifically asked for a breakdown on the increased army estimates, and she received one that showed the Prussian Army had increased by 60,000 men in the past five years. With the mobilization of a reformed *Landwehr* (the equivalent of a modern territorial army), it would total 357,000 men in time of war.[6] Queen Victoria now knew what the Prussians could deploy against the Danes and the French. She was better informed than her daughter in Berlin.

Her son-in-law, of course, made no mention of the new Prussian military arrangements; he was discreet about them now, even when alone with his wife. Queen Victoria, however, was flattering him by asking him to take her dead husband's place at public ceremonies. She had ordered a full year of mourning for her children, so that the Prince of Wales could not stand in for his father at the opening of the second Great Exhibition. She begged for the loan of the Crown Prince for another occasion in 1862. He had already agreed to come to Princess Alice's wedding to Prince Louis of Hesse. 'I cannot demand the sacrifice of yet another journey in the same year,' she wrote to the King of Prussia. 'On the other hand, you will understand how important it is to me that this Exhibition in which my dearly-beloved angel took such a keen interest, should pass off brilliantly in every way. . . . Fritz's presence, both as your son and ours, will have a most important effect on the Exhibition at such a gloomy time.'[7]

The King of Prussia felt obliged to agree to the widow's plea. His son was obviously being made to stand in for the Prince Consort, in the flesh and in his ideas about Germany. Although the Crown Prince was nine years older than his wife, and did not accept all her views, the Prince Consort had been the first person to recognize his political sensibilities. Now that the Queen of England continued in this recognition and treated him as if he were her support, Prince Frederick William found it hard not to hold to the English example. He was gratified to find himself popular, and widely praised in London, which was scarcely the case in Berlin.

After the magnificent opening of the Exhibition, the Crown Prince stayed on in England to give away Princess Alice at her marriage to Prince Louis of Hesse. The Crown Princess could not travel to join him because she was expecting her third child. Again, he was being used in place of the dead Prince Consort, as if Queen Victoria needed to take over her daughter's husband in recompense for her own. In her letters to the Crown Princess, there was sometimes a note of envy at her daughter having a good husband, even if he could never match up to her angel Albert. A woman in the Queen's position, especially one of her nature, could not stand alone.

Although Queen Victoria's grief seems extravagant now, it was the fashion of the time to mourn long and publicly. The Queen spent as much time and care on the building of a mausoleum for Prince Albert at Frogmore near Windsor as he had on building country houses for her. His bedroom was kept always aired and ready, as if he would drop in. His evening clothes were laid out each night, with a towel and hot water in a basin. His habits were not allowed to die. Daily reminded of him, the Queen, in her widow's weeds, kept his memory alive by the display of her sorrow.

When she examined her daughter Alice's trousseau before the wedding, she found it sad to see nothing but black gowns. The Victorian cult of death affected the royal wedding ceremony. Not only had the Prince Consort died recently, but also the Grand Duchess of Hesse. The ceremony was more like a funeral than a wedding. The Queen wore a widow's cap, and sat hunched on a chair near the altar with her four sons at her side. One of them, Prince Alfred, sobbed dreadfully throughout the service. So did the Archbishop of York, who had just lost his own wife, and whose cheeks ran with tears. Princess Alice, herself, was serious and melancholy, conscious of how unbearable her wedding must seem to her bereaved mother, who must have been remembering her own betrothal. 'A dagger is plunged in my bleeding, desolate heart . . .' the Queen confessed. 'I feel what I had, what I hoped to have for at least twenty years more and what I can only have in another world again.'⁸

In August, the Crown Princess gave birth to her second son, Prince Henry. This time, labour was easy and she recovered quickly. Within ten days, she was walking round the redesigned gardens of the Neue Palais, among the plants and trees which her father had sent to her. She felt as if the renewal of life had overcome the loss of her father. She had everything to hope for in the near future.

It was only a dream. The King threatened to abdicate rather than turn to Bismarck as his last resort. He sent for the Crown Prince, who was at Coburg with his wife; Queen Victoria had come there on a visit of sad remembrance. God and conscience, the King told his son, had made him decide to give up the throne. It needed only one signature to hand over the Crown. The announcement of the abdication had already been drawn up. The King gave it to the Crown Prince to read. He could not give in any more to parliament, he said – although he had hardly given in to anything as Regent or as King. His son urged him to remain on the throne; it would be for the good of the country and the dynasty. The power of the Crown would be diminished if a parliament were able to get rid of a King.

Nevertheless, the King declared that he had made up his mind. The Crown Prince was ordered to remain in Berlin and prepare to take over from his father. He informed his wife in Coburg. With the throne so near, she did not know what to advise. The offer of abdication had come at the worst possible time. She and Queen Victoria were together at Coburg, when the engagement of her brother, the Prince of Wales, to the Danish Princess Alexandra was announced; the proposed marriage seemed to the reactionaries near the King to line up England with Denmark against Prussia. How could the King surrender his throne to a son with an English wife?

Finally, although she was fully aware of the risk, the Crown Princess decided to advise her husband to take the throne. The offer of abdication might be a ploy by the King to discredit his son. It would make the Crown Prince seem to be plotting to take over too soon. It might also be a trick to prove that the King was so desperate that he must send for the dangerous Bismarck. Yet the Crown Princess wanted the influence and responsibility of power. Even though she was only twenty-one, she had stood by for five long years waiting to become the Queen of Prussia. 'I see no way out,' she wrote to her husband in Berlin, 'and consider you should make this sacrifice for the country. If you do not accept, I believe that you will regret it one day.' She did not wish to have the responsibility of advising him against it. The alternative would be much worse for the King. 'To take Bismarck is equivalent to a man, who cannot swim, jumping into the water where it is deepest!'[9]

While the King hesitated, Albrecht von Roon, his Minister of War, appealed to his royal conscience. How could a soldier King give up his command when the battle was going against him; it was a battle to develop the Prussian Army and defend the country. Bismarck must be summoned from Paris. The King appeared to agree. Roon had the vital telegram sent to Bismarck; it was written in Latin and French and signed with a pseudonym. The message read: ' – *Periculum in mora. Dépêchez-vous.*' There was danger in delay; the Crown Prince might become King. Bismarck took the next express train to Berlin.

The Crown Prince heard of his adversary's arrival and summoned him to his presence. Bismarck said little at the meeting and made no commitments. He had already compromised himself with the King, who complained to Roon that Bismarck was no good; he had first been to see the Crown Prince. But two days later, the King ordered Bismarck to come to Babelsberg. There he was shown the letter of abdication. He did not notice whether it had been signed or not. He assured the King that he could form a cabinet, and would force through the reorganization of the army against the opposition of the Liberal majority in parliament.

This was what the King had been waiting to hear. He may have promised his wife and the Crown Prince not to appoint Bismarck as his Minister President. Now he said it was his duty, with Bismarck's help, to try to continue the battle. 'I shall not abdicate,' he declared. Bismarck promised his absolute loyalty in making the King supreme above parliament. He would give the King the army he wanted. He would also defend the royal prerogative that had elevated him to power. He did not, however, promise to carry out the King's ideas on foreign policy.[10] The King, delighted to be promised the army he wanted, suppressed his own doubts about Bismarck's known recklessness and double-dealing in diplomacy. Within the week, Bismarck had told the parliamentary budget commission that Prussia's might would resolve the future of Germany, not its example of liberalism. 'The great questions of the day will not be decided by speeches and majority resolutions – that was the great mistake from 1848 to 1849 – but by iron and blood.'

The King knew that he had misled and offended his son. He feared open opposition from the Crown Prince, but Frederick William had also been trained in the virtues of a Prussian officer. He obeyed his father and kept silent in public. He declared only that any breach of the Constitution would be disastrous; he would not tolerate a royal tyranny. The King replied that he was tired of hearing sermons and dismissed his son. It was the beginning of the long breach between them.

Knowing that any show of opposition would play into Bismarck's hands, the Crown Prince decided to leave with his wife on an extended tour of the Mediterranean. They would sail with the Prince of Wales in Queen Victoria's yacht, the *Osborne*. This dutiful act of withdrawal may have been politic, but it appeared cowardly. The Liberals were left without their royal figurehead to halt Bismarck and the reactionaries. The Crown Prince's discretion may have been the better part of valour, but it was damaging to his cause.

The King of Prussia also feared that Queen Victoria would feel betrayed and turn against him, supporting Denmark on the question of the two border duchies. He went to meet her in Coburg, the late Prince Consort's homeland. He would not talk to her about politics except to complain about the heavy weight of affairs on him. She was too tactful to reproach him with Bismarck's appointment, or the reasons behind the temporary exile of the Crown Prince and Princess. The Queen felt it wise to keep her lines of communication open to the King of Prussia; in the near future, she might need to protect her daughter over there.

The Mediterranean voyage was a time of rest and peace. It also gave the Crown Princess an opportunity to bring her husband closer to her adored brother, the Prince of Wales. They sailed together from Marseilles to Palermo and to Malta, where there was a review of British troops in their honour. It was the first time the Crown Princess had ever seen 'our dear troops without beloved Papa'. She was quite overcome, particularly when the riflemen marched past.[11] They sailed to Tunis, where the Bey presented the two princes with Orders studded with diamonds, but wrapped in brown paper. A howling storm on their way back left the Crown Princess sea-sick for two days in Malta, but she revived on the passage back to Naples.

There, the Prince of Wales celebrated his coming of age. He had endeared himself to his brother-in-law, who had become almost as fond of him as his sister, in spite of his proposed Danish wife. 'Bertie is extremely amiable, accommodating and good natured,' the Crown Princess reported from Naples to their mother, 'and we are as happy as possible together.' He seemed to be enjoying himself very much and making progress. He was taking much more notice of what he saw and heard. The Crown Princess begged her mother not to worry about him, there was so much good to come out of him yet. His consideration and tact attracted everyone. Now that they had no father, it was doubly important that the scattered brothers and sisters should hold together in perfect love and confidence.[12]

The royal party was received in Rome by the Pope. They found him a good-natured and jocose old gentleman, not without dignity, but then, as Protestants, they had no great respect for the Supreme Pontiff. The Prince of Wales had to return to England. Both his sister and his brother-in-law had had plenty of time to put the Prussian point of view concerning Schleswig and Holstein before his marriage to Princess Alexandra. They did not want to be at daggers drawn with him in case of hostilities with Denmark. War had to be kept out of happy families. Queen Victoria hoped that the Crown Princess had 'Germanized' her brother as much as possible, for it was most necessary.

Returning to Potsdam by way of the Austrian Emperor's Court in Vienna, the Crown Princess met the American historian and diplomat, John Lothrop Motley, an old student friend of Bismarck's at Göttingen. He was attracted by her appearance. 'She is rather *petite*,' he wrote, 'has a fresh young face with pretty features, fine teeth and a frank and agreeable smile and an interested, earnest and intelligent manner. Nothing could be simpler or more natural than her style, which I should say was the perfection of good breeding.'[13]

Her grace and good manners did not save her when she returned 'behind the bars' in Berlin. During the six weeks she had been away, Bismarck seemed to have transformed the feeling of the city; it was charged with nervous energy. When her husband went to the barracks, he found morale high, and a sense of purpose and urgency. The King was revitalized from spending so much time with his troops. He considered the new spirit of the forces as a triumph engineered by his chief minister, although the man was a mere civilian. Bismarck had persuaded the army command that he would drive the reorganization and the military budget through parliament, whether approved or not. He was preparing schemes to raise money unofficially, to govern without reference to the elected deputies, to muzzle and direct the press even more, and to develop the spy system which Stieber had created. With a strong army and the Prussian State under his control, there was no telling how far he could go in his pursuit of a greater nation.

The Crown Princess was disturbed by her husband's unwilling approval of what Bismarck and the King were achieving with the army. He shared the ambivalence towards Bismarck which was to emasculate liberal opposition to the Minister President. He approved of Bismarck's measures to strengthen Prussia and make her powerful abroad, but he hated the suppression of rights at home. He wanted to have the power but not at the cost of loss of liberty. His wife saw his dilemma and made one of her rare complaints about her husband to her mother. 'He is not born a free Englishman,' she wrote, 'and all Prussians have NOT the feeling of independence and love of justice and constitutional liberty they ought to have.'[14]

Like every one else in Prussia, liberal or conservative, the Crown Prince would respond to the ha-ha of the trumpets and the neighing of the war-horses. He waited for Bismarck to start the war.

Bismarck was only forty-seven and had scarcely been trained to be the leader of Prussia. He was known to be forceful, opportunistic and solitary; devious, quick to move and ruthless. Yet he could charm as well as bully, persuade as well as command. To keep power, he depended wholly on the King, but his remarks about iron and blood had made his master doubt him. During a train journey to Berlin he was summoned to explain himself, and was accused of being another Strafford, who would be executed together with his monarch, playing King Charles I of England. 'They will cut off your head,' the King said sadly, 'and a little later mine.' Like Strafford Bismarck ended by asking what death could be better than in the struggle for the King's rights granted by the grace of God?[15]

By a bold piece of trickery, Bismarck did secure for the King the budget for his reorganized army. He influenced the Upper House to pass the budget although the Chamber had rejected it. The State, however, collected taxes directly without depending on annual grants from parliament. In an impasse between the Upper House and the Chamber, Bismarck claimed that the King had a duty to spend the tax money on the army in order to defend the State. Through this hole in the Constitution, Bismarck could give the King what he wanted, and govern without reference to the liberals.

This was not the *coup d'état* that the Crown Princess had feared, but an intolerable state of dangling and indecision, with Bismarck holding the strings and the power of the executive. 'We live with a sword hanging over our heads,' the Crown Princess wrote to her mother in England, 'and it will fall when we least expect it and on the innocent ones.'[16] She, herself, thought it very possible that there might be another Radical explosion as in 1848. Her husband soon began to look even more ill than his father, who now seemed to flourish, even in the dreadfully hot rooms and crushes of courtiers of the Berlin winter season. If the Crown Prince became ever more pallid, his aged father seemed to become infused with the desperate energy of his new minister and the growing force of his new-model army.

Berlin was very much a city of uniforms, investitures and parades. Everywhere were spiked helmets and flat caps, white tunics and dark-blue field dress, epaulettes and Iron Crosses, swords in long scabbards, racket of drum and trumpet and fife. If society did not change much, the guard was changed daily, loudly and ceremonially. Berlin often appeared a barracks in a country that was an armed camp. In the face of such military presence, peace seemed a mere truce standing sentry on the next war.

During this anxious time, the Crown Prince and Princess and their eldest son William came to England again for the wedding of the Prince of Wales to the Danish Princess Alexandra, whose charms had grown on the Prince until he had proposed to her. Protocol and family feeling decreed that they attend, but politically it was ill advised. Bismarck would represent the journey as disloyalty to Prussia, an indication that the Crown Prince sided with the Danes over the vexed question of Schleswig and Holstein. The Crown Princess's frequent trips to England had begun to worry even her Liberal supporters. 'She has nothing to do there and nothing to seek,' complained one of them.[17] Even their close adviser, Max Duncker, thought that their English parliamentary ideas could not be applied in Prussia.

When her eldest daughter arrived for her brother's wedding, Queen Victoria found her very pretty, so young and fresh and slim.[18] The Queen knew perfectly well that she was playing with German politics by asking for the Prussian Crown Prince to attend her eldest son. 'On account of the Danes,' she confessed to her daughter, 'I am so anxious that he should be there.'[19] She hoped to prevent a war between Denmark and Prussia, by having the Crown Prince attend the wedding of the heir to the English throne.

This obvious diplomacy through royal marriage aroused great suspicion in Bismarck and in other Prussian nationalists who saw it as yet another extension of Queen Victoria's influence. She might seem to remain secluded and in her widow's weeds, but the letters, with the suggestions for shaping policy, still flowed to her relatives. As Lord Rowton pointed out, the Queen selected throughout Europe, the most intelligent member of each royal family, 'on any question, domestic or foreign, which arose, she obtained by letter an opinion.'[20] No statesman could hope for better information.

The marriage of Queen Victoria's heir into the Danish royal family had spread the network still farther. The Greeks were looking for a king who would bring with him an English connection and the friendship of the British Navy. Their first choice was Queen Victoria's second son Alfred, but she wished him to become Duke of Coburg on the death of her brother-in-law Ernest. The second choice of the Greeks was Duke Ernest himself, but eventually he decided to stay in his German duchy rather than risk the violent politics of Athens. Finally, Prince William of Denmark, the seventeen-year-old brother of Princess Alexandra, was chosen. Through the marriage of her eldest son to Alexandra, Queen Victoria had now cast the meshes of her relations over the royal families of two maritime nations, both of which had excellent ports for the British Fleet.

Bismarck was right to be suspicious. A royal wedding was both a form of alliance and part of an Intelligence system. A royal death could still cause a war of succession. The King of Denmark, whose ancestry had sustained a tenuous claim to rule Schleswig and Holstein, could not live for ever and had no direct heir. If Bismarck wanted to shape Prussia's future by iron and blood, Queen Victoria wanted to preserve England's security by gold ring and blood royal. To her, marriage, not war, was diplomacy by other means.

Bismarck's first crisis in foreign affairs found him wanting, and he was fortunate to survive it. The Poles rebelled against their Russian occupiers. Although aware of French and English sympathy for Polish liberty, Bismarck decided to help the Russians to put down the rebellion which menaced East Prussia and his own estates. He was, in any case, a Junker and regarded the Poles as little more than peasants. He had four army corps sent to seal the frontier, describing this extreme act as a simple police measure. He also allowed the Russian troops to pursue the rebels in Prussian territory.

The Russians were grateful and began to put down the insurrection brutally. The French Emperor threatened a war on the Rhine, and Lord Palmerston in England blustered about helping the Poles. There was another crisis in Berlin with rumours of Bismarck's fall. Queen Victoria was so alarmed that there might be war on the Rhine that she would not allow her second daughter Alice, who was expecting her first baby, to return to Hesse-Darmstadt. 'We must, on NO account,' she declared, 'let ourselves be dragged into what may be a war with Germany! The Queen shudders at the very thought of what, if we are not very careful, and very guarded in our expressions to France, we may find ourselves plunged into!'[21]

The Queen's intervention played its part in keeping her divided Cabinet neutral. The Government adopted a policy of hands off, refusing to join with the French in another Crimean War. Bismarck survived in Berlin. So Queen Victoria had indirectly helped her daughter's adversary in Prussia to weather his first diplomatic blunder. England had also set a precedent for not intervening. Perhaps the British Fleet might not assist Denmark, despite the Prince of Wales's marriage to Princess Alexandra. It was common knowledge that Queen Victoria preferred her eldest daughter to her eldest son. If she wished to avoid war with Germany at all costs, she might hamper Lord Palmerston enough to prevent his sending the navy to Copenhagen.

The constant worries of the political situation did not lessen the

Crown Princess's anxiety over the condition of her first-born's neck and arm, which had been damaged at his birth. Prince William's left arm was bluish and useless, while his neck was angled as a result of constricted muscles. The German doctors wanted him put in a machine to straighten the neck. A belt at his waist would hold an iron rod up his back to support something like a horse's bridle. The boy's head would be strapped into that and turned as required by a screw. Seeing her child treated as if deformed was very hard for the Crown Princess, but of course, she would submit to all that was necessary for his good. Yet she found doctors very odd sometimes.[22]

They were odd and the treatment was odder; it made the child odd and angry. Prince William hated the torments inflicted on him and reacted savagely to them. Slowly he learned to deny his deformity, but he never learned to live with it. Obscurely in his heart, he blamed his mother who, in fact, was blameless and suffered with him. Although she tried to hide her pain, her heart bled to see him tortured. When writing about his early life, he accused her of having been wrapped up in the husband she adored. She was the wife rather than the mother, and her three elder children had a stern upbringing. She turned to the nursery only with her younger children, who enjoyed her tender heart and care.

So it seemed to the eldest child. The truth was rather different. The Crown Princess was devoted to all her children, but while she was still young and her husband was engaged in immediate politics, she had to devote herself to him and his affairs. The boy William gave his affection to his father, who was religious and kind-hearted, so tender as to be almost soft. The huge military figure had a genuine sympathy for any form of suffering. He was friendly, full of jokes and a great tease, but he was taught to respect authority and would brook no opposition. He was subject to fits of depression, a *Weltschmerz* that seemed a presentiment of the long-drawn tragedy to come.[23]

The curtain was already going up for the first act of that tragedy. The members of the Lower House remained intransigent with regard to the military budget. In an Address to the King, they went so far as to threaten him with revolution. A chasm separated the advisers to the Crown from the country, they warned; it could be bridged only by a change of cabinet and by a change of system.[24] If the King would not abdicate and allow the Crown Prince to succeed him, the Liberals wanted the Crown Prince to challenge Bismarck before he turned the government into a tyranny.

The King and his Minister President had their reply. Parliament was dissolved again.

Bound by obedience to his father, the Crown Prince remained silent. His wife, Queen Victoria and the British Government urged him to speak out and assert his liberal principles. 'We want a Frederick the Great now!' the Crown Princess declared. 'When will there be another?' A pitched battle was taking place between the Chambers and the Government, she told her mother. Many believed there would be a revolution; she did not share this opinion. The King was determined to uphold Bismarck, the author of all the mischief.[25]

Pressure at home and from abroad forced the Crown Prince to speak his mind too soon. On 19 May 1863, the Crown Princess told Queen Victoria that her husband would protest in writing, if the Government did anything unconstitutional. Queen Victoria passed on this information to her Cabinet. In a significant reply to the Queen, Lord Palmerston praised the Crown Prince's intention to protest as wise and satisfactory. The Prime Minister found it painful to see the unconstitutional course taken by the King of Prussia and his advisers. He echoed the King in comparing it to the career of Charles I of England, who had lost his head for it. If persevered in, it must be ruinous to the King.[26]

Bismarck knew of the English and Liberal pressure on the Crown Prince to declare himself as leader of the opposition. He had already placed his agents in the Prince's household. The Crown Princess was fairly sure that their letters were intercepted and read before being passed on. She warned her mother to keep all details for the royal messenger who came to the Neue Palais twice a week.[27] With Bismarck as the adversary, nothing was safe.

Bismarck believed that the outspoken Liberal opposition menaced the security and reputation of Prussia. It showed a divided and ungovernable nation. He asked the King to use his emergency powers to silence the opposition's press by royal edict. Such a strong measure would smoke out the Crown Prince who, if he wished to retain the loyalty of his supporters, would have to declare himself against such acts performed in his father's name. He had already been ordered to leave the capital and proceed through East Prussia and Poland. This would separate him from his Liberal advisers and from the Berliners. It would also associate him with the reactionary Junkers and the army garrisons he was being sent to inspect.

In this crisis, the Crown Prince depended chiefly on the advice of his

English wife and her counsellors. Bismarck's suspicion of foreign influence was well-founded. The Crown Princess was working all the time for her husband, copying out drafts and letters because no one could be completely trusted. Before he left on his tour of the eastern marches, the Crown Prince wrote a long letter to his father the King, saying that he had no intention of meddling in things which did not concern him. Yet he could not see the danger the King was in without warning and imploring him never to give his consent to any unconstitutional measure being adopted as the only way out of a difficulty. Such a measure would endanger the dynasty and the peace of Prussia; nothing could possibly be improved by it. If it were taken, it would be the Crown Prince's painful duty to protest. He could have nothing whatever to do with it. He hoped it would not come, but could not share in the responsibility.[28]

That same day the press edict was issued in the name of the King. The Crown Prince immediately wrote to Bismarck, declaring the edict to be a disaster for the Crown and for the country; he would not be a party to it. He failed to see that Bismarck had provoked a response from him, causing a rift between father and son, between Prussian nationalism and English example. The Crown Prince's courage and obstinacy would make him blunder further into the trap. Two days later, he wrote to his father: 'I owe it to you as your son and your first subject to tell you frankly when I differ from you, and when my views disagree with those of your Government.'

This was hardly what the King wanted to read. He remembered his own painful obedience to his father and the sacrifice of his first Radziwill love to his sense of obligation. Filial duty was a primary requirement in royal sons. The King was even more angered by receiving another letter from the Crown Prince the following day, again opposing the press edict. Then on 5 June, the Crown Prince ignored a warning from his father. He repudiated the edict at a reception in the town hall of Danzig, following a parade of the garrison there. He told the Mayor and the guests that he was astonished at the edict, which had been issued in his absence from Berlin. He had nothing to do with it, but he urged every one to have confidence in the excellent intentions of the King.

He had fallen victim to Bismarck's provocations; he had declared himself, publicly, to be in opposition to the King's will. Taking Bismarck's advice, the King accused his son in harsh terms: 'You have now spoken quite frankly that you are opposed to my system of Government. What therefore will be your attitude towards me and my Government in the future? ... Any one who does not wish this disgraceful press to be kept within bounds also desires the downfall of the Monarchy.'[29]

The King ordered his son never to make any such indiscreet statement on any occasion in the future. Supported by his wife in his defiance, the Crown Prince replied that he could not take back the words he had spoken in Danzig. He offered to resign his commission in the army and his place in the King's Councils. He said he would retire and live apart from politics. He begged his beloved father's forgiveness for the pain caused by his disobedience and convictions. He was, as the Crown Princess told her mother, in a state of perfect misery. She hoped Queen Victoria would make his conduct known to her ministers and all their friends in England. They felt dreadfully alone, without a soul to give them advice, but her husband's necessity and duty were so plain that they required no explaining or advising.[30]

So the Crown Princess owned to her responsibility in her husband's brave charge at the guns like the charge of the Light Brigade at Balaclava. It was magnificent, but it was not war against Bismarck. She persisted in thinking the Liberals to be more powerful in Prussia than they were. The Chambers were not the same as the English House of Commons and the House of Lords. Their powers were more limited and recent. Authority in Prussia was still enshrined in the tradition of a King ruling through his chosen ministers – Stuart England rather than Victorian. The Crown Prince was fettered by tradition and training from committing any major act of defiance. His independence and pride had been moulded and controlled since his childhood. Whatever his mother or his wife urged, his father would deny and make him suppress. Resistance only increased his psychological turmoil and prolonged melancholies.

Prussia was still Prussia; it would not change for the English Crown Princess. As she was alone with her husband in the east during his repeated acts of defiance, she had to take the responsibility for aiding and abetting him. Certainly her mother and the English ministers egged him on to further opposition. 'Let Fritz be firm!' Queen Victoria wrote. He must not shrink from separating himself from all his father's unhappy acts. 'I know Papa would have said the same.' During the crisis, she praised her daughter more than she had ever done, saying that the Crown Princess was taking the Prince Consort's place – his child in mind and genius.[31]

Her daughter's error was in exposing herself as the present influence on the rebellion of the Crown Prince. She had been used as the go-between to carry angry letters from the King to his son. Bismarck had succeeded in making the Crown Prince and Princess rebel in the wrong place at the wrong time. They were surrounded with spies, who watched all they did, the Crown Princess reported from Königsberg on 11 June. All was fed back to Berlin to checkmate everything they attempted. They had no final answer from the King.[32]

Their fate was being settled in Berlin. There was no one close to the throne to help them except the Queen of Prussia, and the King would not listen to her. Field Marshall Wrangel wanted the Crown Prince put in a fortress and the Crown Princess exiled, but Bismarck was too clever for that. He knew that the making of martyrs was a political mistake and proposed a merciless clemency. The King should not accept his son's offer to resign from the army and the Councils, but should let the Crown Prince's resistance wear itself out in minor duties. Bismarck knew the Crown Prince's weakness, which had been instilled rigorously in him since his boyhood – his absolute belief that he should obey his father the King. Only the thought of his father made him feel powerless, the Crown Princess wrote of him to her mother. 'Think if it was your father,' he asked her, 'would you like to disobey him and make him unhappy?'[33]

This was the crucial question. In obedience to her dead father's training of her beliefs, the Crown Princess had encouraged her husband's rebellion. Her mother and her mother's Government had stood behind her while the Crown Prince charged towards his defeat. 'You are the best and wisest adviser he could have,' Queen Victoria assured her daughter, 'and the worthy child of your beloved father who will look down approvingly on you.'[34]

As with many a crisis, there was no solution; only a definition of attitudes, the search for a small common ground of truce and compromise. The heir to the throne could not be replaced. He was kept from power only by the good health of the King, who had now gone to Karlsbad to take the cure. Bismarck moved quickly to increase the isolation of the two rebels, to let them know that he had saved them from prison and exile – his political genius enabled him to thwart his opponents' plans while making them grateful for his personal forbearance.

Acting on Bismarck's advice, the King sent his son a severe reprimand, but did not strip him of his offices of state. He made it plain that the English influence was to blame for the Crown Prince's public indiscretions. 'You inform me,' he wrote to his son, 'that those statements were made intentionally and, as Vicky writes to Mama, after due deliberation with her.'[35] The Crown Princess was guilty together with the Crown Prince.

Their chief supporter, Queen Augusta of Prussia, was encouraged to pay a long visit to her friend Queen Victoria, in order to explain the King's position on the reform of his army. But her visit to England compromised her as another pawn in the great game played from Windsor and the Foreign Office. Bismarck was reckless enough to assert to the British Ambassador in Berlin that the Crown Prince's speech would encourage an assassination attempt on the King by radical exiles enjoying asylum in London. Moreover, Bismarck added, the Prussian Court believed that the Crown Prince had been acting on advice from abroad, channelled through young Stockmar.[36]

Bismarck was not entirely wrong. 'Be quite easy about Fritz,' the Crown Princess wrote to her mother, 'he will do all he should, he will let himself be guided by Stockmar and you will see that all will go right.'[37] Bismarck told one of his agents, the sly Moritz Busch, that the trouble with having foreign princesses at the Prussian Court was that they brought their nationality with them and retained it, preserving their foreign interests.[38]

The indiscretions of some of the Crown Prince's liberal advisers, and the intervention of The Times, played further into Bismarck's hands. Gustav Freytag had versions of the correspondence between the King of Prussia and his son published in two liberal German papers, and copies of the important letters were received by The Times from an unknown source. As the Crown Princess herself could not be accused of the leak, Ernest von Stockmar was held guilty, and was pressed to resign from the Crown Prince's household. Bismarck was determined to eradicate the Coburg influence as far as possible.

The articles in The Times infuriated the King. They pointed out that the King was at Karlsbad in Austria, while Queen Augusta was at Windsor and the Crown Prince touring the far frontiers of the kingdom. All three were separated, intent on different policies. Fuel was added to the flames when The Times praised the Crown Princess for her liberal views and support of her husband's protests. Nothing could have caused her more embarrassment. She was thought now, she told her mother, the 'genius of evil'. With the Stockmars and Robert Morier, she appeared to be at the head of the Anglo-Coburg influence near the Crown Prince.

It hurt her, of course, to be thought so powerful and dangerous. She felt she had to give advice as positively as possible, but it was disagreeable to be thought meddlesome and intriguing. Politics was not a ladies' profession. She would like to live in peace with everyone, but that would mean having no opinion or policy of her own. She could not be a free-born Englishwoman and Queen Victoria's child if she were silent. She was very ambitious for the country, for her husband and the children, so she determined to brave all the rest.[39]

Of course, the Crown Prince and Princess had their chosen advisers and sources of information, just as Bismarck had his own growing network of financial and secret agents. He treated as an intimate Gerson Bleichröder, Rothschild's representative in Berlin. He needed the shrewd and capable banker to finance the State and the army when parliament would not authorize funds for Prussian expansion. He knew too, that Bleichröder would pass on information immediately to the Rothschilds in Paris and London – and so it would reach the French Emperor and the English City and Cabinet. As Bleichröder's distinguished biographer says, the banker was supplied with bits of selected truths. The full truth, as always, Bismarck kept to himself.[40]

For secret operations necessary to his policy, Bismarck was again using the spymaster Stieber despite the King's distrust of the man. A newspaper proprietor, August Brass, a fiery democrat who had fought the authorities in 1848, had founded the radical *Norddeutsche Allge-meine Zeitung*, with the socialist William Liebknecht as his chief assist-ant. Bismarck decided to use, rather than suppress the paper. Brass became one of his chief supporters, the mouthpiece of many of Bismarck's planted stories and insinuations. He also introduced Bismarck to Stieber as a reliable counterforce to conspirators at home and enemies abroad. Stieber would be used against the new Crown Prince as he had been against the old one.

Badly advised, the Crown Prince decided to continue his attack on the Minister President. He sent Bismarck a memorandum on government which questioned his honesty; people who advised breaches of the con-stitution were the most dangerous advisers to Crown and country. Bismarck scribbled the phrase 'Youth is hasty with words' in the margin. His comment on the Crown Prince's justification of his defiance of his father was even more pointed – the one word 'Absalom!'[41] He sent the annotated document to the King, making him even more angry against his son.

In retaliation, Bismarck encouraged the King to start a witch-hunt over the leaks to *The Times*. He loosed Stieber and his police agents. All leading liberals were under suspicion, particularly the circle round the Crown Prince. Young Stockmar's health gave way under the pressure, and he had to retire to a spa. Max Duncker was turned slowly until he came to believe in Bismarck and agreed to act as his informer. The Crown Princess was scared enough to feel guilty about sending Queen Victoria copies of the correspondence between her husband and his father. Perhaps, inadvertently, her mother had been the source of the leak which now threatened their future.

'There has been a regular inquisition about it which has caused us the greatest annoyance,' she wrote to her mother. The King said he would not rest until he had found out the guilty people.[42] Queen Victoria replied that the letters had been absolutely safe with her. What the Crown Prince had done and said had been no secret. As for the leak, the King should look nearer home.[43]

The death of old Baron Stockmar in July was an unexpected help to Bismarck and a sad blow to Queen Victoria. The Prince Consort had depended on his advice. With Stockmar's son now separated from her daughter, the Queen felt bound to try and fill the breach herself. She travelled to Coburg, officially to visit Stockmar's grave and see her dead husband's birthplace. Actually, she wanted to intercede with the King of Prussia on behalf of her daughter and the Crown Prince. If they were to be forced into retirement, she wished them to join her in England; a married daughter and grandchildren would keep her company.

Two of the wiser members of the Anglo-Coburg group did not support the Crown Prince's defiance of his father. Robert Morier thought that this was no way to fight Bismarck. The Crown Prince had already been enmeshed before he was provoked into playing Absalom. Every kind of calumny had been spread about the Prince's friends. Spies had been placed over him in the shape of aides-de-camp and chamberlains; conversations had been distorted or invented, until the Danzig episode had brought matters to a climax.[44] In Morier's opinion, Bismarck had caught the Crown Prince in a snare; he could now remove the heir to the throne from all policy making.

The oldest Coburger of them all, King Leopold of the Belgians, took Queen Victoria gently to task for her interventions. 'I think that you have a sort of right to interfere in an amicable way,' he wrote to her. The King of Prussia was more likely to forgive his son at her request than for any other reason, but there was the fifth commandment: 'Honour Thy Father and Thy Mother'. Queen Victoria's daughter could not alter the law or the traditions in a foreign land. In her own position, the Queen of England could not promote the disobedience of her children.[45] As King Leopold knew well, she had her problems with the Prince of Wales.

When she arrived in Coburg in August, Queen Victoria's intercession with the King of Prussia did clear the air. The King respected her as a widow, and as a monarch more powerful than he. Without hesitation he gave her what she chiefly wanted; a visit to Balmoral by the Crown Prince and Princess. But the policy which she had hatched with her daughter was unsuccessful. She asked the King to attend the current Congress of German sovereigns at Frankfurt. This had been called by the Austrian Emperor, who came personally to invite the King to attend, but the King still would not go, and the reason was Bismarck. The Minister President had to argue half the night with his master, until the King was sobbing uncontrollably and Bismarck was smashing glass bowls to relieve his feelings. But the point was won. The King did not go to the Frankfurt Congress, which was stillborn without his presence.

Bismarck was not wrong in aborting the Congress. Queen Victoria's observer, the urbane Lord Clarendon, likened it to a team of thirty horses, some half-bred, shambling and vicious; some Shetland ponies; with two great dray horses always kicking and biting at each other. The German Confederation did not work and reform would not make it work.[46] There had to be another solution. Bismarck hinted as much to Lord Granville, saying that a civil war between Germans would be a relief. Good with terror was better than terror without good.[47]

At Coburg yet another solution was urged on the King of Prussia by Queen Victoria. With her two married daughters and their children living in Germany, she did not want war there. She asked the King whether he would accept what the Crown Prince and Princess had suggested he might accept – equality with Austria in managing German affairs. 'But how?' the King asked, reeling off a list of slights and disagreements with Austria. Queen Victoria would soon be meeting the Habsburg Emperor. She asked if she might tell him of Prussia's wish for a good understanding, on the basis of complete parity. The King took his leave, saying, 'I recommend my interests to your care.'[48]

The meeting was a personal triumph for Queen Victoria and threw Bismarck into a fury. The King of Prussia was allowing the Queen of

England to represent him with the Austrians. It was too much. Bismarck hid his anger and returned to Berlin with the King, who was very kind to the Crown Princess and 'as jolly as possible'. Her mother met the Austrian Emperor three days later, feeling like a child – unprotected, unsupported. 'I took care to say what you wished,' she wrote later to the Crown Princess. She kept on telling the Emperor that Prussia had to be treated as an equal by Austria. He assured her that this was his wish, that there was no other wish anywhere in Germany, and that she could repeat this to the Crown Princess. He only regretted that the King of Prussia had not come to the Frankfurt Congress, but laid the blame at Bismarck's door.[49]

The Crown Princess was delighted to be able to tell the King of her mother's diplomacy. 'How kind and good of you to say what I begged to the Emperor of Austria – ' she wrote to her mother, 'I am sure it will have done some good.' The King of Prussia was touched and grateful that Queen Victoria had spoken as she had.[50] He did recognize the occasional value of the English relationship and influence which Bismarck wished to destroy.

The opportunity to retaliate came with another paper from the Crown Prince protesting against another quick dissolution of the new parliament. Bismarck enjoyed mocking the Crown Prince about what was constitutional, and what was not, saying that he had sworn to observe the constitution conscientiously – but what if his conscience told him not to observe it?[51] In his comments on the Prince's paper, Bismarck played on the King's fears and suspicions. The witch-hunt over the leaks of the royal letters to *The Times* was continuing. The King went on blaming foreign influence for his son's opposition. He had threatened the Crown Prince, saying: 'I shall deal very severely with whoever it is who puts these ideas into your head.'[52] If the Crown Prince were invulnerable because he was the heir to the throne, his advisers were not, nor was his wife entirely.

Bismarck struck swiftly at the heart of the matter. At one stroke he could discredit the Crown Prince and destroy the King's respect for Queen Victoria's meddling in international diplomacy. He inserted a comment on the Crown Prince's paper, accusing him of being too indiscreet through his marriage and his English relatives. He knew too many state secrets and told them to his wife, who could pass information to her mother and so to the British Government. It would be wise, Bismarck wrote, not to trust the Crown Prince and Princess in confidential matters until they realized that in Reigning Houses their nearest relatives were not always their fellow-countrymen, but had to represent other interests than those of Prussia. It was hard when a country's frontier was the boundary of interests between mother and daughter, between brother and sister, but to forget that spelt danger to the state.[53]

The accusation was true. The question of Schleswig and Holstein was already dividing mother, son and sister in Queen Victoria's family. Bismarck was also firing the opening salvo in his war to subordinate the international royal Intelligence system to the security needs of the new nation state. He could never allow Prussian interests to be represented by a foreign queen, even if she called the King of Prussia 'Brother'. Equally, he had to stop official secrets reaching the wife of the heir to the throne, because she had been born in an alien land where half her heart remained.

So Bismarck worked on the King's fears and won an easy victory. The Crown Prince had been indiscreet and was in opposition to his father's wishes. It was simpler to blame foreign influences than German liberals, although they too were blamed. At the end of September, the Crown Prince and his whole family were packed off to Balmoral for a long stay. This would give Bismarck time to turn the King finally against his son and convince him that the Crown Prince should be excluded from the councils of state for fear that he might betray his country's secrets to his mother-in-law in England.

What Bismarck had predicted occurred at Balmoral in November. The problem of Schleswig and Holstein split the family. The Danish King was trying to incorporate Schleswig into Denmark through a new constitution. The Crown Prince and Princess were dead set against it; the duchies lay across Prussia's access to the North Sea and were essential to its future strength. There was bickering among Queen Victoria's children, some siding with Prussia, others with Denmark. Open quarrels broke out with the sudden death of the Danish King in mid-November.

This was a major international crisis. The King had no direct heir. Princess Alexandra's father was proclaimed King Christian IX and immediately signed the new constitution incorporating Schleswig into Denmark. The Local Assembly in Holstein appealed to the German Confederation to send as their ruler Frederick of Augustenburg, a liberal Duke. The conflict was fought over at Balmoral, where, for the first time, the Crown Prince stood up to Queen Victoria. Prussian interests could not be reconciled with Danish or English ones.

Queen Victoria complained to her uncle, King Leopold, that her son-in-law was very violent on the subject. She trembled at what he might say to the Prince of Wales and his Danish wife. She was miserable, wretched, almost frantic without the Prince Consort to stand by her and put the others down and in their right place. No respect was paid to her opinion now. This helplessness almost drove her wild. In the family, his loss was more dreadfully felt than anywhere. 'It makes visits like Fritz and Vicky's very painful and trying. Oh! God, why, oh! why was all this permitted?' And now that everything that the Prince Consort understood so well was taking place, he was not there to help them and write those admirable papers which were gospel now.[54]

With the Queen's family divided among itself and the Anglo-Coburg group in disarray, Bismarck continued to widen the rift between the Crown Prince and the King. The Prince was recalled to Berlin and told that he should keep away from all state councils; that he must give up any sign of opposition in public; and he must be careful not to disclose official or army secrets to anyone at all. This last warning was obviously directed against the Crown Princess, who was still in Scotland.

So Bismarck ended the year triumphant. He was preparing to unite Prussia by a short sharp war against the Danes. A glorious victory would change the mind of parliament about the need to strengthen the army. It would even change the mind of the Crown Prince, who was first and foremost a soldier. In one year of office, Bismarck had confused and scattered his opponents at home and abroad. The Crown Princess and Queen Victoria's efforts at diplomacy in Germany seemed futile. In fact, Bismarck could be grateful for the English Queen's interference. She had also advocated a good understanding between Prussia and Austria. Why not? At least, until the Danes were beaten and the duchies regained. Then the victors could fight over the spoils.

CHAPTER FIVE

To Us Germans

THE CROWN PRINCESS stood on her balcony in Berlin. Below her, the grey and blue soldiers were marching away, rank upon rank, to Schleswig. On 1 February 1864, a combined force of Prussian and Austrian troops had crossed the border into Schleswig. The Crown Prince was going with them to join the forces under the old Field Marshal Wrangel. Parades had always excited the Crown Princess; the prospect of war overwhelmed her. 'Our dear troops', she called the Prussians now. Until the war against Denmark, 'our soldiers' had always been British ones, but the sound of boots and drums in Berlin had made the Crown Princess identify herself with her adopted country at last. There was no problem about Schleswig and Holstein for her. It was 'to us Germans plain and simple as daylight and one for which we would gladly bring any sacrifice.'[1]

Bismarck had provoked the war. Technically, the Danes were in the wrong. The new constitution signed by King Christian IX broke the terms of the London Treaty which had defined the extent of Danish power in Schleswig and Holstein. When Bismarck's ultimatum was rejected, Prussia and Austria could claim the right to intervene on behalf of the German Confederation. While the smaller German states wanted a new independent duchy set up on the borders under Frederick of Augustenburg, Bismarck wanted Prussia to annex enough territory to secure access to the North Sea. At a Crown Council, he reminded the King that each of the recent rulers of Prussia had increased its size. The King thought that Bismarck had been drinking, the Crown Prince raised his hands to heaven as if Bismarck were mad, and the other ministers did not know what to say.

The invasion was a bitter blow to Queen Victoria, who had to struggle for six months to keep her Government from helping the Danes. Lord Palmerston told the Queen that the Germans were acting like bullies, but in real life as in romance, the wicked giant sometimes found that his intended victim met with unexpected support.[2] The Queen replied that England must play a passive role. She lobbied other Cabinet Ministers to keep her country out of the war, but in fact, the Cabinet was divided on the issue and came to no decision.

The conflict in the royal family was bad enough. The Queen's eldest daughter and the Crown Prince had supported the King in wanting to go to war. Both of her German sons-in-law were army officers and had left for the front. 'I had hoped that this dreadful war might be prevented,' she wrote to the Crown Princess, 'but you all (God forgive you for it) would have it!'[3] Her heart and her sympathy were all German, but she had to think of the whole family. The Prince of Wales was frantic, thinking that everyone wished to crush Denmark. His young wife Alexandra was in a terrible state of post-natal depression after the birth of her first child. Her father and brothers were fighting against their German cousins. 'Oh! if Bertie's wife was only a good German and not a Dane!' the Queen wailed. It was not so much the politics, but that the peace and harmony of the family were being destroyed. It was terrible to have the Prince of Wales supporting the wrong side. It aggravated her sufferings greatly.[4]

The Crown Princess had no special reports on what was happening in the war. Bismarck kept most of the confidential information from the Crown Prince, and the King had again warned his son not to reveal state matters to his wife. Bismarck did not even tell the King much of what he was planning or doing. As he admitted later, with the risks he was taking, he was beginning to live as close to the gallows as to the throne. He was chiefly fretting about having to pay for the war illegally from Prussian treasury reserves. He was not getting the quick cheap victory he needed. The outnumbered Danes fought well, withdrawing slowly, so that it was not until 18 April that the German troops were able to storm the trenches at Düppel and force the Danes to accept an armistice.

The action had been preceded by the bombardment of the town of Sonderburg, which caused an outcry against Prussian brutality from *The Times* and in the British Parliament. Inspired by growing Prussian patriotism, the Crown Princess was indignant. The bombardment of the town had been necessary in order to take Düppel. The constant meddling and interfering by England in other people's affairs was exciting ridicule on the Continent; it made her own position in Prussia intolerable.[5]

Attacks on Queen Victoria began appearing in English newspapers. She was accused of embarrassing the Government by her pro-German views. Lord Palmerston sent her one critical editorial, and accused persons close to her of being indiscreet about her opinions. 'Pilgerstein is gouty, and extremely impertinent,' Queen Victoria complained, giving a nickname to her Prime Minister. Yet when Lord Ellenborough attacked her in the House of Lords for her German sympathies, she was grateful for Lord John, now Earl Russell's defence of her and for his claim that the Government alone took the responsibility for British foreign policy.

The same sort of thing was happening to the Crown Princess in Berlin. People there said she was unhappy at the success of Prussian arms. Court circles regretted having an Englishwoman in the royal family. New rumours spread that she had discovered secrets from a Crown Council and had telegraphed them to Lord Palmerston, who had immediately threatened Prussia. 'I feel as if I could smash the idiots,' the Crown Princess declared, 'it is so spiteful and untrue. I am sure that I would almost quarrel with my real and best friends in dear England rather than forget that I belong to this country.'[6]

On the advice of her Foreign Secretary, Queen Victoria wrote twice to her 'Dear Brother', the King of Prussia. In her first letter, she congratulated him on his victorious army. (Her son-in-law the Crown Prince was soon to be given command of the Second Army Corps.) The agitation in England was only because people wrongly believed that Prussia wanted to annex Schleswig and Holstein. She did not believe this and could not believe it of the King. In her second letter, she begged him to show generosity to the weaker party and not ask too much of the Danes.

Her letters had little effect on the King. Victory had made him stubborn. He wanted ports and fortresses on the Baltic and the North Sea, and he wanted the greater part of Schleswig. The armistice negotiations were broken off and the war was resumed. Because of Field Marshal Wrangel's advanced age, the Crown Prince was becoming the effective commander of the army. His tact and leadership saved many lives during the inexorable progress through Denmark. If there were any credit to be had from such a one-sided contest, it went to him.

Feeling for brave little Denmark was so strong in England that the sending of the fleet to help her seemed probable. Earl Russell proposed this, but was opposed by the Queen. At two critical Cabinet meetings in June, the peace party only just prevailed. The navy would not be sent to help the Danes unless Copenhagen were threatened or Denmark, herself, was in danger of being destroyed.

It was a close-run thing. The Queen's unwavering support for Germany, her insistence that she would not agree to a war in which English interests were not directly menaced, had just prevented intervention. 'After a week of the greatest anxiety,' she wrote to her uncle, King Leopold, 'the only wise and reasonable course has been pursued; and this country is safe.' She felt that Prince Albert had blessed and guided her. His ideas still worked on for everybody after his death. 'It IS satisfactory to see that my efforts were not unavailing.'[7]

The King of Prussia thought so too. Although he was exasperated by the threats issuing from Palmerston and Russell, he was conscious of the Queen's role in helping to keep England out of the war. He never missed an opportunity of telling the Crown Princess how much he owed her mother for keeping the peace. What tormented the Crown Princess was the feeling of animosity between her two countries. It was dangerous and harmful; it was kept up by foolish trifles and could be avoided. Aware that her soldier husband and Prussia were becoming increasingly important to her life, she warned her mother: 'Now dear Papa is no longer here I live in constant dread that the bonds which united our two countries for their mutual good are being so loosened that they may be in time quite severed!'[8]

Queen Victoria would not admit to that possibility. She would not permit any break in relationships, so long as the Crown Princess could keep open her sources of Intelligence from Prussia. She would use that special knowledge to prevent a rupture between the two countries. Unfortunately, at the moment, public opinion in England was ungovernable because it was thought that Prussia wanted to seize both Schleswig and Holstein. The Queen, however, had taken to heart Lord Palmerston's accusation about the indiscretions of those close to her. She told her daughter never to say that the Queen's opinions were in opposition to her Government's – which they often were, which she sometimes told her daughter they were, and which her daughter used to excuse England's behaviour to the King of Prussia. It was only a constitutional hypocrisy to say that they never were.

The resumed war did not last long. The Prussians and Austrians pressed forward in Jutland, there was a change of government in Copenhagen, and the Danes sued for peace. They were ready to concede both Schleswig and Holstein to the German Powers. When the Prussian and Austrian representatives met to agree a division of the spoils, Bismarck demanded the two duchies for Prussia. The Austrian Foreign Minister was prepared to accept this, if Prussia would guarantee to help Austria to reconquer Lombardy. Bismarck agreed, only to find that the King of Prussia's sense of honour would not allow him to seize the duchies. He had no right to them, he said.

So Bismarck had to accept a joint occupation of the duchies by Prussia and Austria. It was not an alliance, but an increase of opportunities for misunderstanding. It was the prelude to a civil war in Germany.

During the war, the love between the Crown Prince and his wife grew deeper and stronger. Although the fighting took her husband away from her, the Crown Princess recognized that it brought out the best qualities in him. She envied him because he won the love of his troops. Only when he was away did she realize how much she was disliked in Prussia. His love and presence usually protected her. Now she felt she could do nothing right. Her husband reassured her that they were made for each other. He joked that he did not understand how a gifted woman like her could put up with an inferior fellow like him.[9]

The Crown Princess had become pregnant again, but her mother did not approve. She ought to have had two good years' rest before she began again, Queen Victoria declared. Her own example could not be cited against her; she had begun three years later than her daughter had. She had also never suffered in the same way, even if it had done her nerves terrible harm.[10]

With her nine children, Queen Victoria was in no position to complain about her daughters having too many children themselves. The offspring would increase her family and her influence. Now that Alice was also pregnant again in Hesse-Darmstadt, the Queen could look forward to having enough grandchildren to fill the thrones of many more kingdoms and principalities.

Although the Crown Princess was not allowed to travel to England because of her condition, she wanted her eldest son, Willy, to go. The sea air at Osborne would do him good, and English doctors could look at his bad arm. The King was reluctant to give permission for his grandson to visit England. As the Crown Princess herself admitted, feelings in Prussia were so violent, that anything which seemed to point to her English sympathies could damage her and her husband's position very much. Yet she could not help thinking how natural it was to send a little child away for the good of his health and to see his grandmother who, personally, was most popular in Germany.

The trouble with her son Willy was that, in a sense, he was public property, the next in line to the throne after his father. 'We have to consider all these things,' she told her mother, 'particularly as there is such a jealousy about me as a stranger – and such a fear that I have a bad influence and would wish to bring up the children as foreigners.'[11] She did not wish to give useless offence to good, if prejudiced people, but she ended by doing so. Willy was sent over to see his grandmother, because the King was grateful to Queen Victoria for having helped to keep England out of the war.

The Queen of England immediately wrote to her friend, the Queen of Prussia, to say how pleased she was at her grandson's arrival. He felt quite at home and was a dear, sweet child, affectionate to her and, more important, tactful enough to remember his grandfather. She herself felt terribly sad. It reminded her so vividly of the happy summer three years before, when the Prince Consort had been alive and had doted on his grandson at Osborne. 'Now everything is as it was then – and everything in ruins!'[12]

During that summer holiday, with her Prussian grandson to herself, Queen Victoria formed a special relationship with him. He felt so certain of her affection that he would turn to her all his life, even when he was at odds with his mother. This special feeling between the aged Queen and her grandson who was to become Kaiser, was a factor in keeping the peace between the British and German empires at the turn of the century. He could never quite ignore his love and awe of her, while she could never quite forget how she had cared for him when he was alone in England.

Willy's education worried the Crown Princess. As he would probably inherit the throne from his father, he must be influenced in the right way. She wished him to become a great man, a second Frederick the Great or Prince Albert. With his father, he would have so much to do in rebuilding what was being destroyed by the 'powers of darkness' presently ruling Prussia.[13] She wanted to bring him up with a British feeling of independence and common sense. Her mother agreed with her. 'Bring him up simply, plainly,' she stressed, 'not with that terrible Prussian pride and ambition, which grieved dear Papa so much.'[14]

Hopes were one thing, practice another. Steps were being taken to select a tutor who would be right for Willy. Trusting Robert Morier's recommendation too much, the Crown Princess chose George Hinzpeter as the man who would instruct her son. He was a pedant and a bore, who believed in discipline and high principles at the cost of compassion and understanding. Unfortunately, Morier had praised Hinzpeter's morals and political principles – not exactly the qualities needed to deal with a wilful and difficult child like Willy, who was being even more tormented by electric shock treatment for his withered arm. Young Stockmar, still clinging to his post in the Crown Prince's household, distrusted Hinzpeter, finding him heartless and too Spartan. But Hinzpeter was to keep his position for thirteen years, in spite of Willy's mother wishing to study her child, herself, and judge what was best for him.

In September, the Crown Princess gave birth to her third son Sigismund, whom she particularly adored for his sweet and loving nature. She seemed to delight more and more in domesticity, seeing in it a private blessing, a compensation for her public misfortunes. As distrust of *die Engländerin* grew, and as Bismarck managed to keep her husband more and more in quarantine, she concentrated on making a happy home and a large family for him. She looked for a quiet country house near Potsdam where she and the children could retire from the suspicious atmosphere of court circles. In the little village of Bornstadt, she found a deserted house in an overgrown orchard. Surrounding it was a broken-down village where poor peasants slept like their own beasts on straw beds. The place would be a haven and an experiment in reform. The family could live simply and be happy there.

The playwright, Gustav zu Putlitz, for a time a chamberlain to the Crown Princess, drew an illuminating portrait of her in the first summer of her quarantine under Bismarck. He found her wonderfully well-read, more cultivated than any other woman of her years. She debated like a historian with judgement and discrimination. Above all, with her candour and simplicity, she had the gift of putting people at their ease. Sometimes she wore a plain woollen dress and sang songs as she sat at a spinning-wheel. She devoted herself to making a home for the Crown Prince, where all might feel secure from intrigue, and where frankness and clear intelligence were prized.[15]

Robert Morier found the Crown Princess's island of security and straightforwardness more at risk. He saw the couple soon after Bismarck had finally forced young Stockmar to leave their service. This ended all direct Coburg influence and eliminated one of Queen Victoria's two main sources of Intelligence. Bismarck's diplomatic victories had not affected the Crown Prince or his wife. They told Morier that they were disgusted at such successful brilliance. They stood like a dead wall against the cynical sophistries of Bismarck.

Morier thought that the Crown Prince's defiant speech at Danzig had made Bismarck think twice about attacking the Constitution again. The continuing passive opposition of the heir to the throne was paralysing Bismarck's illegal activities. The fact that the two young people had remained unscathed was a credit to them. Now that Stockmar was gone, there was not a single person in their entourage who was not a devoted Bismarckian. The two men closest to the Prince were Bismarck's creatures body and soul.[16]

Beset and marked out, the Crown Prince and Princess stood firm. Bismarck kept up the slights upon the Crown Prince in the hope of eroding the wall of his resistance. The King's displeasure at his son's persistent opposition was shown in the most public way; the Crown Prince was forbidden to be in Berlin to take the salute of the victorious troops returning from Denmark. This made him sad, but left him stubborn. The hardest thing, his wife admitted, was not an open struggle, but coping with the constant little annoyances and persecutions. They were allowed to meet the Prince and Princess of Wales at Cologne, but it was a stiff and awkward encounter. The Prussian Prince could not hide his pride at his recent victories in Schleswig. He flaunted a very objectionable campaign ribbon – Queen Victoria was told by her son – which he had received for his deeds of valour against the unhappy Danes.

The only refuge from the pinpricks of the reactionary court, and the attentions of Bismarck and his spies, was in the family. The greatest achievement of Queen Victoria in the rearing of her children had been to keep them close-knit and loyal to her – they would tell her everything without much discrimination. The special quality in her huge correspondence with her daughters in Germany lay in the mixture of the personal and the political, the trivial and the secret, as if all matters were equally important. Babies teething and rumours of war, difficulties with nannies and Bismarck's intrigues, gossip about relations and possible royal marriages, all were given the same space and weight – a ragbag of inside information which the Queen of England could pick from at her leisure, sending on selected paragraphs to her Foreign Secretaries for the good of her country, and reserving the rest to treasure as a mother and as the centre of her powerful family.

The flow of political information from Berlin diminished with the new year of 1865. Bismarck's quarantine was taking effect. Very little news of any importance, and no state secrets were reaching the Crown Princess. She had to make do with stories about her children to amuse her mother, who was now reverting to seclusion and detachment after her six months' burst of activity in helping to prevent her country from going to war with Germany. The Crown Princess wrote to her mother about an argument between Willy and Charlotte on the nature of the Divine. Charlotte had said she thought that God was in her heart; Willy had disagreed, saying that she was sometimes naughty, so God had come into him. 'Yes, but I am not naughty now,' Charlotte had replied, 'and God will not fly away to you.' Yet Willy would not give up. If his sister had God, he had Jesus in him. When his governess had tried to point out that God was powerful enough to be in the hearts of both the children at the same time, and that He was really the same as Jesus, Willy had protested: 'Oh no, *mademoiselle*, Jesus and God are not the same thing. Jesus Christ has some whiskers, I saw it in my book, and I am sure *der liebe Gott* has no whiskers.'[17]

'Now you are head of all the family,' Princess Alice wrote to her mother Queen Victoria, 'it seems incredible, and that dear Papa should not be by your side.'[18] With the terminal illness of her uncle and father-figure, King Leopold, the Queen of England found herself the elder statesman of them all. Bismarck was manœuvring to swallow up the two duchies and provoke Austria into a losing war. Queen Victoria and the Crown Princess were set on a collision course with Bismarck over the best way of uniting Germany. It was to be the last year of the long Coburg dream, for Germany would be united soon by iron and blood.

To Bismarck, the English Queen's trump cards, the marriages of her children, seemed to be played as deliberate provocations. Her third daughter Princess Helena now needed a husband. The Queen chose Prince Christian of Schleswig-Holstein, an intimate of her eldest daughter and the Crown Prince. He was the younger brother of Frederick of Augustenburg, the pretender to the two duchies, backed by the smaller German states. At the end of the Danish war, Bismarck, furious that they would not surrender their rights, had deprived both brothers of their army commissions and their property. At the Convention of Gastein in August, he arranged that Holstein should be administered by Austria, and Schleswig by Prussia; the Augustenburg claims were ignored.

This agreement with Austria, Bismarck sneered, was papering over the cracks. He took Queen Victoria's choice of a husband for her third daughter as a slap in the face, and a reminder that she did not expect Prussia to gobble up smaller German states and eliminate their rightful rulers. The fact that both the Crown Prince and Princess supported Prince Christian as Helena's husband, calling him the best creature in the world, made them greater offenders in Bismarck's eyes. They seemed to enjoy thwarting him.

Queen Victoria's visit to Coburg that summer also seemed to be a demonstration of her support of the lesser German states against Prussian aggrandisement. Officially, the Queen went to Coburg to unveil a statue of her beloved husband, but she was joined by all of her nine children and fifteen of her princely German relatives at the 'beautiful, touching and solemn ceremony'. It was an impressive display of the Queen's influence – a reminder that the Queen was deeply concerned with the future of Germany. At Coburg she was showing that she would do her best to carry out her husband's policies, which Bismarck was determined to deny.

For the first time, Queen Victoria's letters began to take on a bias against Prussia. 'Prussia seems inclined to behave as atrociously as possible, and as she always has done,' she declared. 'Odious people the Prussians are, that I must say.'[19] Bismarck's policy of aggrandisement had changed Queen Victoria's belief in the necessary alliance of the two great Protestant powers. She did not even want to meet the King of Prussia during her visit to Germany, but she felt she had to see him after a plea from his wife, who claimed that the King's personal feelings for Queen Victoria were what they had always been, but sadly he was under the influence of a clever, unprincipled man who had completely changed him. When Queen Victoria did meet the King, it was clear that he had been told to remain as silent as possible. He talked about the weather and left after half an hour.

The Queen could do nothing to help her eldest daughter against the ascendancy of Bismarck, who had been created a Count by the grateful King after the Convention of Gastein. The Crown Princess continued to send her mother stray pieces of political information, but nothing of great importance. Surrounded by Bismarck's spies, she knew the danger of criticizing the Minister President in writing. From Schleswig in August, she dared to send a letter by ordinary post instead of waiting for the royal messenger. In it, she declared that Bismarck was a reckless adventurer. She added that if the letter were opened by the postal officials, she would be accused of high treason – but that she was as loyal as anyone.[20]

Bismarck took pleasure in having the Crown Prince shunted aside to become the honorary Protector of Public Museums. The new *realpolitik* was consigning the antique decency of the Crown Prince and his Coburg friends to a repository of the past. 'The Crown Prince occupies himself with politics he does not understand,' Bismarck jeered to a French diplomat, 'talks of things of which he knows nothing, and opens books which he does not read.'[21] He was almost irrelevant to Bismarck's unfolding plans to make Prussia into Germany – unimportant as long as he could not rally the Liberal opposition and did not inherit the throne. The Prince still performed his military duties, for example, visiting the great Krupp works at Essen, where ten thousand workers were turning out the breech-loading needle rifles for the Prussian Army. But he had effectively been put out to grass. Only if Bismarck were to get the war he wanted against Austria, would the Crown Prince have his opportunity to command.

The fact that the army reforms were being carried out and paid for, increased Bismarck's dominance over the King. The Chambers continued to refuse to vote funds for the military budget, and they continued to be dissolved by Bismarck; he preferred to rule without the nuisance of having to consult a pack of deputies. Yet he found the money to pay for more troops and munitions, and to line a war chest for the coming war against Austria. His financier was still Bleichröder, who arranged for the illegal sale of the Prussian State's interest in the Cologne–Minden railway for thirty million *talers*. This would pay for the mobilization of nine army corps, and would keep them in the field for a month, without touching the reserves in the state treasury.

So Bismarck was acquiring the sinews of war, but he was not sure about its outcome. Financing was one thing, fighting, another. The leading strategist Moltke continually reminded him that war was uncertain. Austria was held to be more powerful than Prussia. What had to be avoided was a war on two fronts, with the French attacking across the Rhine. Bismarck went to Biarritz and saw the French Emperor, who alone in Europe was as enigmatic and reckless as himself. He hinted that if Napoleon III stayed on his side of the Rhine during the coming German war, France might be compensated with parts of Belgium or Luxembourg. Also, Italy would be able to seize Venetia from Austria and round off her kingdom below the Alps. The Prussians would do the fighting, the French and their allies would reap some of the harvest. When Bismarck left, he had promised nothing definite, but he had neutralized Prussia's western flank. 'Napoleon will dance a cotillion with us,' he boasted, 'without being clear in his mind when it will begin or what figures it will include.'[22]

Bismarck's brilliance at this time even seduced the new British Ambassador to Berlin, Lord Napier, who reported that Bismarck had some great and generous qualities even if he were indiscreet and unscrupulous in pursuing his aims. The Prussian minister intended to quell all opposition at home by his success abroad. Finally, Napier confessed to a peculiar sympathy for Bismarck's strange, impetuous, desultory, domineering, aspiring, humorous character. He was a man who should not be in government in Berlin, but should live in London with free spirits and men of letters.[23]

To have a British ambassador being as cynical and realistic as Bismarck was too much. Napier was replaced by a previous ambassador to Berlin, Lord Augustus Loftus. Queen Victoria would not have as her representative in Prussia any one who seemed to side with Bismarck against her daughter. The Crown Princess still thought that Bismarck and a small reactionary clique were the villains who perverted and misrepresented all. Like Lord Napier, the King of Prussia had been turned. He had agreed to take over Schleswig and the naval base at Kiel. He had put aside his deep beliefs in the sanctity of hereditary right, in order to gain more land and power for Prussia. His honour now seemed to consist in accepting what Bismarck achieved for him, without inquiring too closely into how it was done. The Minister President's most dangerous quality was his ability to attach people to the tail of his comet. Where he blazed, they were dazzled and drawn on. In admiring his successes and his genius at diplomacy, they stifled their doubts about his morality and methods.

The Crown Prince and Princess seemed old-fashioned. Their liberalism, once a revolutionary force in Europe, appeared dated and futile beside the new thrust of national diplomacy. Their pious judgements seemed insupportable and irrelevant, an intrusion on what had to be.

Even their moral rock, the values and example of Queen Victoria, was slippery beneath their feet, for she was becoming involved in the only scandal of her private life. She had taken to herself a permanent Highland servant, John Brown. Having been alone too long, she needed the devoted and comforting support of a strong man. Brown cleaned the Queen's things and did odd jobs, put her on her pony and took her off, fussed over her welfare and shielded her privacy – and even interposed his body between her and attempted assassins.

The Queen's Highland servant was five years younger than she, a handsome brawny man with a curly beard and bright blue eyes. He had a trenchant manner which could offend; he was liable to call the Queen 'Wumman' and tell her how to behave outdoors. The Prince of Wales thought him a boor and an intruder. Yet Brown could be so tender, particularly about the Queen's grief for her dead husband, that she was touched to the heart. In her most illuminating story about her new relationship, she told the Crown Princess about Brown's first visit to the Mausoleum at Frogmore near Windsor.

When he came to her room later, he was much affected. He looked at the Queen with pity, while tears rolled down his cheeks. In his simple expressive way, he said: 'I didn't like to see ye at Frogmore this morning. I felt for ye – to see ye coming there with your daughters and your husband lying there – marriage on one side and death on the other. No, I didn't like to see it. I felt sorry for ye. I know so well what your feeling must be – ye who had been so happy. There is no more pleasure for you, poor Queen, and I feel for ye but what can I do for ye? I could die for ye.'[24]

The Queen was deeply moved by this emotional speech from her blunt hardy man, her child of the mountains. She grew to depend on his care and judgement. His constant presence by her and her continuing refusal to make public appearances led to rumours and jokes that she was 'Mrs John Brown'. She would try to dismiss these insinuations as ill-natured gossip among the aristocracy, because she could not be forced out of her seclusion.[25] But she could not stop the deterioration abroad of her image of strict morality, particularly where viperous tongues were stinging the King of Prussia's ear.

Queen Victoria's character and dignity made it unbelievable that she could be John Brown's mistress or his secret wife. She wanted security and devotion, no more than that. But her fierce defence of Brown's position so close to her person, her refusal to listen to the wise advice to shed him for the sake of her reputation, damned her in the eyes of the gossips and intriguers against the Coburg influence and the English alliance. What Queen of England could complain of immoral behaviour by foreign diplomats when she was so close to a body-servant? Those who lived in glass palaces could not throw stones.

CHAPTER SIX

❧❧❧

To Win, To Lose

'YOU ARE AMBITIOUS to be a king,' the Crown Princess mocked Bismarck in 1866, 'or at least President of a republic.'

She was half-joking, half-serious. Her so amiable and condescending manner irritated the Prussian minister. She had that touch of ironical superiority which Bismarck remembered from his one meeting with Queen Victoria at Versailles. The English Queen and her daughter seemed reluctant to be unfriendly to a man they clearly found unsympathetic and eccentric.

So Bismarck replied in the same semi-jocular tone. He was more confident now, and even more powerful, for he had achieved his war with Austria, and the Crown Prince had helped him to win it. Yet he still feared the potential influence of the alien Crown Princess who was so intelligent and provocative that she could dare to fence with him.

'I am personally spoilt for a republican,' Bismarck told her. He had need of a monarchy for his well-being on earth. He thanked God he did not have to live like a king, constantly on show. Until his death, he was fated to be the King's faithful subject.

The Crown Princess continued to look mockingly at him as he protested his loyalty. He was forced to change tack. He said that not everyone thought, as he did, that the monarchy would last. There would never be a shortage of royalists, but there might be a shortage of kings. 'To make a stew, a hare is needed. To make a monarchy, a king.' The next generation might be republican, if there were no king who wanted to be king. The heir to the throne made him anxious; he did not seem to respect monarchic traditions.

The English princess refused to be drawn. She kept up her ironies and her pleasantries, giving Bismarck the impression that she was merely teasing a political opponent. She seemed to like provoking his patriotism by playful criticism.[1] It was a policy which she had learned from Bismarck himself, who had taunted the opposition at home, and tormented Austria until she had been driven into mobilization. Now he had become too powerful for the Crown Princess to do more than taunt him.

The Crown Prince had been the leading supporter of peace with Austria and fair dealing over the independence of Schleswig and Holstein, so Bismarck had attacked his motives by way of his wife's relatives. When the betrothed Prince Christian and Princess Helena had proposed to spend part of their honeymoon in the Augustenburg's family castle at Gravenstein, they were forbidden to do so by the King of Prussia on Bismarck's advice. The castle was in occupied Schleswig; Prussian troops held the ground; might displaced right. Queen Victoria could think the King's behaviour a gross insult; the Crown Princess could be dreadfully hurt and shocked, calling it monstrous for the King to forbid a prince to go to his private property, but politics came before property. When Queen Victoria insisted that the Crown Prince show his father an outraged letter from her, it merely made the Prince seem more in the wrong, and under his mother-in-law's thumb.

Bismarck knew his worth to the monarchy, yet he knew he might be dismissed when the Crown Prince became King. He told Count Robert von der Goltz, his ambassador in Paris: '*Après moi le déluge.* The Crown Prince can never govern the country.'[2] In a Cabinet council, he accused the Crown Prince of being personally antagonistic to him, and pernicious to Prussia. He had the Crown Prince called to the deathbed of a leading Junker who used his last breaths on a paean of praise of Bismarck: as the ablest pilot of the State, worthy of all support. Similar sentiments poured from the lips of the Mayor of Berlin, who interrupted a business interview with the Crown Prince to laud and magnify Bismarck's name. These did not convince the Crown Prince, who also resisted veiled threats. When the Mayor of Magdeburg pointed out that Bismarck's power would be gone when the Crown Prince took the throne, Bismarck replied that he would succeed in annihilating that opposition before it became dangerous to him. Manteuffel, the previous Minister President, spoke in much the same way.[3] The Crown Prince was kept in a state of siege and alarm. 'I am the only one who is not told even an iota about political affairs,' he wrote in his diary. 'Everyone is thinking of war with Austria which Bismarck wants at all costs.'[4]

Bismarck intended to drive the Crown Prince into openly declaring his opposition to the coming war. On 24 February, after they had refused to vote for an expanded military and naval budget, Bismarck had the Chambers closed yet again. He wanted no elected deputies present to witness his handling of the conflict. 'Look what a lamentable pitiable spectacle we are,' the Crown Princess complained to her mother, 'with worse than no constitution, a prey to the caprices of a bad and dangerous man! One feels so sad – so ashamed and so helpless.'[5] Four days after the closure of parliament, the Crown Prince was summoned to a critical Crown council, where all were bound to an oath of secrecy. Moltke and the General Staff were there with the court's military advisers; the War Minister, Roon, the Finance Minister, Bodelschwingh and Bismarck were present; so were Goltz and the King. All the generals favoured a war with Austria that spring. Bismarck recited a catalogue of Austrian perfidy and insults of the past fifty years, and claimed that it was Prussia's mission to unite Germany. He also agreed with Moltke on the need for an alliance with Italy so as to involve Austria in a war on two fronts.

Not every one agreed. Knowing that the Prussian treasury could not support a campaign of more than a few weeks, the Finance Minister was hesitant and favoured a last attempt at peace. The Crown Prince stood firmly against a war, declaring that when brother fought brother in Germany, only the French would profit on the Rhine. He knew nothing of Bismarck's dealings with Napoleon III, which were intended to neutralize him. All he had done was to expose himself as a pacifist, although he might well be given command of a Prussian army in the event of war.

The King listened and finally spoke. His conscience and his God demanded justice for Prussia even at the price of a war with Austria, but he would not allow an unjust war against fellow Germans, so peace with honour would still be preferable. He approved of Bismarck's working for French neutrality and a military alliance with Italy. By accepting a conflict which was inevitable sooner or later, the King left its timing to the generals. They and Bismarck thought he meant to fight, but they could not be sure. So secret was the meeting that even the Crown Princess heard no word of it from her husband. The new British Ambassador, Lord Augustus Loftus, could only report that it had taken place, and that a campaign had been planned to annex the Danish border duchies.[6]

In early April, Bismarck achieved a military alliance with Italy. If war were to break out within the following three months, Italy would attack Austria in Venetia. While Italy committed herself, Napoleon III pursued his ambiguous neutrality, negotiating with Austria so as to become the arbiter of a struggle in Germany. The winner would have to pay him off in the Rhineland as the price for keeping the French out.

The Austrians were sufficiently provoked into taking elementary military precautions against a surprise attack. Their army needed seven weeks to mobilize, the Prussians, after the King's military reforms, only three. Forced to play Bismarck's game, the Austrians felt obliged to reinforce their fortresses in Bohemia and Moravia. With intelligence sources reporting every detail of these troop movements, Bismarck could represent defensive measures as aggressive ones. The strengthening of a fort against a sneak attack was made to seem a menace to Prussian borders. The King was persuaded to send troops and munitions to the southern frontier, yet he still would not call up the reserves.

While Bismarck pursued his policies, the Crown Prince and Princess tried, with Queen Augusta, to prevent the war. At a reception given by Bismarck in the middle of March, the new British Ambassador managed to have a long conversation with the King. Unexpectedly, the King responded to an offer of British arbitration between Prussia and Austria. He declared that he did not want to push things to the extreme. Then for the first time, he spoke to his son about the political crisis, asking him to write to Queen Victoria and offer her the agreeable task of mediating between the two German powers. This was a strange about-face and a blow to Bismarck's methods of diplomacy. As the British Ambassador said, the question for Bismarck was: Would he carry the King with him? If the British could get the wedge in, Bismarck would find it more difficult.[7]

'You again, dearest Mama,' the Crown Princess wrote in elation, 'may be the means of averting a European conflagration.' England's interference had often been untimely and unlucky, but this time there was every chance of success. Bent on war for his own 'wild, mad purposes', Bismarck probably knew nothing of this new policy of the King's. It was in Austria's interests not to fight. All now looked to Queen Victoria as their good genius.[8]

When he heard of it, Bismarck was appalled by such direct royal intervention. He immediately lodged a protest through Count Albrecht von Bernstorff, the Prussian Ambassador in London. The Crown Prince should not have sent the King's message to Queen Victoria; it should have gone through the Prussian Embassy. Lord Clarendon, now the Queen's Foreign Secretary, was himself annoyed at rival royal negotiations. Yet he defended the Crown Prince, saying that if he had not passed on the message, or had modified it, he would have been blamed by the King.[9]

'The wicked man' Bismarck was frantic, the Crown Princess wrote to her mother. He said that the alternative royal diplomacy would not do. It crossed his plans; it was a useless interference. In short, he was very angry. He would now do all he could to pin the King to his policies and paralyse any intervention. She thought Queen Victoria should know this without delay even though it might appear like an intrigue, which she hated.[10]

The Crown Princess knew the risk she was taking. If Bismarck laid hands on any message to her mother that revealed a state secret, he could utterly destroy her and her husband. 'Please pray do not betray me,' she implored her mother early in April. 'I am not supposed to know anything contained in the Despatches, but as I did hear this I thought I would tell you.'[11] Needing to protect herself from Bismarck's increasing surveillance, she asked her mother for more secure and quicker methods of communication. She did not even want the British Foreign Office to know what she was telling Queen Victoria; her mother would not betray her, where an ambassador might.

'Will you not arrange a cipher between me and you?' she asked her mother in England. 'When I want to use it, I can send the figures to Lord Augustus Loftus. Nobody here will know that he is not telegraphing something of his own. The Foreign Office can pass on the figures to you without knowing what they are. I think this might be very useful, and if you approve, no time ought to be lost about it.'[12]

Queen Victoria knew the limits of royal diplomacy far better than her daughter did. She told her Prime Minister immediately of the information in her daughter's last letter, but she did not think an offer to mediate between the two German powers would work. It was made superfluous by Bismarck, who had already sent a long letter to Count Bernstorff saying that such an attempt would all end in smoke. Her own Foreign Secretary, Lord Clarendon, was being disagreeable and unmanageable, resenting her efforts to intervene. Earl Russell was still anxious that she should do all she could.[13] But Bismarck's insistence that all the faults lay on Austria's side meant that her good offices would require her to persuade the Habsburg Empire to surrender to his demands.

Bismarck followed up his instructions to Bernstorff by making it clear to Lord Augustus Loftus that Prussia meant to fight unless Holstein, and control of the whole of north Germany, were delivered on a plate. He declared that Prussia was only responding to Austrian military preparations. 'What would you do,' he asked Loftus, 'if you found a violent man in the street threatening the public security and peace?' Loftus replied that he would call for the police who, in this case, were the great powers of Europe. 'But if it were the case of a gentleman,' Bismarck countered, 'you would give him your card' – and fight a duel to the death.

The truth, Loftus stated, was that Bismarck had fully made up his mind for war. He had gone so far that he must either carry out his hazardous policy or resign.[14] This bleak assessment stunned Queen Victoria, but Earl Russell was of the same opinion. As the Crown Princess admitted to her mother, trying to stop a war without the Prince Consort's help was a nervous business. Queen Victoria was prostrated by one of her worst headaches when she heard from Queen Augusta that there was no time to lose. She must reply to the King of Prussia's offer to accept her mediation; he seemed a good deal hurt that she had made no response.[15] She could not tell him that, because of the reactions of Bismarck and her own Foreign Secretary, her mediation would prove unacceptable, and was foredoomed. She was forced to agree with Earl Russell's diagnosis. There was but one remedy, one certain path of preserving peace. If any patriots close to the throne could persuade the King to dismiss Bismarck, all might come right.[16]

So began the 'Coburg intrigue', the last-ditch effort of the surviving believers in old Stockmar's plan to unite Germany. Not entirely in jest, Princess Helena had asked her eldest sister, the Crown Princess, to send as a wedding present – Bismarck's head on a charger. He must go, or sister would be set against sister in Germany, brother would fight brother in Bismarck's civil war.

Queen Victoria initiated the 'Coburg intrigue' by suggesting that Bismarck was treacherous. Replying to the King's offer to accept her arbitration, she wrote to the Crown Prince that the course pursued by the Prussian Government made it difficult, if not impossible, for England to intervene. The annexation of both duchies, despite the known feelings and wishes of the people there, violated English principles. The Queen then attempted to drive in the wedge further between the King and his Minister President, by revealing that Bismarck had sent to Paris an account of the King's private conversation with Lord Augustus Loftus at the reception. He was abusing his Master's confidence, she said, in order to defeat the pacific views of the King.[17]

When the Queen's letter arrived safely in Berlin at the end of March, the Crown Prince sent its contents in a personal message to the King, but received no reply. Meanwhile the Crown Princess, ignoring her delicate situation, replied to her mother's inquiries about the extent of Prussian mobilization: five of the Prussian frontier forts had been fully armed; four army divisions had been put on alert.[18] This military information reached Queen Victoria before she heard of it from the Foreign Office.

It was now the turn of Queen Victoria's brother-in-law, Duke Ernest of Coburg, to intervene. He secured a letter from the Austrian Foreign Minister declaring the Emperor's wish for peace, and travelled to Berlin personally to see that it reached the King of Prussia. No one wished for war – the Duke reported from Berlin – neither the King nor the princes nor any mortal; the fault rested singly and solely with Bismarck.

This comment was ingenuous. The general staff wanted war, as did many of the Junkers and reactionaries at court. It suited the war party and the King to put all the responsibility for Prussia's policy on Bismarck, who wished only to unite Germany in the way Italy had been united. It suited the Coburgs and the peace party around the Queen of Prussia and the Crown Prince to cast Bismarck as sole and total villain, misleading the righteous King. The Tsar now intervened, sending his uncle, the King of Prussia, a peace proposal through Baron Schleinitz, an ex-aide-de-camp of the Crown Prince. But the proposal was ignored. The Duke of Coburg and the rulers of the other small German states were now worrying about a circular from Bismarck which demanded to know who would fight for and who against Prussia. In the Duke's opinion, only a serious warning from England and France together would deter Bismarck from his disastrous course.[19]

While English diplomacy was trying and failing to secure French support against Bismarck's war, the King made a move of his own. He proposed to send General Münster on a special secret mission to Vienna to see if disarmament were still possible. Bismarck dissuaded him by offering his resignation if his policy were not followed. The King yielded, breathing peace and war alternately to different people. Ever vacillating, his anger towards Austria remained constant. Bismarck was intent on war, Lord Augustus Loftus reported, and war he would have if he remained in office. In short, the King had to choose between Bismarck and peace.[20]

The joint strains of stimulating the King to fight and frustrating the 'Coburg intrigue' were telling on Bismarck. He was tired of foreign monarchies trying to stick a finger into the national omelette. He hardly ever left his official residence, and was said to be ill or dying. There, the Austrian Ambassador found him lying on his red sofa like a wounded boar – in agony, but a threat to any hunter who came into his lair. He was suffering from indigestion, neuralgia and varicose veins. In the mornings, he was usually bilious and hung-over. Rumours of his resignation were widespread in early April. In an endeavour to steal the Coburg clique's thunder and attract liberal and national support for Prussian policy, he had boldly proposed that the German Confederation at Frankfurt be ruled by deputies elected by national male suffrage. But the idea of one man, one vote offended the King. He told Bismarck: 'What you are proposing to me is revolution!'[21]

The contradictory swerves in Bismarck's policies baffled his supporters as well as his enemies. At this low point of his unpopularity, Queen Victoria struck her hardest blow. She sent a personal letter to the King of Prussia through Lord Augustus Loftus, who handed it to the King in the royal railway carriage. The British Ambassador told the King that the letter was the private act of Her Majesty and did not involve her Government. Then and there, the King read the letter with interest and attention, while Loftus watched him. The letter ran:

BELOVED BROTHER,

At this fearful moment I cannot be silent, without raising my voice earnestly, and in the name of all that is most holy and sacred against the threatened probability of war. It is in your power to avert the calamities of a war, the results of which are too fearful to be even thought of, and in which thousands of innocent lives will be lost, and brother will be arrayed against brother.

War is ever fearful, but when it is begun for mere objects of ambition, for imaginary affronts and wrongs, it is still more fearful. You are deceived, you are made to believe that you are to be attacked, and I, your true friend and sister, hear your honoured name attacked and abused for the faults and recklessness of others – or, rather more, of ONE man!....

Ever your affectionate and unhappy Sister and Friend

Victoria R.[22]

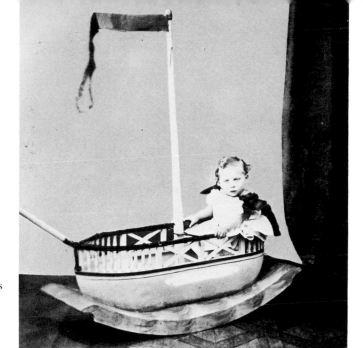

Victoria and Frederick's eldest son, Prince William, showing a precocious interest in ships, December 1860.

The Crown Prince and Princess with their children Prince William, aged two, and Princess Charlotte, aged one. Winterhalter.

The Crown Princess and
Prince William mounted,
June 1863.

Crown Prince Frederick
with Prince William at
Balmoral, October 1863.

Queen Victoria with her grandson Prince William of Prussia in 1864.

The Crown Princess with her sixth child, Prince Waldemar, in November 1868.

Emperor William I with Bismarck, Moltke and their entourage at the Battle of Königgrätz, 1866.

Emperor William I and his son the Crown Prince receiving garlands under the triumphal arch at the victory parade, 16 June 1871.

The Crown Prince and Princess with some of their children, (*left to right*) Princesses Charlotte, Victoria (*seated*), Sophie and Margaret, and Prince Waldemar, August 1874.

The Crown Princess with Prince William, February 1876.

Crown Princess Frederick,
c. 1878.

Four generations: Emperor
William I (*seated*), Crown
Prince Frederick (*left*),
Prince William and his baby
son Prince William, in June
1882.

Louis, Grand Duke of
Hesse-Darmstadt, with
Victoria's sister, Princess
Alice, and three of their
children shortly before
Princess Alice's death from
diphtheria. Von Angeli,
signed 1879.

Emperor William I at his desk in
September 1884.

Emperor William I and Empress
Augusta, Coblenz, 1885.

After reading the letter, the King told Loftus that the latest Austrian dispatch had made it difficult for him to hold back from war. Loftus answered that, as the Emperor of Austria desired peace as much as the King said he desired it, there must be a way to accomplish it. But the King replied, 'I do not see how it could be effected.'[23]

In fact, the King had not read the latest Austrian dispatch; it had been misrepresented to him by Bismarck. This gave the Coburg intriguers their opportunity to drive home the wedge between the King and his Minister President. The King had forbidden Queen Augusta to approach him directly with political matters because of her intrigues against Bismarck, but she sent a copy of the Austrian dispatch to the Duke of Coburg, who had it printed in the state *Gazette*. Once printed, the Queen could lay the full text in front of the King. His anger at having been tricked by Bismarck into thinking it offensive was very great. Queen Victoria's allegations in her letter had been proved true.

The Duke of Coburg had asked his influential contacts in Vienna to verify whether Austria wanted war or not. The answer was that Austria wanted peace and was scarcely arming. Full details of all Austrian military movements were sent to the Duke of Coburg, who had them passed to the King by the trusted Schleinitz.[24] Again Bismarck's assertions regarding Austrian mobilization were exaggerations; the Crown Prince called them 'frivolous frauds'.

At this time, the fall of Bismarck became a real possibility. Austria prepared to withdraw her reinforcements from Bohemia and Silesia. If this were done, the King declared, Prussia would begin disarming the day after Austria began. Bismarck seemed too ill to protest. 'My illness and death might prevent the war,' he said. 'If I had been in health, I would have insisted on it.'[25]

Now the secret pact with Italy saved him and restored the King's faith in him. He persuaded his ally to move most of her army towards Lombardy. The Austrians could not leave Venetia undefended against such a threat, and on 21 April the Austrian Emperor felt obliged to declare a partial mobilization for his southern army. This made it seem as if he had been deceiving the King of Prussia about disarmament and wanting peace. As Bismarck asserted, war with Austria was necessary.

It was the end of the 'Coburg intrigue'. The King again trusted Bismarck's tactics and sources of Intelligence. Far from dismissing his Minister President, the King feared that Bismarck might resign if his recommendations were not followed. Bismarck knew that Austria could hardly commit her armies to an Italian campaign without first deploying defensively against a stab in the back from Prussia. Her slow process of mobilization, twice as long as Prussia's, meant that she must make her preparations first. So six days after the partial mobilization in the south, the Austrian Emperor reluctantly ordered the mobilization of the northern army in Bohemia. Even if this were to provoke a full Prussian response, there seemed nothing else he could do.

Bismarck had got what he wanted, an apparent Austrian threat against Prussia. His health suddenly and wonderfully improved. To the Crown Princess, he seemed dangerously well, and his audacity was rising with his spirits. Lord Augustus Loftus confirmed her view. When peace seemed likely, Bismarck would be down and depressed, but with the revival of his war policy, he too revived. Sooner or later, war would be inevitable because of him. As he joked to the British Ambassador, he would prefer to descend to posterity in the character of Attila.[26] There would have to be a conflict to remove so dangerous a man – or an assassination.

On 7 May, a fine spring day, the Minister President left his red sofa to confer with the King at the palace. He returned on foot and unguarded along the Unter den Linden. A student from Tübbingen, Ferdinand Cohen-Blind, stepped from under the trees and fired five shots at Bismarck at point-blank range. The minister gripped his assailant and handed him over to a couple of passing guards. During the struggle, the revolver was pressed against Bismarck's thick coat, which was pierced by two bullets, one of which bruised his ribs without breaking the skin. Bismarck told the King that he was wearing a breastplate of silk and wadding, which had saved his life. He told his political secretary that the shots had little effect because the gun was against his coat and the bullets had little velocity.

The assassination attempt was strangely timely, as it provoked the first demonstration in favour of Bismarck. A crowd assembled in the Wilhelmsträsse and cheered him until he appeared on his balcony. The would-be assassin was the Jewish stepson of Karl Blind, a socialist revolutionary from southern Germany, then in exile in London. Bismarck's spies immediately linked the attempt to a secret society of republicans in Württemberg who planned to murder the King of Prussia and leading members of his Government. The King was confirmed in his fears of revolutionaries and in his dependence on Bismarck's agents, while the British were linked with the conspiracy. Cohen-Blind had hoped to escape to London, and had sent on his bags in advance. The Prussian police retrieved the luggage receipt and a police officer left for London to recover the bags hoping to find papers which would incriminate the members of the secret society. British police cooperation was demanded.[27]

The timing of this attempt on Bismarck's life was perfect for him. It rallied popular support for his policy against the enemy within as much as against the enemy outside. The fact that he was wearing a thick coat or padded breastplate on that day was very fortunate. The identity of his assassin was a godsend, a Jew and a radical, connected with two opponents of Bismarck's diplomacy, Württemberg and England. The quality of the revolver used in the attempt was incredibly poor. Bismarck's explanation of the bullet-holes was improbable. Bullets fired at point-blank range have more power, not less; a murderer would prefer to hold the muzzle against his victim to make sure of his death.

The sequel was extremely odd and made the attempted assassination seem even more spurious. Cohen-Blind cut his own throat in his cell that night. He was either murdered by police agents or had been given a razor and encouraged to commit suicide. It was beyond belief that such an important witness should not have been kept alive, unless there were good reasons to shut his mouth. As it was, he could never now disclose the identity of those who had placed him in Bismarck's path, armed with a revolver so defective that it was little better than a popgun.

In Berlin, however, even Bismarck's critics thought that the attempt on his life was genuine. They could not believe that a gullible youth could have been found to act out a fatal part in a political charade. The Crown Princess called the dead man a poor, well-meaning, mistaken, short-sighted wretch. It was better that Bismarck should live to see the consequences of his reckless madness than die a martyr.[28] Her mother was more vengeful and more sceptical. She could not quite agree that it was better that Bismarck had not been shot. 'Here people think it was all got up on purpose and don't believe that the man really tried to shoot Bismarck – else why did he not succeed?'[29]

The temptation to kill Bismarck was very great, for Prussian aggression threatened to swallow up all the small independent German states such as Württemberg. On 2 May, Bismarck's Cabinet sent a unanimous resolution to the King, asking for full mobilization against Austria. The next day, the Crown Prince was summoned to a secret meeting of the Crown Council, at which it was decided to put the four army corps on alert for a full war footing. The news that Hanover, because of her connections with the British Crown, would not support Prussia and was arming against her, made Bismarck savage. The entire Prussian Army and the reserves were called up. Bismarck intended to cut the Gordian knot of Germany with the sword.[30]

That May, as Austria and Prussia and Italy prepared to fight, the feeling of helplessness among the Anglo-Coburg group gave way to despair. Everybody was arming against somebody – Queen Victoria recorded – and everybody declared they wanted to attack nobody.[31] At least, she was on the sidelines of the war, involved only through her children and cousins. The Crown Princess was threatened with worse than the end of the Coburg dream: her own husband might have to try to kill her sister's husband in Hesse, and her close relatives in Hanover and Coburg.

It was all absurdity and horror. Wretchedly low and depressed, she dissected daily her family's ruined future, contrasting it with the castles she had been building in the air for eight years. Her husband had been given command of a major Prussian army. The King had never been in better spirits. He might not wish for a war any more than the Crown Prince, but his passion for soldiering put other considerations in the shade. 'I fear,' the Crown Princess told her mother, 'it is a characteristic trait of the whole family, you know.'[32]

She was writing in reply to one of Queen Victoria's more absurd suggestions. Her mother wished the Crown Prince to be firm and to say that he refused to take part in such an iniquitous war. This would raise him in the eyes of all the world.[33] That might well have been true, but it would also have put him inside a military prison on a charge of treason. Queen Victoria would not admit what her daughter knew very well: the Crown Prince thought of himself primarily as a soldier and a Prussian commander. He would not be such a fool as to appear a traitor when the tide of Prussian nationalism had begun to run so strongly. Better to accept the gift of an army than to serve time as a public enemy.

The Crown Princess's blood relations forced her to divide her loyalties. Nearly all the people close to her in Germany belonged to princely families in the south. They would necessarily side with Austria. Her sister Alice's husband, Louis, and his youngest brother, Wilhelm, would have to support the Grand Duke of Hesse-Darmstadt against Prussia.

Yet the second brother, Heinrich, was in command of the 2nd Prussian Lancers and would have to fight with the Crown Prince, perhaps against Hesse. The family might be killing one another. The Crown Princess assured Alice that, whatever happened, she would always love and help her. She passed a message of personal support to her cousin, the King of Hanover.

The defection of Hanover particularly enraged Bismarck. The state was in northern Germany and should have been within the Prussian sphere of influence. Bismarck saw its opposition as a dying kick of the Anglo-Coburg conspiracy. The blind King George showed courage and put his small forces in the field against a Prussian invasion. He might reasonably have expected support from England because of his dynastic connections with the throne, but Lord Clarendon put a stop to that. He advised Queen Victoria that the fact of the King of Hanover's being a member of the English royal family did not mean that she should take any special measures in the event of Hanover being invaded by Prussia.[34] The Queen of England could not risk the storm of unpopularity if she tried to involve her country in a war abroad, to protect her German cousins or her own daughters.

The greatest instinct for survival was shown by the leading Coburg intriguer, Duke Ernest himself. Certain that Prussia would win the war, he applied for a command in its army. Although he thought Prussia was in the wrong, he joined Bismarck's side to preserve his Duchy. His lack of courage displeased Queen Victoria. He could have agreed to be neutral – that might have been necessary, but to change colours, she could not think right.[35]

Austria now made the mistake of repudiating the agreement to split the Danish border duchies with Prussia. In reply, the King sent Prussian troops into Holstein. The Austrian forces would not fight, but withdrew over the border into Hanover. Not a shot had been fired, and peace was still just possible. But on 14 June, Austria called for the mobilization of all the smaller German states against Prussia. Most of them wished to be neutral, but they were caught between the hammer and the anvil. They agreed to mobilize, but only to defend their individual frontiers. Their weak decision meant that Prussia could gobble them up piecemeal. Bismarck immediately sent an ultimatum to Hanover and Saxony: they must allow Prussian troops to march through their territory or be destroyed. The two states rejected the ultimatum and prepared to fight the war that was being forced upon them.

The war was coming at the worst possible time for the Crown Princess. In April, she had given birth to Victoria, her second daughter. In Darmstadt, Princess Alice was also having another child. Both the sisters needed their husbands' support while recovering from their pregnancies, but the two men were called to arms on opposite sides: the Crown Prince was ordered to take command of the 120,000 men of the Second Army in Silesia, while Prince Louis was sent to command a Hessian Brigade of Cavalry. The Crown Princess was left to overcome her fears and her nightmares alone.

'Last night I dreamed of a battlefield where nothing but heads and arms and legs lay about,' she wrote to her husband in the field. 'I was so glad when I woke up and thought: Thank God, it was only a dream. But how soon may it become a reality?'[36]

All too soon, death in the family became a reality: her son Sigismund, not quite two years old, died of meningitis while his father was away on campaign. He had been her adored child, her special love. Four weeks after the joyful christening of the infant princess Victoria at Potsdam, a funeral procession followed Sigismund's little coffin. Too old to go to war, Field Marshal Wrangel bared his head to the dead child, who would never serve as a Prussian prince.

The Crown Princess was overcome with grief, and had nobody to comfort her. 'What I suffer none can know –,' she wrote to her mother. 'Few know how I loved! It was my own happy secret – the long cry of agony which rises from the inmost depth of my soul reaches Heaven alone.'[37] She was so pierced to the heart that she devoted herself more and more to the nursery. Her younger children now had the full benefit of her love, which had been mostly given to her husband.[38] Her eldest boy, William, noted the change in her, but then, he was always jealous for his mother's love.

Sigismund died as Prussian troops were marching, virtually unopposed, into Saxony and Hanover. At Langensalza, the brave, blind King George ordered the Hanoverians to fight, but they were swept away. By the end of June, most of northern Germany was in Prussian hands. One army was striking south to punish Frankfurt for having decided to mobilize the smaller German states. The First Army, under Prince Frederick Karl of Prussia, was moving to join another army on the Elbe and engage the Austrians. The Second Army, under the Crown Prince, was advancing through Silesia. The Austrian General Benedek wanted to defeat the Prussian armies separately, but Moltke had planned that a three-pronged force should converge to attack and put the enemy to rout. All depended upon the Crown Prince breaking through a number of scattered Austrian corps and joining the other two armies in time for the vital battle.

Now that he had what he wanted, Bismarck had become superfluous. He could do nothing to influence the conduct of the war, but could only observe the military forces which he had raised and equipped. Wearing the long grey cloak and pointed helmet of a cavalry major in the Landwehr, he sweated it out with the King in Berlin until the news came that the decisive battle was imminent. Then he joined the royal retinue in the six special trains commandeered to take the great and the curious to the front line. Not for them the rigours and rehearsals of war. Only the grand finale.

The Crown Prince had a hard time of it, advancing through Bohemia towards his rendezvous with the First Army. He won three engagements on three successive days at Nachod, Skalicz and Schweinschädel. Benedek's outlying corps desperately tried to hold him off; the Austrian commander wanted to provoke the First Army into attacking him on its own. His defensive position was near the village of Sadowa, only seven miles away from Frederick the Great's old headquarters at Königgrätz, where a fortress now dominated the junction of the Alder and the Elbe Rivers.

The Crown Princess could not hide her pride at her husband's bravery, energy and modesty. His troops cheered him whenever they saw him and were said to adore him. He was often thirteen hours in the saddle at a stretch, but he never complained. Sensitive man that he was, he found the fatigue as nothing to the mental excitement and exertion of directing so dangerous an undertaking. Above all, he felt himself pulled apart by the violent emotions of the fighting and the dreadful horrors of the battlefield. 'To one so kind,' the Crown Princess said, 'I know what the shock to his nerves must be.'[39]

She herself felt the most conflicting emotions. She wrote to Queen Victoria imploring her to understand her feelings, which had to be on the side of her country and her husband. Of course, she was in despair at being forced to think of other Germans as her enemies and wish for their destruction. Yet she had death in her heart, the death of her darling Sigismund.

'I can only regret that I did not die before all this,' she wrote to her mother, 'or was born after it comes to an end. And what the end of it will be – Heaven knows! I cannot describe what a cruel contradiction of feelings one had to pass through – but over all sounds my darling's last cry – and the tears that I shed for all the poor fallen and wounded and their afflicted families flow over his little grave.'[40]

As her husband moved his army towards his reckoning at Königgrätz, she put aside her grief and began to think about the casualties. She worked hard to scrape together necessaries for the field hospitals, now full of Prussians, Austrians and Saxons. She begged her mother to send sponges and old linen; Princess Alice was asking her mother for the same – to nurse the retreating Hessians serving in the Federal Army.

With the Crown Prince rode Colonel Walker, a British military attaché. The position of military attachés was curious at this time. If ambassadors were sent to lie abroad, attachés were sent to spy abroad, but they were official spies, licensed to inform. The Crown Prince wanted a British colonel, whose reports on his behaviour and successes would go directly to Queen Victoria. He had waited so long to do something of consequence which might win her admiration. He knew that the value of Walker's reports in terms of propaganda and deterrent effect, would outweigh the disclosure of Prussian war secrets. If the colonel could give detailed accounts of the effect of the needle rifle and the Krupp rifled cannon, he could also point out how formidable the Prussian armies were. The King and Moltke would want that.

Walker was with the Crown Prince when the news came that Prince Frederick Karl's First Army, which now incorporated the smaller Army of the Elbe, was to engage the main Austrian and Saxon forces near Königgrätz on 3 July. The Crown Prince was in the position of Blücher at Waterloo. If he could not reach the battlefield in time, Prince Frederick Karl, playing Wellington, might be defeated by Benedek. The Crown Prince's army was encamped many miles away. At midnight on the eve of the battle, he was ordered by an officer of the general staff to make for the flank and rear of the Austrian position. Rousing his weary troops he set off in the night towards his destination. His energy and example were extraordinary; he kept his men on the move for the next twenty-four hours.

Nearly half a million men were engaged in the Battle of Königgrätz: a greater concentration of troops than in the Napoleonic wars. It was the herald of the triumph of the railway carriage over the horse-drawn wagon. It would decide the future of Germany, which had been so long confused with the Holy Roman Empire and its usual emperors, the its outcome would decide finally whether Germany was to be ruled by Habsburgs, who had unfortunately looked more towards the Danube and the Mediteranean than to the Rhine and the Elbe. The battle would decide whether Germany was to be united at last by a greater Prussia, or whether the Austrian Emperor and the King of Saxony and the gaggle of minor German princes leading the Federal Army in the south-west would keep Germany as divided and impotent as Italy had been before the Austrian defeat there.

Staying close to the King and his military advisers, Bismarck watched the battle from the hills behind the Prussian lines. Mounted on a large strawberry roan, he became saddle-sore and blistered during the eight hours of the struggle. Austrian shells passed unpleasantly close, and he scolded the King for taking unnecessary risks. The staff officers thought that he was really afraid for his own precious person, but the King listened to him and sought a less exposed position from which to view the battle below.

It was not going too well. The Saxons fought valiantly, led by the two sons of their king. Benedek's men checked the advance of Prince Frederick Karl's troops and put them on the defensive. The Austrian cavalry was massing for a charge which might end in a Prussian rout. Then, towards one o'clock, Bismarck saw five miles away 'a line of grey trees' advancing from the east. It was the Crown Prince's army making for the Austrian flank and rear, exactly where it should be.

Heavily bombarded by the Austrian artillery, the Crown Prince's advance guard stormed the village of Chlum and threatened Benedek's line of retreat to the south through Königgrätz. The Austrian commander sent in his reserves to retake Chlum, but the Crown Prince held on, pushing up more and more of his men. Benedek had to fall back or risk the loss of his whole army. Through the courage of his rearguard and the Saxons, he managed to escape with 180,000 men, leaving 40,000 dead or wounded or taken prisoner. The Prussian cavalry, which had not been used in the action, failed to charge in hot pursuit to break up the routed Austrians. Benedek still stood with a large army between the Prussians and Vienna.

Bismarck was depressed rather than elated by the carnage. He was thinking that his serving son, Herbert, might be among the piled dead. He rode into a nearby village in the dark, broke into a cottage to spend the night there, and fell into a manure pit. This was a watershed in European history, for if that pit had been twenty feet deep and full, Bismarck reminisced later, they would have had a long search next morning for their Minister President.[41]

In Colonel Walker's opinion, the First Army had been very hard-pressed before the arrival of the Crown Prince. His judgement and decision, firmness of execution and calmness could not be surpassed.[42] Of course, Moltke's strategical planning had aimed to bring the Prussian armies together at Sadowa, but he depended on the vigour and skill of the field commanders, particularly of the Crown Prince. The princes had relied on the fighting qualities of their men, who were armed with the needle rifle against stubborn opponents more used to the bayonet. At the first sight of the Crown Prince's men, Moltke's reliance on strategy prompted him to declare: 'The campaign is decided. Success is total. Vienna lies at Your Majesty's feet.' The King was very angry at such a preposterous statement. His commanders must still lead his men to victory. War was more than communications; it was will and timing, iron and blood.

For once, the Crown Prince had done the right thing in the right place at the right moment, and he had done it in front of his father at the most decisive battle in Europe since Waterloo. When the Papal Secretary heard of the Austrian catastrophe, he said, 'The world topples.'[43] The King of Prussia was overwhelmed by the Crown Prince's superb display on the field. He personally placed the coveted ribbon of the *Pour le Mérite* around his son's neck, and embraced him among the dead and the dying.

The outcome of Königgrätz turned a disgraced and isolated Crown Prince into a national war hero. Ironically, it made the dangerous policies of his chief enemy, Bismarck, seem the superhuman statesmanship of a genius. Victory changed all and hallowed all. The past was shriven. The Crown Prince and Bismarck were now the joint saviours and makers of the new nation.

As if to show this, they formed a misalliance of convenience against the King. The extent of the Prussian victory had gone to His Majesty's head. He wanted to march into Vienna as a conqueror, then annex great sections of independent Germany and Austrian Silesia. William I of Prussia, Loftus wrote gloomily, would prove as ambitious and audacious as Napoleon the First, and put all Europe in a blaze.[44]

The King's aggressiveness did not suit Bismarck, who clearly saw new dangers for Prussia. The victory had been too quick and too great, but not great enough. Benedek still had a large army in the field. He might not be able to defend Vienna, but he could still retire to the east. The allied Federal Army in southern Germany was still intact. The French and the Russians were waiting to intervene. Only a swift and moderate peace would prevent the other great powers from interfering. Bismarck also knew the danger of a war of revenge. If the peace terms were too harsh, Austria would be bound to ally herself with France so that she could reconquer her lost territories. Better to make a future friend of a foe, than a certain enemy through greed.

The drama between the King and Bismarck was played out in Deitrichstein Castle at Nikolsburg. Finding the King obdurate, Bismarck threatened to resign, and sent for the Crown Prince to support him. Surprised at this appeal, the Crown Prince wrote to his wife that he might now be able to act on her ideas. As usual, he agreed with her views down to the last detail. 'If God is as good to us as He has been so far,' he declared, 'Germany's renaissance may really be achieved in spite of Bismarck.'[45]

Moltke was waiting for the Crown Prince when he walked up the hill to the castle. Things were in a terrible state. The King and Bismarck would not even see each other. The French Emperor was threatening to come into the war, if his peace proposals were not accepted. These were very much what Bismarck wanted: Austria was to cede no territory, but was to be excluded from Germany; Prussia was to get Schleswig and Holstein and a large indemnity; France would receive Venetia and hand it over immediately to Italy. Nothing was to be agreed about northern Germany. There, Bismarck and the King were to have a free hand. Prussia could swallow up the small states in due time; not at a gulp, but slowly, bite by bite.

The Crown Prince partly agreed with Bismarck. The 'Coburg' plan had always sought the unification of Germany by Prussia, but sadly, it was being achieved by the drawn sword, not by the liberal word. Germany was going to be merged into Prussia, as Bismarck wished; Prussia was not going to be merged into Germany, as the Crown Prince and his wife wished. Yet Bismarck seemed to want to conciliate his old opponents. His proposed North German Confederation would have a Reichstag, or elected parliament, as a figleaf over naked Prussian control. The Crown Prince hoped against hope that Bismarck's show of moderation would prove to be more than show, but he was watchful of his unlikely ally. As he wrote in his diary, he would not allow himself to be led astray.[46]

He, alone, tried to induce the King to accept the reasonable terms of peace. For three days, he was the sole contact between his father and Bismarck, and when he finally persuaded them to meet, he shocked his father by supporting the Minister President. 'It is a topsy-turvy world,' he had to admit. 'For the last three days Papa has said such things to Bismarck that he actually cried last evening and was really afraid to go in again. I had to calm down both of them.'[47]

Bismarck was so depressed by the resistance of the King and the generals that he contemplated throwing himself from the window of his room on the fourth floor. As he stood in front of it, he heard the door open behind him, then felt a hand on his shoulder. 'You know that I was against this war,' the Crown Prince was saying to him. 'You considered it necessary, and the responsibility for it lies on you.' But, the Crown Prince continued, if Bismarck thought it was time for peace, then there would be peace. He would go to see his father once more, and he did so. He returned to Bismarck's room within half an hour. 'It has been a very difficult business,' he said, 'but my father has consented.'

So the Crown Prince saved Bismarck and his policy twice over; once by his determined march to Königgrätz, and again by his persuasion of the stubborn King. Bismarck could never have done it; in time of war, he was a despised civilian. But the Crown Prince was the hero of Prussia's great victory, and it was this which finally made the King give way and stop his army fighting in the middle of another battle. He hated to do it. He had seen himself entering Vienna at the head of his troops. Now he was to be deprived of that triumph. He wrote a bitter note in the margin of Bismarck's last memorandum to him, accusing his minister of leaving him in the lurch in the face of the enemy by threatening to resign. He could not replace Bismarck at that moment. His son supported Bismarck's opinions. So he found himself reluctantly compelled, after such brilliant victories on the part of the army, to bite this sour apple and accept so disgraceful a peace.[48]

The fighting was not yet finished. By making a separate peace with Prussia, Austria had left her German allies in the lurch. All the Prussian armies could now turn and crush the small states. In Hesse-Darmstadt, Princess Alice wrote despairingly to her mother that all the bloodshed had been useless – which made it harder to bear. The small countries would have been wiser to submit sooner, as their enemy was too mighty.[49] Robert Morier was commanded by Queen Victoria to make his way through the fighting and see how Princess Alice was faring. She broke down completely in front of him. She did not know what was happening to her husband Prince Louis who was with the Federal Army. His cavalry brigade had already suffered severe losses at the hands of the Prussians. The Federal soldiers were living on raw potatoes and green apples, while Prince Louis himself had survived for two days on one piece of black bread.[50]

The Federal forces were saved from annihilation because the states began to defect from the common cause and submit to Prussia. Bavaria was the first to make a separate peace, followed by Baden. The other minor German states soon gave up the fight and trembled to think what their fate might be. All of Queen Victoria's German relatives appealed to her to intercede with the victors. Hesse-Darmstadt was occupied by the Prussians, and faced the prospect of losing the largest and oldest part of the state. 'If we lose it,' Princess Alice complained, 'we shall not only be very poor, but may as well give up the name of Hessian.' It was a thankless task, but if her mother could write to the victorious Crown Prince of Prussia to use his influence for them, she would be deeply and truly grateful.[51]

There were other pleas to Queen Victoria, particularly a noble and moving one from the King of Saxony. He had felt that he had to defend the independence of his country. His troops had been loyal and courageous. He could say with the clearest conscience that he could not, he ought not, to have acted in any other way than he had.[52] Queen Victoria could only reply to him that her heart bled for his country, a land to which she was tied by ancestry and affection. But she could do nothing for him. The policy of her Government was to keep out of any situation that might involve England in the war.[53]

The case of Hanover was the closest to home. Queen Victoria's soldier cousin, the Duke of Cambridge, was next in line of succession to the throne after the blind king and his son. He wrote in great distress to the Queen. The stoutest heart shuddered at the bare thought of all their old German associates being knocked on the head, and their friends and relatives scattered to the winds. His feelings went out chiefly to the poor Hanoverians. What would the Queen do?[54] Little, she answered, beyond expressing her deep interest in Hanover's integrity and welfare. She had heard, anyway, that there was no intention of annexing it.

She had heard wrong. Bismarck needed Hanover in order to strengthen Prussia's new position on the North Sea and to act as a buffer in case of a French invasion. He also wanted to lay his hands on the Hanoverian King's treasury which would give him a secret fund to use on influencing the Press and his Intelligence system. Stieber had formed a counter-espionage group, ostensibly to protect Prussian headquarters, but actually so as to keep Bismarck informed about military opinions. He would be as useful after the war as he had been during it.

Queen Victoria tried to plead for her German relatives through her son-in-law, the Crown Prince. She expected he could do little and admitted that she wrote only to ease her conscience. She knew that such a total victory had given Prussia the power to annex by right of conquest. All kingdoms had been assembled by the Queen's method – royal marriage, or by Bismarck's method – war.

Her feelings about Prussia's victory were ambivalent: she did believe that Prussia should unify Germany, and she was influenced by her eldest daughter's pride in the Crown Prince's success and example on the battle-field. Her son-in-law seemed such a splendid contrast to her eldest son, who appeared to live only for pleasure. She had Colonel Walker's reports praising the Crown Prince sent to the Prince of Wales in the hope that they would inspire and 'Germanize' him.

In fact, they enraged him. Prussia's outright annexation of Schleswig and Holstein had made him angry; it was a serious blow for Denmark and his wife's family. Unlike his mother and his elder sister, the Prince of Wales did not believe in the Protestant alliance between England and Prussia. He believed that England needed an alliance with France – and even with the old enemy Russia.

Because Queen Victoria's Government did not protest about the annexations, the old feeling of respect for England began to revive in Berlin. It made life easier for the Crown Princess. Her flexible nature enabled her to rejoice in her absent husband's triumphs and to forget, at least for some of the time, the loss of her child. The war had confirmed her in her new-found Prussian patriotism. 'I am NOW every bit as proud of being a Prussian as I am of being an Englishwoman and that is saying a very great deal,' she wrote to her mother, who knew what a 'John Bull' she was and how enthusiastic she was about her home. Yet now she praised the Prussians for their intelligence and humanity; their only fault lay in Bismarck's conduct. Their army had behaved excellently, but she could never believe that the war was justified, although good for Germany might come out of it.[55]

If she could not justify the war, she could justify Bismarck's harsh policies towards the conquered German states. Her memory of her husband's danger, her pride in him, her anguish at the loss of her child, her pain at seeing the wounded in the hospitals, these had given her a new maturity and clarity. At this sad time, she told her mother, she must separate entirely her feelings for her relatives from her judgement of political necessities.

Bismarck's voice might have been speaking from her. The success of his diplomacy had already turned the Crown Prince to support him against the King. Now it was turning the Crown Princess, his former enemy. She was talking of political necessity, not of moral judgement and family feeling. Of course, she assured her mother, she and her husband were not giving up their liberal principles. But as Queen Victoria knew, political events had their own imperative. Those rulers who were now threatened with annexation might have foreseen what danger they were running into; they had been told beforehand what they could expect. They chose to go with Austria, so they had broken their own necks.[56]

Such political realism finally persuaded Queen Victoria to make the best of a bad job. Prussia had won. Like it or not, Germany would be united. This was the main thing and a good thing. If it were not being done the Coburg way, it was, nevertheless, being done. The Crown Prince would inherit that which he had won with the sword Bismarck had put in his hand. If the present were brutal and in Bismarck's grasp, the future was bright and would be in the hands of her son-in-law and her daughter.

So the Queen compromised with the dead Prince Consort's gospel about Germany. She praised her daughter's strength of mind. She could see in every one of her Vicky's letters how her great mind and large heart were developing. 'How proud adored Papa would have been of you,' she wrote to the Crown Princess. 'But, oh! if only Papa's great maxim of Prussia becoming Germany and a great German empire could be realized.'[57]

It was already being realized in Bismarck's way. All were following where he led the King of Prussia. His critics suspended judgement for the time being; they called it the logic of events, not the power of the one man. Even his enemy, Robert Morier, had to admit that Bismarck was a man of genius, although he was still the unprincipled scoundrel he had been before the battle of Königgrätz.[58]

On 10 August, the Crown Prince came home from the war. His wife took the children in a carriage and drove out to meet him in a wood. He looked well, but thinner, bearded and serious. He was depressed, not only by the death of little Sigismund. The scenes of war and the loss of tens of thousands of lives hung heavy on his soul. All the struggle and the suffering, what were they for? Nothing had really changed for him in his own country. Do what he might, so long as Bismarck and the King remained as they were – the good of Germany and Prussia never could be secure.[59]

CHAPTER SEVEN

Waiting On Ceremony

THE VICTORY PARADE was led by the King on horseback. At his back rode the Crown Prince, bearded and erect, every inch the Teutonic hero. Bismarck had been made a general of Landwehr cavalry. Pale-faced beneath his helmet, he rode along the Unter den Linden, a garland of flowers round his neck. The strain of the past months brought about a nervous collapse immediately after the parade; he called it a softening of the brain.

It certainly led to a softening of his hard line at home and abroad. When he had recovered, he made his peace with the right wing of the Liberals. His years of governing unconstitutionally were forgiven by an Indemnity Bill, which was passed by a vote of three to one. The King was opposed to asking for absolution from the Chamber, but again the Crown Prince gave Bismarck his support; even among the liberals, Prussia's victory had tossed a halo over the spike of Bismarck's helmet. The angel of darkness, wrote Liebknecht, had become the angel of light. Before him, the people lay in the dust and adored.[1]

A further softening revealed itself in Bismarck's policy towards the smaller German states. With the assistance of the Crown Prince's former adviser, Max Duncker, he created a North German Confederation above the River Main. Its Reichstag had few powers. In it, the new National Liberal Party continued the compact with Bismarck, who became Chancellor. The National Liberals supported their old oppressor because they thought that a strong and united Germany should come first. Personal liberties could wait. There was no hurry to assimilate the whole of Germany. It would take years for Prussia to digest the petty northern states; the different and difficult Catholic states of the south could wait.

The seventy-year-old King agreed with Bismarck's softer policy. He went out of his way to assure the British Ambassador that he did not expect to see the unity of Germany in his lifetime. It would not be carried out by force, but would be left to time and public opinion.[2] Neither he nor the new Chancellor trusted the support of South Germany. If there were to be a war with France, Bismarck would rather have the southern states as enemies. 'It would be necessary,' he said, 'to place a Pomeranian behind every Bavarian.'[3]

By waiting too long, Napoleon III had gained nothing from the German war. He began to press for the frontier fortress of Mainz or of Luxembourg, both garrisoned by the Prussians. There was no question of Mainz being yielded, but Luxembourg was another matter. Bismarck favoured giving a sop to the French Emperor while Prussia consolidated her gains. He helped to persuade the indebted King of Holland, the nominal sovereign of Luxembourg, to sell the buffer duchy to France. It seemed a satisfactory arrangement to everyone.

Yet Bismarck had sown the dragon's teeth. The Prussian generals and the King would not allow the French Army to have a base so close to the heartland of Germany. War loomed and both countries armed furiously. Even the Crown Princess clung to her new allegiance. She told her mother that Bismarck was not in the wrong. The aggression came from France; it was there they wished for war. For her part, she thought it better the war should be now rather than later – horrible as it was. The great united empire of Germany would never consolidate itself in peace until the power of France had been reduced.[4]

Queen Victoria was shocked at her daughter's belligerence. Bismarck seemed to be leading her on as well. Queen Augusta of Prussia was quite right in wishing for no war; that was what every woman should do. Bismarck was wrong because he had encouraged the French Emperor to believe he could get Luxembourg. As for reducing the proud old State of France to a second-rate power, when Prussia herself had only become a great power recently, that was a sorry thing to say. 'I am afraid the time may come,' the Queen wrote prophetically, 'when Europe will wish France to be strong to keep the ambition of Germany in check.'[5]

She had already put the blame of trying to start a new war on to Prussia alone. Writing directly to the King, she had taken the side of Napoleon III, who was only asking now for the disarmament of Luxembourg. An imperious refusal to make this small concession would put

Prussia in the wrong. The French Emperor, Queen Victoria asserted, was very anxious that peace be maintained. The British Government would arbitrate. It rested entirely with the Prussians whether there was to be war or not.[6]

This surprising letter from Queen Victoria did much to prevent the outbreak of hostilities in 1867. Prussia could not risk having England support France against her, so Bismarck accepted a meaningless collective guarantee of Luxembourg's neutrality from the British Government. The Prussian garrison was withdrawn, the fortifications were razed, and the duchy was left with the King of Holland. Napoleon III had opened one of the gateways into Germany without having had to capture it.

Queen Victoria was praised by both the King of Prussia and the French Emperor for keeping the peace between them. It was not flattery. In the world of royal diplomacy, she had acted as an honest broker between the rival rulers. She had made her reluctant government negotiate a piece of paper that saved face and allowed Prussia to back down with honour. The Crown Princess also had played her part in keeping the peace. She had even dared to discuss politics with Bismarck. With her usual candour, she told the Chancellor that she was no blind admirer of his, but he would increase her admiration if he could preserve peace. He replied that the French were rearming so fast that Prussia must rearm against them. She then proposed mutual disarmament, but he would not give her an answer. She could not fathom what he intended to do. She had heard that he was disinclined to go to war, but she never could know what he really meant.[7]

She was so afraid that her candid letters might fall into the hands of Bismarck's spies that she asked her mother to burn them. She knew that they revealed state secrets which might reach the ears of the German Embassy in London through the indiscretions of British ministers briefed by her mother. But Queen Victoria thought the letters of such importance that she kept them to use in her own diplomacy. The royal group of Coburg sympathizers still survived, although it was reduced to Duke Ernest, Queen Augusta of Prussia, the Crown Prince and Princess, King Leopold II of the Belgians and the Grand Duke of Baden. All of them had worked hard to keep the peace.

The entente in Europe enabled the Prussian royal family to come, with the Russian and Austrian imperial families, to the World Exhibition in Paris. It was a lavish and exhausting occasion, marred only by an attempt on the lives of the Tsar and the Tsarina. A refugee Pole shot at them, but only wounded an attaché's horse. Their consternation was obvious to the Crown Princess. The Tsarina cried all the evening and would not be comforted; the Tsar was as white as a sheet. Both said they regretted that the French Emperor had not been touched.[8]

To royalty, assassination seemed a form of sacrilege. Regicide was worse than a murder in the family – it was unholy. Although the Crown Princess rather admired Cromwell, Queen Victoria would never forgive him for having had Charles I's head cut off. Shortly after the Paris Exhibition, when revolutionaries executed the Emperor Maximilian in Mexico, the Queen of England was shocked and outraged; it was too awful. 'How dreadful that we can do nothing to avenge this horrible murder –' she lamented to her eldest daughter, 'and that the days of chivalry have passed away.'[9] Their Coburg cousin, Charlotte, had married Maximilian; she went mad with worry and grief.

The temporary understanding helped to heal the wounds within Queen Victoria's own family. The process began during the Prince of Wales's visit with his wife to Berlin. They were returning from the wedding of his sister-in-law, Princess Dagmar, to the Tsarevitch. Queen Victoria had not wanted her eldest son to go to St Petersburg. She objected to his remaining so little at home and always running about.[10] But he went all the same, for his mother would give him nothing of consequence to do in England. From a diplomatic point of view, this was an important marriage. The new royal alliance between the Danes and the Russians was a further guarantee against Prussian expansion. 'A young life is thus being sold and sacrificed,' the Crown Princess wrote of Dagmar, 'to the doctrines of the great conventions.'[11] She could have said the same about her own marriage, although it was a love match.

The Crown Prince was sent to the wedding celebrations as Prussia's ceremonial representative. He took the opportunity to try to persuade the Danish princesses and their husbands, the heirs to the English and Russian thrones, to accept Prussia's friendship. The Prince of Wales was too good-natured and diplomatic to hurt his brother-in-law. He was friendly to the Crown Prince in St Petersburg, and on his return journey to England, he found himself welcomed by the Prussian Court. Like the Crown Prince, he looked ill from the long nights spent in railway carriages, followed by interminable receptions and banquets in overheated palace rooms. For both of them, representing their countries abroad was bad for their health and a quicker way to the grave.

Bismarck seemed to adopt a policy of slowly weakening the Crown Prince by ceremony, travel, political isolation and kindness. The long court Season during the Berlin winters was a trial by heat and cold, etiquette and rigour. The Crown Princess found it more and more intolerable for her and her husband. It nearly killed them, but it renewed the vigour of the couple they were waiting to replace – the King and Queen of Prussia. 'I am quite knocked up by all the Balls,' the Crown Princess complained to her mother in March 1867. 'I have been out every night since Sunday and rarely home before two. I cannot stand it. My digestion, my hands, my eyes – all suffer. But the King and Queen so delight in it that they seem to go out oftener and stay longer every year.'

The Queen of Prussia had a passion for the Season. She dressed in the height of fashion like a young girl of twenty, and wore a new gown each night. The Crown Princess did not understand how a woman in her late sixties could care so much for the *grande monde*. Fritz looked pale and ill. He complained of feeling always tired from the unremitting social round.[12]

Every now and then, the Queen would decide to leave a Ball before the late supper. Then she would make her daughter-in-law take the place of honour and receive everybody in her place. 'I wish she had a heap of daughters and daughters-in-law,' the Crown Princess wrote in desperation. 'Then she would not always want me for everything.' The Crown Princess was sure that people were sick of seeing her so perpetually; she almost felt inclined to beg their pardon for boring them so often.[13]

The winter Seasons were now more glittering and prolonged because Berlin was becoming an international capital rather than the chief city of a major German state. Details of the North German Confederation had still to be settled. The foreign affairs, inevitable for a new great power, must be discussed. The ceremonies of the court were also occasions of diplomacy, when negotiations were conducted discreetly. At those, the King showed favour to one country or another by choosing to speak to a particular ambassador. Royalty in Berlin communicated as well as condescended. The King saw to it that every important person knew his shifting place. The interminable balls were not so much a dance of wasted time as a game of musical chairs.

For five winter seasons after the defeat of Austria, the Crown Prince and Princess were forced to keep their stance just behind the throne. This ceremonious lingering was contrary to their natures and cost them dear. By May 1870, the Crown Princess was extremely worried about her husband's health. '*Soirées* follow one another daily,' she reported to her mother. 'You would be sorry to see Fritz so pale and yellow. I really feel quite anxious about him. The Queen has no mercy. This week she has not been in bed once before 2 o'clock, and on the move all day long. I wonder it does not kill the King outright. As for Fritz, it is injuring his health, and I have no means of stopping it.'[14]

Dancing attendance at court wore down the Crown Prince less than his protracted foreign missions. Apparently Bismarck wished to prolong the King's life by keeping him at home. The Crown Prince would be exposed to risk and possible scandal if sent abroad, and would also be kept away from the influence of his English wife. In 1868, he was sent to Turin to represent the Prussian royal family at the wedding of Prince Humbert to Princess Margherita of Genoa. The following year, he was delegated to attend the opening of the Suez Canal.

On both occasions, the Crown Prince furnished ammunition for Bismarck's propaganda machine. In Turin, he was on good terms with Prince Napoleon and seemed to be appeasing France. In Egypt, he was photographed with the Emperor and Empress of Austria – a peaceful picture that suited Bismarck well. The Chancellor wanted Austria as a friendly power in the forthcoming war against France to complete the unification of Germany. The outbreak of the conflict had only been postponed. When it came, Bismarck wanted all the other powers as allies or neutral.

The Crown Princess found her husband's long absences difficult to bear. He had come to dominate much of her life. Command in war had given him confidence in his own judgement; his wife now looked to him for advice as once she had to the Prince Consort. 'It is extraordinary how Fritz has grown mature of late years,' she told Queen Victoria. 'I often tell him he is not only Husband but Father and Mother to me now.'[15] To write this was heresy, but the Crown Princess meant it. She was determined to be a good Prussian now. She knew her mother did not like Prussia at the moment because of Bismarck's treatment of the Augustenburgs and the King of Hanover, but she could do nothing about that. Her heart was thoroughly with the interests of her new nation, her work was for its future.[16]

For three years, the Crown Princess did not come to England to visit her mother. It proved her new commitment to Prussia. On the anniversary of her mother's wedding, she gave birth to another son, Waldemar. He seemed sent to her to assuage the ache in her heart left by the loss of Sigismund – heaven forbid that he too might be taken from her.

Her large family as well as her political sensibility kept her at home. Eventually at the end of 1868, she and her husband paid a two-month visit to Queen Victoria, who made them feel that England was a second home. They stayed for Christmas, and were rebuked by the King of Prussia for missing the opening of the Berlin Season. The trips to England always caused bad blood between father and son.

Ever since the victory at Königgrätz, the King had been kind to them so long as they did not talk to him about politics. There seemed to be none of the anger and suspicion of the years before the war. The King knew that his son was waiting for his place on the throne. The unspoken compromise between them was that, while the father lived, the son would not speak out. Even so, the Crown Prince and his wife were required to remain close to the court for most of the time. The Crown Princess knew that whenever they were away from the King, ill-wishers would find a way to make him dissatisfied with them.[17]

She was spied upon in her own household. The ladies-in-waiting and the Prince's aides were often Bismarck's creatures in Liberal disguise. Lady Ponsonby was horrified at the espionage and intrigues which surrounded her. The Princess had grown indifferent; she expected nothing else in Prussia. Bismarck was so clever, she told Morier, that she expecting to find herself preaching his gospel one day without realizing it. She still had the trustworthy Countess Blücher to help her with the household, and she had engaged Count Seckendorff, a thrifty and honest man, to be Court Chamberlain. Bismarck had accepted this appointment in the belief that he would be able to turn Seckendorff too, but he never succeeded. The Chamberlain remained loyal to the Crown Princess to the end, reserved, fastidious, devoted to a platonic love of her.

Bismarck continued to isolate the heir to the throne from his advisers. Those who were not suborned were removed. The trusted Professor Geffcken was exiled to England, where the Crown Princess recommended him to her mother. He had been the object of a special vendetta by Bismarck, who persecuted him until he was obliged to leave.[18] Young Stockmar spent more than two years recovering from his nervous collapse which had been brought about by Bismarck's pressure. He clung to solitude as the best way to avoid persecution.

Her loss of advisers induced the Crown Princess to commit a political indiscretion. Sir Robert Morier was especially feared by Bismarck, because he was as capable at intrigue as the Chancellor and had formed a network of his own spies and informants in Germany. The

Crown Princess asked her mother to have Morier recalled to Berlin as Secretary of the Embassy there. He would be the right man in the right place,[19] to provide the Crown Princess with the secret Intelligence, of which Bismarck had deprived her.

Queen Victoria was grateful for the services Morier had given to the Coburg group and to her family. She used to receive him privately at Windsor when he brought the latest Intelligence and confidential messages from the Crown Prince and Princess. The Queen urged his appointment in Berlin, and Sir Henry Stanley, who was now Foreign Secretary, seemed ready to accept Morier's transfer until he learned of Bismarck's absolute opposition. The fact that Morier felt so warmly and strongly about German politics caused him to think of himself as a German politician. His ideas were directly opposed to Bismarck's. If he meddled in political matters in Berlin, England would lose all her influence there.[20]

Queen Victoria did not press the matter; wherever Morier was, he would still serve her and her daughters. The Crown Prince and Princess continued to use him as adviser and agent. Their movements in Germany were now being restricted by the King and Bismarck, but they could not be stopped from visiting the spas in the spring and summer. The whole court and the financiers went there to take the cure and exchange confidential information. At Karlsbad and at Gastein in 1869, the Crown Prince and Morier drank the waters together and discussed politics in the Crown Princess's rooms at night. Between them, they tried to decide what Bismarck would do next. A war with France seemed the likely course of action.

Another weapon in Bismarck's arsenal against the influence of the English royal family was the use of scandal, and the most obvious target was the Prince of Wales. 'There is not a horror in Germany that is not told of Bertie,' the Crown Princess informed her mother in 1866, before her brother's visit to Berlin. He and his wife were represented 'as a wretched couple and you as a most unhappy mother.'[21] When, four years later, the Prince of Wales would be falsely accused of adultery by the hysterical Lady Mordaunt, he would be condemned in his own country even though the lady would be found to be insane. In Berlin, he would be utterly vilified. Queen Victoria believed in his innocence, but recognized that his name ought never to have been dragged in the dirt or mixed up with such people.[22]

The Crown Princess was not spared from scandal. For the next thirty years, she would be falsely accused of taking her Chamberlain, Count Seckendorff, as her lover. When the Crown Prince was at Suez and she travelled to Cannes with her enormous caravan of baggage and children, she put propriety above inconvenience and expense. 'It would not be proper for me to be in a hotel in a foreign country with only one gentleman,' she wrote to her mother, '– besides Count Seckendorff is much too young for that.'[23] She knew that in the Prussian Court, like Caesar's wife, she must be above suspicion.

Unfortunately for the Crown Princess, one of her favourite ladies-in-waiting, Walburga, Countess Hohenthal, fell in love with a Count Üxküll. A duel was fought, and she eloped from Cannes as the Count's mistress. She completely broke away from her family and friends, telling the Crown Princess only that she wished to retire from court life. A dreadful scandal was certain to be made of it; the Crown Princess dreaded going back to Berlin more than she could say. She was pregnant again, and felt unfit to face her mother-in-law's anger at letting down Prussian standards.

Queen Augusta was furious. She ordered the Crown Princess to install a *Grande Maîtresse* to supervise the ladies-in-waiting and their morals. The Crown Princess, she said, was obviously incapable of keeping up a decent household for her husband. The Crown Princess could not accept this. Another spy planted on her by the Prussian Court would be intolerable. She said she would rather her husband had brought back one of the overseers from the harem in Constantinople.[24]

The Crown Princess wanted a domestic life with as little ceremony as possible. Her family was large, and growing larger. Another daughter, Sophie, would soon be born to join her five brothers and sisters. Even Queen Victoria, with her nine children, thought it all too much; she had never shared her eldest daughter's devotion to infants. 'Very few worship babies as you do,' she reminded the Crown Princess. Children were far more of a terrible anxiety than a pleasure.[25] She could not see that children were a compensation for her daughter. During the four years of her greatest political activity, the Crown Princess had had only one child, the dead Sigismund. She had come from a large and happy family herself, and to re-enact that happy state helped her feeling of impotence in public affairs. She felt the need to create a small world of her own.

She was strict about the education of her two elder boys, believing firmly in the merits of a Spartan self-discipline. At whatever cost to her tender heart, she chose to ignore William's disabled arm. He must learn to live with it and ignore it himself. Sympathy would only encourage self-pity in him. She and her husband showed no signs of noticing the pain suffered by their eldest child during his fearful riding lessons. His riding master put the boy on his pony without stirrups and made him take the reins in his right hand. When the pony trotted, the boy fell off. The master picked him up and put him back again. The boy fell off again. The master mercilessly ignored the child's prayers and tears and put him back on the pony after each tumble, until he could stay there. By the age of ten, he had normal Prussian cavalry practice and could ride in a victory parade.

In the schoolroom, however, he showed the same defect as the Prince of Wales: he could not concentrate. No severity of Hinzpeter could turn the child into a scholar. He had an elusive and disobedient nature, full of pride and self-will. He was not developing into the son his mother wanted. As she wrote to Queen Victoria, she was looking for her children to grow up 'like my Fritz, like Papa, like you and as unlike the rest of the Prussian royal family as possible'. Then they could be good patriots and useful to their country – call it Prussia or call it Germany. Their education was by no means an easy task.[26]

William felt more and more that his mother was cold, and his father distant towards him. His harsh schooling seemed to prove their indifference. He was to remember a joyless childhood in which renunciation was the law. It was dry bread for breakfast and no praise; duty was all.[27] Although his father taught him German history and took him on long visits to castles and parks, he did not rescue him from Hinzpeter's severity. He wanted his son to be a soldier and a ruler, despite his handicap.

Finding little tenderness or encouragement in his life, William began to react against his mother. He felt inadequate because of his arm, then blamed his feeling of inadequacy on her. It was her fault that he was a cripple, not his own. She had made him so. She was also a foreigner who was always praising the stoic virtues of the English gentleman, not the Prussian officer – which, like his father, he would soon become.

He did not feel the same when he visited his grandparents, the King and Queen of Prussia. They sympathized with him and encouraged his love of soldiers and uniforms. The King saw in the boy a way of transmitting his own royal traditions to the future, untainted by the heresies of his son and daughter-in-law. He encouraged William's childish self-assertion and resistance to his mother's ideas.

The Crown Princess hated the fact that her eldest son already had a military tutor, von Schrötter, and was being trained as a recruit in the Grenadiers; a Sergeant Klee was teaching him to beat march time on a drum, in preparation for his tenth birthday, when he would be made a Lieutenant in the 1st Regiment of Footguards. He was deeply impressed that the King would present him with the Order of the Black Eagle; it would be like receiving a knighthood. When his mother saw him wearing his little uniform, she thought he looked like some unfortunate little monkey dressed up and standing on top of an organ.[28]

The Crown Princess knew the ceremony marked the turning of her eldest son away from her. 'It will go hard with me to make an amiable face,' she confessed to her mother, 'when I see William seized upon – and all sorts of nonsense talked to him – which I have carefully kept from him till now. It cannot fail to make the child quite confused. He will receive his commission from the King, put on his uniform, and report himself to all sorts of military superiors. The King and the whole family are delighted. They fancy the child will be quite one of them from that day forward.'[29]

William was becoming one of them, together with his younger brother Henry. Both loved military and naval games. In his first letter to his grandmother, Queen Victoria, William told her of having a large mast set up in the garden at Potsdam. He climbed to the foretop with a real Captain to look down on the whole deck plan of a ship, laid out on the ground below: 'We play in it, and about it and enjoy ourselves famously.'[30]

Most impressive of all was a visit to the largest ironclad in the world, the *König Wilhelm*. The boy looked up at the rows of huge guns with their heavily polished muzzles. Sailors manned the rigging; his father and himself were piped aboard. They were given rich, and forbidden, cakes in the Admiral's cabin, fitted-out in the solid English style. The boy thought what a joy it would be to command such a fine ship. The memory of it left him no rest.[31] It recurred again and again to him as a way to challenge his mother's authority and superiority. She was always telling him that the British Navy was the best of them all. She would see.

France and Prussia continued to arm against each other. They would go to war soon if they did not disarm. Depending on the victor, Germany would be united or dismembered. Mutual disarmament would be the solution, but this could not be achieved. For the King of Prussia was devoted to his army. Queen Victoria's new Foreign Secretary Lord Clarendon agreed to ask the King to disarm, but he knew he would fail. The King did not desire war, Clarendon observed to Queen Victoria, but his army was his idol, he would not listen to any proposal to reduce it. He would make no changes to the Prussian system which compelled every man to serve.[32] And as for Bismarck, his maxim had always been: When travelling in dangerous company, the only thing to do is to carry a revolver.[33]

Nevertheless, Bismarck laid the British proposals for disarmament before the King, who was annoyed by them. They seemed to have been dictated by the French, and embodied the policy of the King's enemies in Germany. In Bismarck's opinion, they were merely the act of a cool friend.

'Put yourselves into our skin,' he said. 'You would then think – you would then act – differently. What would you say, if we were to observe to you that your Navy was too large? That you did not require so many ironclads?'[34]

There was no answer to that.

CHAPTER EIGHT

Empire

'WE COULD NOW fight France and beat her too,' Bismarck told his chief propagandist, Moritz Busch, in February 1870. 'But that war would give rise to five or six others.'[1] He was waiting for his opportunity to make France seem an aggressor. Time and Spain delivered that chance into his hands. The throne of Spain was vacant; as usual, a German prince was the traditional choice to fill it. The Spanish Parliament and its leader, General Prim, asked for a Hohenzollern prince to accept their crown. To France, this overture could seem to be a Prussian plot. In the event of war, Louis Napoleon would have to divide his armies to guard against a stab in the back from across the Pyrenees. But how could he protest against the offer? How could a civilized modern country still go to war for dynastic reasons? 'Please see that this theme, a new war of succession in the nineteenth century,' Bismarck scoffed to Busch, 'is thoroughly threshed out in the press.'[2]

When the Spanish offer came to Prince Frederick of Hohenzollern-Sigmaringen, Bismarck encouraged him to accept it. As head of the royal family, the King of Prussia would have to give his consent. Bismarck sent him a strong memorandum, favouring a Prussian prince on the Spanish throne. Prussia would benefit, France would feel threatened and humiliated. The King did not agree. Ignoring all advisers except the Crown Prince, he refused to give his permission. There might be too much trouble for too little gain. No Hohenzollern would take the Spanish throne, even if Bismarck wanted it.

The Crown Princess sent this information to her mother; her husband had asked her to do so in his name. In fact, it was no business of hers. It should have been kept most profoundly secret, because nobody wanted the French to know. The Crown Prince and the King were confident that Queen Victoria would inform Lord Clarendon confidentially. Would the Queen give her own and her government's opinion on the Hohenzollern candidature as soon as possible? 'Perhaps you would write it in German to Fritz,' the Crown Princess concluded, 'as it is particularly disagreeable to me to be a medium of communication in things so important and serious.'[3]

It was more than disagreeable. The King was using her in this secret negotiation with England in order to counter his own Chancellor. The diplomacy came to nothing, because Lord Clarendon would not permit Queen Victoria to give any advice on the matter, and because Bismarck would not take no for an answer. Although Prince Frederick was persuaded by his father to refuse the offer, Bismarck sent a trusted agent and a military representative to Madrid to urge General Prim not to give up the idea of a Hohenzollern candidate, but to accept the Prince's elder brother, Leopold. He could change royal minds as he had often done before. By the end of May, Prince Leopold had decided that he would be a candidate for the throne, if the offer were made to him.

Bismarck sent the news by cipher to Madrid early in June. He had carefully calculated that, because of the summer recess, nobody would interfere with his planning. The King was taking the cure at Bad Ems and Moltke was in Silesia, while he himself had retired to his country estate at Varzin. It would be difficult to convene a Crown Council to prevent anything that was taking place in Spain. In any event, Bismarck claimed the matter had nothing to do with him; it concerned the King in his private capacity as head of the family. The King could neither grant nor refuse permission, Bismarck told the British Ambassador. The Hohenzollern Prince was in the same position as any other Prussian subject who wished to emigrate.[4]

This was a specious argument. Bismarck certainly protested enough when one of Queen Victoria's children and relatives made a marriage or took a throne that seemed to threaten Prussia's interests. He knew that there would be a furore in France when the secret was out. A plebiscite had confirmed Napoleon III's tenure by a huge majority. As his new Foreign Minister, he had chosen the Duc de Gramont, who mistakenly believed that he could count on Austrian support in a war against Prussia. When, at the end of June, the French discovered that General Prim had asked the Spanish Parliament to 'elect' Prince Leopold as King, all hell broke loose in Paris. And when the Hohenzollern Prince accepted the Crown and the King of Prussia gave whatever consent he could, de Gramont's fury was even greater than the national anger. He made an inflammatory speech in the French Parliament on 6 July, threatening war if the Hohenzollern candidate did not refuse the Spanish throne.

French belligerence began to change the Crown Princess's mind just as it changed the King's. On the day of de Gramont's speech, she was thinking that Prince Leopold's acceptance was a sad mistake. But two days later, she was reflecting court opinion by saying that she did not see why the French were complaining. Prince Leopold had made an independent decision; it was really nothing to do with the government or the King.

Her ingenuousness was a consequence of Bismarck's shrewdness in staying away at Varzin. Nobody knew that his agents had been working to persuade General Prim to offer the crown again to a branch of the Hohenzollerns. But his astute leave of absence almost proved Bismarck's undoing. Count Benedetti, the French Ambassador to Berlin, was sent to speak directly to the King at Bad Ems. There was no Chancellor to protect His Majesty and interpret messages from France. Although Bismarck later blamed the King for dealing directly with the French in his absence, he had decided to stay away and allow French belligerence to lead to the necessary war. Absent from Bad Ems, he could not speak for his master.

As it was, the King saw the French Ambassador on four successive days at Bad Ems. He was surprised at the violence of French reaction to the Hohenzollern candidate, which Bismarck had always undervalued to him. He made grave diplomatic errors, which Bismarck would not have done. He admitted he had authorized Prince Leopold to accept the Spanish throne, but had done so only as head of the family, not as sovereign – a meaningless distinction to the French. And he properly reported that Bismarck was aware of his grant of royal consent, which proved to the French that the whole affair was a Prussian plot. They demanded that the King withdraw his consent to Prince Leopold's candidature. This the King refused to do.

In an endeavour to secure peace, the British and French again used the system of royal communications. The French Emperor wrote to King Leopold II of the Belgians to put direct pressure on his friend and namesake, Prince Leopold. Queen Victoria was asked by her new Foreign Secretary, Lord Granville, to exert her influence by writing to Prince

Leopold's brother-in-law, Philippe, Count of Flanders. She asked him to tell his relative that the Queen of England begged him to withdraw and maintain the peace of Europe. For whatever reason, Prince Leopold did renounce the throne as a personal decision. King Leopold claimed all the credit; he needed to boast in order to win friends for his country, which might be engulfed in a war between its two powerful neighbours.

The apparent success of royal diplomacy once more seemed to postpone the outbreak of war. Prince Leopold's renunciation was represented as a private decision influenced by pressure from friendly European sovereigns. It was not the result of a command by the King of Prussia, although he had listened to the entreaties of his wife and had sent a military aide from Bad Ems to advise Prince Leopold to withdraw. De Gramont remained bitter. The cause of the quarrel had been removed, but the original insult of Prussia's secret backing of the Hohenzollern candidate rankled.[5] The French Foreign Minister demanded more than a diplomatic victory. He required the public humiliation of a rival power which had sought to humiliate France by means of a dynastic device.

Benedetti was sent with further demands. The King of Prussia ordered Bismarck to come back and accept responsibility for Prussian policy. The Chancellor also had to try and unravel the royal peace-making, which he had allowed by his studied absence. As usual, his first thought was to offer his resignation rather than accept a diplomatic defeat at the hands of France. But the War Minister, Roon, and Moltke and his secret agents all advised him that this was a good time for Prussia to fight. France's new weapons, the *chassepot* rifle and the *mitrailleuse* machine-gun, were not yet operational. So Bismarck sent a message to the King, urging him to recall the Prussian Ambassador, Baron Werther, from Paris, and to demand an explanation for de Gramont's belligerence. This would greatly increase the chances of an ultimatum from the French who, Bismarck thought, were running amok like a Malay who had got into a rage and was rushing through the streets dagger in hand, foaming at the mouth, stabbing everyone who happened to cross his path.[6]

Meanwhile, de Gramont was pushing his diplomatic luck too far. On 12 July, he instructed Benedetti to ask the King of Prussia to declare his approval of Prince Leopold's withdrawal. The King must also refuse to authorize the Hohenzollern Prince to accept the Spanish crown, if it were offered to him again.[7] The King hid his anger at being pestered again on the promenade of Bad Ems. He turned down the new French demands, but said he would consider the matter. His touchy sense of honour had been provoked.

Nevertheless, the draft of his written reply to Benedetti did not break off negotiations with France. Using firm and moderate language, the King refused to bind himself for the future. He denied Prussian complicity in Prince Leopold's decisions. He also declared he would have no further direct dealings with the French Envoy; in future, Benedetti might only approach one of His Majesty's aides. Now that Bismarck was again in Berlin, the King sent him the draft letter by cipher telegram, with authority to release the text at his discretion.

Strategically and politically, Bismarck had decided that this was the time to unite the German nation. Bavaria and the southern states were bound by a military alliance to support Prussia, now threatened by a foreign ultimatum and invasion. So Bismarck edited the King's text, cutting it until it became a curt refusal to negotiate in the face of French aggression and insolence. When he read the changed text to his dinner guests, Roon and Moltke, they became cheerful.

'It sounded before like a parley,' Moltke said. 'Now it is like a flourish in answer to a challenge.'

'Our God of old lives still,' Roon added, 'and will not let us perish in disgrace.'

Bismarck may not have directly provoked the war by editing the King's draft reply, but he was responsible for releasing the brusque text to the Press and the foreign ambassadors. Because the French demands were excessive and the King's refusal reasonable, Bismarck could brand the French as aggressors. As he told his two dinner guests: to stop other great powers from intervening, it was important that Prussia should be the party attacked;[8] the edited Ems telegram made it appear so.

De Gramont made a further error by proposing that the King of Prussia write a letter of apology to the French Emperor. Baron Werther, the Prussian Ambassador, was stupid enough to forward this proposal to Berlin. When the King heard of it, he was so angry that he agreed to recall his Ambassador. It seemed as if he were breaking off diplomatic relations with France. Bismarck, of course, was still posing as the injured party. He told the credulous Lord Augustus Loftus that the ambassador's recall was a personal matter, not a rupture with France. Prussia still desired peace, he said.[9]

Werther's recall finally convinced the French that the Prussians would rather fight than admit that they had plotted to install the Hohenzollern candidate on the Spanish throne. Both nations began to mobilize, and the French also called up their reserves. Remembering the victories of the first Napoleon, most people, other than Bismarck and the general staff, thought that the French had the superiority in numbers and weapons. The Crown Princess became hysterical at the very idea of possible defeat. On 13 July, she suffered a violent headache and a choked throat, because she thought that the French were well-prepared and the Prussians not at all. Three days later, her mind was rambling and incoherent, because her nerves were so shaken. She thought that Prussia faced devastation, ruin and perhaps annihilation. Yet she was totally convinced by Bismarck's insistence that the French had shamefully forced the Prussians into war. It was a crying injustice. There was a universal cry – 'To arms' – to resist an enemy who had so wantonly insulted them.[10]

The Crown Prince kept his head, while his wife was losing hers. He had seen Bismarck on the crucial 13 July, and had been hoodwinked by him. The Chancellor had told him that, since Prince Leopold had renounced the throne, peace was assured. 'He gave me the impression,' the Crown Prince wrote in his war diary, 'of being taken completely unawares by the sudden and threatening turn of affairs in France.' Two days later, when war was almost certain, Bismarck, Roon and Moltke revealed to the Crown Prince the truth which they knew, that the French Army was less strong and prepared than the Prussian Army. They went to Brandenburg together to meet the King returning from Bad Ems. He was surprised to see them, but was soon convinced of the need to mobilize the army. The Crown Prince urged him also to mobilize the Landwehr and the Fleet. The King consented, and embraced his son with emotion. They would fight together again. This was the true bond between a Prussian king and his heir.

They had never been more popular with the Prussian people. So dense was the crowd in front of the Royal Palace, the Crown Prince recorded, that he and his father had great difficulty in pushing their way through to the terrace, which was packed with officers. The cheering never stopped. Again and again the King had to show himself. The multitude sang 'Die Wacht am Rhein' with one voice, and in that moment, all realized the full significance of the words.[11]

Queen Victoria was convinced that Prussia was wholly in the right and France absolutely in the wrong. Three of her closest German male relatives were in the army, her Coburg brother-in-law and her two sons-in-law, the Crown Prince of Prussia and Prince Louis of Hesse. She pressed her Liberal Government to intervene, but her Prime Minister, Gladstone, would not listen. England must continue its policy of strict neutrality, whatever the Queen might feel about her kith and kin in Germany. In a summing-up for the Queen, the Foreign Secretary, Lord Granville, assigned the blame for the war with elegance and prescience, knowing very little of Bismarck's hand in provoking it.

'The last week seems like a feverish dream. The result today is dreadful. Every one seems to have been in the wrong. The King of Prussia probably did not give his consent to the candidature of Prince Leopold without the knowledge of M. Bismarck. The latter must have known how distasteful it would be, rightly or wrongly, to the French. The secrecy of the negotiation, and the suddenness of the announcement was discourteous. The violent language used by the French Ministry was undiplomatic and unstatesmanlike. France is morally unpardonable, but perhaps militarily right, in making such haste. But it is inconceivable that, in the present state of civilization, hundreds of thousands of Frenchmen should be hurled against like numbers of Germans, on a point limited to a matter of etiquette.'

In Lord Granville's opinion, Her Majesty the Queen had done all that she could have done to make Prince Leopold withdraw. Her Majesty's ministers had done all they could do to keep the peace. So they could do nothing more but rest on their oars.[12] Bismarck was right. Britain was a happy island which could afford to coast along and keep out.

Britain's refusal to come into the war was taken badly in Prussia. In the previous war against the first Napoleon, the British and the Prussians had fought together. Even now, the consensus of informed opinion was that Prussia could not fight alone. Although the combined German forces numbered 1,500,000 men and 400,000 could be mobilized and sent to the front within four weeks, the illusion of French superiority was still paramount. The odds were fearfully against Prussia in the awful struggle, the Crown Princess informed Queen Victoria. 'There is not a family that is not torn asunder, not a woman's heart that is not near to breaking and for what?! Oh that England could help us.'[13]

England could, but England would not. Queen Victoria passed on her eldest daughter's impassioned plea to her ministers, but they would not budge. England would stay out, and her Queen would have to hide her partiality. 'Can there be a more cruel position than the unhappy

Queen's?' she complained to Lord Granville. 'She knows what her duty is and will do what must be done, but she will suffer dreadfully, and were Germany, dear Germany, the land of her Husband and her Mother – of her only Sister and Brother – to be crushed, she hardly knows how she could ever get over it!'[14] She confided to the Crown Princess that her whole heart and her fervent prayers were with beloved Germany. She would suffer cruelly for all of them. Her dead husband would have gone to fight for Germany if he could.[15]

While revealing her private feelings, the Queen did not forget to ask about Prussian plans of defence and attack. But the Crown Princess knew little of her country's strategy. Her husband was ordered to lead the Third Army in the south. Known for his tact as well as for his military skill, he was always given the most difficult post. His Second Army at Königgrätz had been full of dissident Poles. His new one would be full of south Germans, who had fought against the Prussians four years before. Two Prussian divisions would stiffen the forces of Bavaria, Württemberg and Baden. They were expected to hold off a French invasion from across the Rhine until the main Prussian armies could assemble. The Crown Prince did not think much of their chances, but he would do his duty.

The sad christening ceremony of his infant daughter, Sophie, seemed more like a farewell party than a festival. Afterwards, he left for the front without telling his wife. The thought was kind, and yet she felt as if her heart would break. He was gone without a kiss or a word of farewell. She did not know whether she would ever see him again.[16] He did not know whether his south German troops would fight alongside the Prussians. It might be a just war, but the Crown Prince had not yet tested national feeling in the states near the Rhine.

Bismarck wished to play the injured party in public, and use propaganda to win allies abroad. He gave a long interview to William Russell, the famous war correspondent of *The Times*, although its editor, Delane, was no friend of Prussia, and was putting his bet on 'Casquette against Pumpernickel'. The Chancellor was so reckless and indiscreet during the interview that Russell felt his hair curling tighter and tighter with alarm. The war correspondent's position was privileged. He was attached to the Crown Prince's headquarters together with the British military observer, General Walker, and most of the commander's old Anglo-Coburg group: Duke Ernest himself, the historian Freytag, the Baden Minister Baron Roggenbach and briefly, Morier, who came to glean what information he could. Morier was on his way to Darmstadt to check on Princess Alice's well-being, and to watch the Hessian troops march off to become part of the Prussian advance guard – a military detail, which Morier cabled in cipher to Lord Granville.[17]

Although the English were favoured in the Crown Prince's Army of the South, they were hated elsewhere. Before leaving to join his armies, the King of Prussia informed both the Crown Princess and her mother that he was deeply grieved by a secret Intelligence report from London. England was supplying France with shipping coal for her fleet, horses for her artillery, and millions of cartridges. Was this neutrality.[18] Morier confirmed the national feeling against England. Many sons of Germany might now be killed by English bullets. He knew England believed in free trade and could not control her exports. Yet how could such an explanation convince in time of war, when England's neutrality seemed biased and little less than desertion?[19]

It was Bismarck who was orchestrating the anti-English campaign, and the task was not difficult. As the Crown Princess told her mother, the King and Queen of Prussia believed the innuendoes against England because, with a pistol to one's breast, no one was inclined to investigate much.[20] A supposed gaffe of the Prince of Wales's – that he hoped Austria would join France, and that Prussia would fare ill – was publicized everywhere. Bismarck also alleged that there were treasonable foreign intrigues going on in Hanover – ironically, its treasury was now the 'Reptile Fund' used by him to bribe the Press. He saw no harm in inflaming German newspapers against England while encouraging the English Press to support Prussia in the war.

He had a fresh weapon of communications to hand. In 1869, he secretly gave government funds to Bernhard Wolff, in order to prevent his news agency, the Continental Telegraph Company, from being taken over by its rivals, Reuter of London and Havas of Paris. Wolff was given a virtual monopoly in Germany so long as all telegrams of a political nature were immediately reported to government agents. Bismarck also had the right to censor or to originate all news stories that were sent by telegraph to all local German newspapers. This was a fundamental way to influence the Press, through the only rapid method of transmitting news.

Bismarck always saw the Press as a dangerous and despicable opponent, to be bullied or bought or cowed. Although he despised journalists, he was conscious of their power. His sensitivity to criticism in print and his ruthlessness in dealing with it were extraordinary. 'Every Press attack must be smashed,' he once declared, 'every insult must be avenged.'[21] In war and peace, he used Busch and Stieber to run a central clearing-house for government propaganda, and for countering hostile sources of information.

It was the beginning of a modern system of media manipulation in the interests of the State, compared to which, the old royal system of suggesting or planting an occasional article was inefficient and out of date. In the greater Prussia he was creating, Bismarck's methods overwhelmed the few newspaper articles which the Anglo-Coburg group could arrange to be printed. Most of its scribes had now joined the Crown Prince with the Third Army. Even he believed Bismarck's accusations against Lord Granville and the British Government. He told General Walker that the English governing class was blindly hostile to Prussia, and that all hope of a good understanding between the two countries had broken down.[22] Temporarily, the Crown Prince felt isolated and betrayed by his life-long support of his wife's homeland.

He had also become Bismarck's ally in the great emerging vision of a united German Empire. The extraordinary welcome he had received in Bavaria and Württemberg had persuaded him that even the people of the southern states felt German above all. 'The Union of Germany is effected,' he confided to Morier, 'and it is the people of Germany by whom it has been effected.' It was a national feeling, not mere hatred for the French. He had pledged himself to lead the combined German forces to victory in order to create a united Germany with his father as Emperor. 'If you hear after some great battle of my suddenly quitting my army,' he told Morier, 'do not think I have run away. I shall have gone straight to headquarters to urge and plead this cause with the King. I shall have Bismarck on my side.'

This assertion startled Morier, who knew of the enmity between the Chancellor and the Crown Prince. The English diplomat realised the significance of their strange alliance. In war, their aims were the same: a moderate peace which would end by uniting Germany. In peace, they were opposed, because the Crown Prince wanted a free Germany. But the heir to the throne could hope to inherit the title which he and the Chancellor desired the traditional King to take – German Emperor instead of Monarch of Prussia.

But first, victories had to be won against France. The Crown Prince thought the Germans would win in the end. Morier was one of the few who thought that they would win in the beginning. He sent back an opinion which the Foreign Office thought ridiculous: the Germans would be at the gates of Paris in three weeks.[23]

Speed of mobilization was all. Three German armies were ready to advance across the Rhine while the French were still straggling towards the front. In the south, the Crown Prince could hardly believe it. There would be no invasion of Germany; he could push forward into Alsace. 'For all the French sabre-rattling,' he wrote in his diary, 'and all their age-long preparation against a sudden onslaught, we must be the aggressors. Who could ever have thought it?'[24]

The walled town of Weissenburg barred the way into France. As the Crown Prince advanced with the Third Army, the French crammed troops into its fortifications. With his usual speed of manœuvre, the Crown Prince launched two simultaneous attacks by the Bavarians and the Prussians. To his surprise, the Bavarians fought well, and the French finally had to flee to avoid being surrounded. The vaunted *mitrailleuse* seemed cumbersome and ineffective, and the intermittent rain of bullets failed to halt the bayonet charges of the German troops.

It was the first German victory over the French for fifty-five years. Even better was to follow. Two days later on 6 August, the Crown Prince totally defeated Marshal MacMahon at Wörth. The French commander had taken up a strong defensive position on the steep slopes of the valley of the Sauerbach, protected by the stream and water-meadows. Improving on the strategy and success of Königgrätz, the Crown Prince deployed his army corps with the centre laid back and the two wings projecting in long horns. He would rather outflank than attack frontally; he would try to cut off, not to batter down.

He might have encircled the whole of MacMahon's army, if the Bavarians had shown more stomach for the fight. Throughout the long day of the struggle, the French held the heights above the town with tenacity and courage. The *mitrailleuses* and the *chassepots* began to thin the Prussian ranks; Zouaves counter-attacked in great leaping bounds down the slope. Towards late afternoon, the Württembergers broke through and threatened MacMahon's line of retreat. Despite a Balaclava-style cavalry attack on the German artillery, the French Army had to withdraw. Soon the retreat became a rout; the roads for miles around were littered with discarded French weapons.

It was hard-won victory. The Germans lost more than 10,000 men, the French, double that number. The annihilation of the cavalry brigade of Cuirassiers was particularly horrible. Their charge at the guns had become entangled in vineyards and orchards, where they had been shot down or taken prisoner almost to a man. General Walker saw the woods and fields covered with breastplates and helmets, swords and lances, heaps of dead horses, their broken riders lying beside them. Although the French had fought well and had been ably led, the Prussians were too quick for them, both strategically and tactically. For once in history, the élan of French troops had been surpassed.[25]

The Crown Prince had won the first major victory over the French, shattering the myth of their superiority. With his speed of attack and ability to inspire his troops, he had proved himself the best of the Prussian field commanders. If the Bavarians had shown more fury, he might have surrounded MacMahon and won a total victory. As it was, he was the hero of the hour. His success heartened the First and Second Armies, which were striking down through Lorraine towards Metz and Marshal Bazaine's forces.

The Crown Prince loved and hated being a warrior. He looked the role, mounted on his bay horse, his yellow beard and whiskers in an aureole under his cavalry cap. The sight of the dead after the battle affected him deeply. The fallen had stiffened in the last spasm of their death agony; their arms and legs stuck out at odd angles, their faces contorted in frozen pain. Set above a mass grave, a simple wooden cross was supported by piles of broken rifles and muskets. 'When once we get back home,' the Crown Prince recorded, 'the Fatherland will be drowned in tears.'[26]

The Crown Princess regarded the wounded as her own special concern. She supervised the building of a temporary hospital of wooden huts in the Kreutzberg at Berlin; it was meant to accommodate 1,600 wounded men. She begged her mother for more old linen. Sending it would hardly be a breach of English neutrality. A wounded man had ceased to be an enemy, she told Queen Victoria, he was only a suffering human creature entitled to every one's help.

She was being accused of supplying her mother with secret information, which the Foreign Office was passing on to the French. So she took care to define her delicate position; the information she relayed was a personal act, not an affair of state. 'I hope I am only doing what you wish,' she confided to Queen Victoria, 'in writing openly what I hear, see and think. I only write as a private individual to you as my dear Mama, at the same time thinking it may be agreeable and useful to you to hear what is thought and said on this side of the water from an unofficial source. Of course I am looked on with suspicious eyes – as England is supposed to be on the other side.'[27]

She was increasingly under suspicion. In time of war, all foreign-born people tend to be accused of being unpatriotic or of sending vital information abroad. Queen Augusta became jealous of her daughter-in-law's success at organizing the temporary hospital in Berlin and wanted to stop her from founding another one at Homburg, but the King permitted it at the Crown Prince's request. He could refuse little to his victorious son, although he too was becoming jealous of the hero-worship of the Crown Prince within the ranks of the German Army. The soldiers seemed to know that the Crown Prince cared for their lives and would win his victories at the minimum cost, but the King and his wife wanted no one to steal their glory in battle or at the bedside of the wounded.

The King's advance on Metz with the First and Second Armies was altogether more bloody. At Gravelotte, the French caught the Prussians in a defile and punished them with *chassepots* and *mitrailleuses*. The King, himself, was in great danger. He won a Pyrrhic victory at a cost of some 20,000 Prussian dead and wounded, while the French retired with lighter losses. An attempt by Marshal Bazaine to break out of the fortress of Metz was shattered in another bloody battle at Mars la Tour, a field where poor tactics allowed much more death than glory.

Here, the leaden rain from the *chassepots* was literally like a hailstorm.[28] The Prussian Dragoon Guards were destroyed in a useless charge, repeating the French mistake at Wörth; the whole ground was littered white and blue with their bodies. Bismarck's elder son Herbert was hit by three bullets and reported dead. Wearing the yellow undress uniform of the Landwehr heavy cavalry, his father rode to look for him and found him wounded but cheerful in a field ambulance station. The American General Sheridan was visiting the Chancellor, and condemned the unnecessary slaughter. 'Your infantry is the best in the world,' he said, 'but it was wrong of your generals to advance their cavalry as they did.'[29]

The Crown Prince never wasted the lives of his men; he manœuvred his army into victory. Now he was ordered to join the King's main army and advance on Paris with 300,000 men. But Intelligence revealed that MacMahon's army was striking along the Belgian border to relieve Metz, which was still being besieged by the dogged Prince Frederick Karl with seven army corps. 'The time is now ripe to set the mousetrap for the enemy,' the Crown Prince wrote in his diary. With his father the King, he swung northward. He pushed MacMahon out of a strong defensive position on the rocky crag of Senuc, towards the border fortress of Sedan. The guaranteed neutrality of Belgium should prevent the French Army from escaping across the Meuse and the frontier.

To stop any such retreat, the Crown Prince once again executed one of his brilliant strategical marches. He sent his two Prussian army corps in a flanking movement across the Meuse. The early morning mists hid the manœuvre. MacMahon's forces thought they were facing only a Prussian and Saxon army to the front and flank. Instead, the Crown Prince's army corps took up their positions in the French rear and blocked the last loophole of escape. Desperately, the French charged with Chasseurs and Cuirassiers, Turkos and Zouaves, but the Prussian needle rifles cut them down. The demoralized French infantry fell back on Sedan in a panic. 'Our plan was being carried to completion with mathematical precision,' the Crown Prince recorded, 'Marshal Mac-Mahon was surrounded!'[30]

Although it had been Moltke's plan, its success was once again due to the Crown Prince's execution of his part of it. When the battle was over, he rode from his observation post to report to the King, who had ordered a short bombardment of Sedan. The burning town of Bazeilles sent up a dense grey-yellow pillar of smoke into the clear air. The setting sun gilded the bodies of the fallen, and the crests of the hills about doomed Sedan, where the French Emperor himself was now thought to be trapped. When the Crown Prince reached his father's side, he heard the news that Napoleon III wished to capitulate with all his army. 'That is a grand success!' the King exclaimed, offering his hand to be kissed by his son. 'I thank thee for thy share in it.'[31]

Once again the Crown Prince had marched his men to the right place at the right time. He had prevented the escape of the French Emperor, whose surrender might well end the struggle. 'The War had reached its culminating point,' the Crown Prince wrote, 'the instigator of the crying wrong was in our power. Peace could not now be long delayed.'[32] Soon a plenipotentiary appeared with Napoleon III's written offer to surrender his sword to the King of Prussia. The King accepted the surrender, using his son's writing-paper and sealing his answer with the eagle signet from his son's holster. Then father and son threw themselves into each other's arms, deeply moved by a victory greater than Königgrätz.

The illusion did not last. Peace had not been won. The King and the Crown Prince were not reconciled. When the Crown Prince begged the King not to humiliate the French Emperor by making him hand over his sword on the hilltop among the Prussian generals, he was thought to be showing too much sympathy with the enemy. At the peace parley in the villa to which the French Emperor had fled, Napoleon III accepted defeat and exile in Germany. But he stressed that he could only speak for himself, not for his Government which might choose to carry on the war. His short and podgy figure made the King of Prussia's tall and commanding form look wonderfully imposing, but when Napoleon III wept and claimed he had never even wanted to go to war, the Crown Prince did not know what to say.

Soon after the capitulation, the Crown Prince was visited by his strange ally, Bismarck. Together they planned how they might put pressure on the King to establish a German Empire. Bismarck now insisted on taking Alsace and Metz from France, even if it meant prolonging the war; the capture of the Emperor, with an army of 80,000 men, had changed the conditions of peace. To the victor belonged the new frontier.

At the time of the battle of Sedan, Bismarck confided to his creature Busch his views of the Crown Prince and his wife. He claimed that he was now quite good friends with the Prince. 'Why should he not be pleased?' Bismarck asked. He was the heir apparent to one of the most powerful kingdoms in the world. He would turn out to be reasonable and would allow his ministers to govern for him. He would learn not to thrust himself too much forward. In general he would get rid of many bad habits that made old gentlemen of his trade rather troublesome.

As for the Crown Princess, Bismarck did not consider that she had too much influence over her husband. He thought she was a clever woman, but far too candid. Because she could not disguise her feelings, she was very vulnerable. 'I have cost her many tears,' Bismarck said. She had been unable to conceal her anger with him at the time of the annexations of Schleswig and Hanover. She could hardly bear the sight of him. She had once asked him to bring her a glass of water. As he handed it to her, she had said to a lady-in-waiting, 'He has cost me as many tears as there is water in this glass.' But, Bismarck said, that was all over now.[33]

It was all over – but only for the duration of the war, which was not all over. Bazaine's army in Metz was still making ever more bloody and futile attempts to break out. A Third Republic was declared under General Trochu and Jules Favre, to forestall a Red revolution in Paris, feared by the Rothschilds and the financiers. With the north lost and the road to Paris open, a *levée en masse* was decreed, in order to create new French armies in the south. It was too little and too late.

The rapidity and extent of the German successes had been incredible. The Crown Prince found them almost terrifying. He took Rheims only four weeks after his first victory at Weissenburg. To his wife, the surrender of the French Emperor at Sedan had a moral. Such a downfall was a melancholy thing, she wrote to Queen Victoria. But it was meant to teach deep lessons. 'May we all learn what frivolity, conceit and immorality lead to! The French people have trusted in their own excellence, have completely deceived themselves. Where is their army, where are their statesmen?'[34]

The inexorable German advance on the French capital caused panic there, and many refugees fled westwards. By 20 September, the blockade was completed with the Crown Prince making his headquarters at Versailles. There was general depression within the besieged city. It was felt, the British Ambassador reported, that while the respectable citizens were on the ramparts, the Reds might pillage the town. Foreign diplomats, however, would stay on in Paris unless it were bombarded.[35]

This was the difficult question. In military terms, there had to be a bombardment to force a surrender, particularly as the French had heavy artillery in their fortifications around the city. But in terms of international propaganda, any destruction of such a centre of civilization would be a fatal mistake. Abroad, anger at the French provocation of the war was already turning into sympathy with their continual defeats.

Many stories of brutalities in the conquered countryside began to circulate. The strategy of living off the land by forced requisitions from Stieber's list of resources involved coercion and violence. Guerilla resistance invited the reprisals Napoleon I had used in Spain. Bismarck had no pity on men caught with weapons and without uniform. He had them shot at once, saying that human life was of little value. 'If we lived four hundred years, it would be another matter.'[36] Even the Crown Prince accepted the necessity of reprisals. If a shot were fired from a house at a

Prussian patrol, it was burned down, or else its owner was flogged and stripped of food and money. It was horrible, the Crown Prince admitted, but consistent with the proclamation of martial law.[37]

Luckily for the field generals, the responsibility for the atrocities landed on the generals of the occupying forces or on the military police led by Stieber. He understood the use of terror in order to control the local population. Any peasant who watched Prussian troop movements was liable to be tortured or hanged as a spy. So was any balloonist who came down while trying to escape from Paris. When the King followed the Crown Prince and set up his headquarters at Versailles for the siege of the French capital, Stieber was always at His Majesty's side, feeding the royal paranoia with stories of hundreds of French spies and assassins. In reprisal for a trivial anti-Prussian demonstration, Stieber threatened to hang ten town councillors. And when an innocent young man on his honeymoon was sentenced to the gallows for keeping a diary, Stieber answered army pleas for clemency with the words: 'That only makes my task the more painful' – and had the young bridegroom hanged all the same.

Security measures and the rigours of martial law had to be applied more and more against a French population, recovering now from the shock of total defeat and adopting guerrilla tactics against the invaders. The Italians took the opportunity to seize Rome from the French, but Garibaldi came to teach the French republican government how to fight using irregulars. A scratch army was put together on the Loire and managed to retake Orleans, while another instant army advanced towards Alsace. Even though Bazaine eventually capitulated at Metz with 175,000 men, Paris still held out, firing from its fortifications at the forward positions of the Germans. The besiegers began to feel as if they were the besieged; a huge force of 300,000 men surrounding an enemy city, but surrounded by a hostile nation. Bombardment of the enemy capital seemed the quick solution.

Bismarck certainly wanted that. Opposed to him were the Crown Prince, now General in command of the siege, and Moltke. From the military point of view, an immediate bombardment would be stupid. The Germans had not brought up the long-range artillery nor the munitions to keep up a continuous shelling of Paris. With the guns they had, they could only hit the rich *faubourgs* instead of the industrial and workers' *quartiers* where a red reign of terror was already said to be starting. The Crown Prince refused to sacrifice his men's lives by storming the fortresses outside Paris, or to waste his few shells on a symbolic bombardment. 'Fritz regrets every shot that is fired,' his wife wrote to her mother, 'and every death.'[38] For four months, he refused all demands to shell Paris until he was overruled by the King. The New Year of 1871 would see the bombardment. Hunger had not forced the city to surrender.

The Crown Prince's stand against the folly of bombarding the French capital led to a vicious smear campaign against him and his wife. 'In Berlin it is now the order of the day to vilify my wife,' he wrote in his diary, 'as being mainly responsible for the postponement of the bombardment of Paris and to accuse her of acting under the direction of the Queen of England. All this exasperates me beyond measure.'[39] Bismarck himself pulled the strings of the campaign, through his wife at home, and recorded the accusation in his memoirs. He found it absurd that Paris should not be treated like any other fortress. Making it into a special case was a notion imported from London by the roundabout route of Berlin – the cant of English public opinion.[40] To Bismarck, heavy artillery and assault must end the siege quickly. With each passing month, intervention was more likely from England, Austria, Italy or Russia.

Bismarck had begun by courting international opinion, but now he did not mind alienating it. He and the King and the Prussian generals became domineering in their victories, demanding a French capitulation. Only the Crown Prince seemed conscious of the shifting tides of opinion. The English and American correspondents at Versailles were now condemning the Germans as a greedy and brutal people – no longer innocent victims but arrogant victors. 'What good to us is all power,' the Crown Prince asked himself, 'all martial glory and renown, if hatred and mistrust meet us at every turn? If every step we advance in our development is a subject for suspicion and grudging? Bismarck has made us great and powerful, but he has robbed us of our friends, the sympathies of the world, and – our conscience.'[41]

So the Commanding General of the siege agonized and was accused of pro-French sympathies under English direction. In point of fact, his mother-in-law, Queen Victoria, was herself being accused of foreign sympathies because she continued to back the German cause when public opinion was swinging to support the gallant resistance of the French. She hated the war because of the intolerable strain it put upon her. She was on the side of Germany but remained Queen of England. These divided interests in royal families were quite unbearable. Human nature was not made for such fearful trials – especially not mothers' and wives' hearts.[42]

In the long struggle to change the King into a German Emperor, the Crown Prince was both instigator and conciliator, soothing the King and the Chancellor when they would not speak to each other on the subject. He had been taught to be an imperialist by Prince Albert, whose dream always was of a free liberal German Empire as the leader of civilization. The Crown Prince wanted a revival of the ancient imperial crown, more than a thousand years old, and in this he was not disinterested; he hoped soon to inherit the imperial title from his aged father. 'The Crown Prince is as stupid and vain as any man,' Bismarck complained. 'He has been made crazy again by all that Kaiser madness.'[43]

Bismarck also wanted a united Germany, and the title of Emperor was a convenient umbrella for it. He hammered out separate treaties with the south German states, and used his 'reptile fund' to pay off King Lugwig II of Bavaria, who sent a letter drafted by Bismarck, requesting the King of Prussia to assume the imperial crown. Although the King protested that it would only be a cross for him to bear, Bismarck and the Crown Prince clasped hands outside his room. This formal request by the leading minor German sovereign would lead to a change of mind. The only thing preventing the actual ceremony was the King of Prussia's desire to wait until he had taken the French capital.

The siege of Paris, however, dragged on into the New Year. The bombardment proved ineffectual, as the Crown Prince had predicted. His wife was more ferocious about it than he, telling her mother that it might annoy the English that *their* beautiful and charming Paris should be battered to pieces, but these were the unavoidable consequences of fortifying the city and prolonging the war.[44] To the Crown Prince, Gambetta seemed a mere butcher, raising scratch armies which could not hope to defeat the professional Prussian corps. The Government of National Defence seemed to Princess Alice of Hesse to be a form of terrorism; the Republic which the English were so enchanted with, was a far worse despotism than that of the Empire.[45]

Under pressure from his Chancellor and his son, the King of Prussia assumed the title of German Emperor in the Hall of Mirrors at Versailles. Paris still would not fall, but the German princes could not hang about at headquarters for ever waiting for the ceremony. On 18 January 1871, all the dignitaries assembled, wearing their military dress uniforms and insignia. The King purposefully wore the Russian Order of St George, while the Crown Prince wore the Garter at his knee to show his love of England.

The Palace of Versailles was packed with Prussian and German officers and troopers carrying their tattered regimental colours. Beneath a central window in the huge Hall of Mirrors the King stood with the royal princes before a field altar. After the Crown Prince had ordered 'Off helmets for prayer!', a chaplain from Potsdam read a short service. Massed military bands then struck up the hymn, 'Sei Lob und Ehr', under the painted ceiling which glorified the triumphs of Le Roi Soleil. The 'Te Deum' was sung and the King proceeded to the Salon de la Guerre, where he read a short Address to the German sovereigns. He was followed by a grim Bismarck, who read another Address to the German people as if he were reciting an agenda. Then the Grand Duke of Baden cried in a loud voice, 'Long live His Imperial Majesty the Emperor William!' Flags waved, huzzas shook the tapestries, the Crown Prince knelt and kissed his father's hand. He was raised up and warmly embraced. He was His Imperial Highness now – which, he claimed, he did not wish to be called.

The new Emperor also claimed he did not want his title. He had fought to be called Emperor of Germany. He had wept and had threatened to abdicate if he could not get his way. But as this title implied a territorial claim, Bismarck had insisted that the King of Prussia be called the German Emperor. 'Delivering the imperial baby was a difficult case,' Bismarck wrote to his wife. 'At such a time, kings – like women – have strange longings.' As midwife at so protracted a labour, Bismarck had felt ready to explode like a shell and blow up the whole palace.[46]

The acceptance of the imperial title was the last great service that the Crown Prince would perform for his father. He had been the major contributor in the winning of three great battles. If the fortunes of war had gone the other way, there would have been no Prussian solution to the German problem. By his military skill, the Crown Prince had helped achieve the Coburg dream of a united German Empire. Despite his enforced co-operation with Bismarck, he secretly wanted to pension off the Chancellor.[47] Bismarck was not eternal, as the Crown Princess pointed out to her mother. She thought he would soon be as quickly forgotten as the Louis Napoleon who had once so frightened Europe.[48] Only the heartbeat of one old man fluttered between the Chancellor and dismissal. Bismarck might try to speak and act like the new German

Emperor, but he could fall as quickly as he had risen. In any event, his power was limited so long as the war continued. When he tried to interfere with military strategy, Moltke quarrelled with him, and the Crown Prince had to try and heal the breach. Moltke wanted a war of extermination against the French, while Bismarck wanted peace, and a resumption of his total control.

The Chancellor won his peace. At Sedan he had played no part in fixing the terms of surrender, but now he was appointed to negotiate for the capitulation of Paris and the ending of the war. He embittered the Crown Prince and the other generals by excluding them from the preliminaries. The French negotiators, Favre and Thiers, stood in awe of Bismarck, and they knew that further resistance was useless. Paris was starving, and the recruits gathered from the *levées en masse* were scarcely more than boys. By the end of February, the French capital had formally surrendered. By the end of the first week of March, the deputies of the newly elected National Assembly at Bordeaux had ratified the peace terms. The war was over.

France had to pay a great price. She lost Alsace and the northern part of Lorraine, including Metz. She also had to suffer a German army of occupation living off the land 'like caterpillars on a tree' until a war indemnity of five billion francs (£200 million) had been paid.[49] Throughout the negotiations, Bismarck behaved like a bully, conducting himself with monstrous and intentional rudeness. At the last moment, he spared Thiers the indignity of submitting the French capital to a German Triumph through its streets. Instead, the new German Emperor twice reviewed 30,000 of his troops on the racecourse at Longchamps. Bismarck had again snatched from him the chance of a victory parade through a conquered capital.

In March, the Crown Prince returned, an embittered victor, to his wife in Berlin. His cousin, Frederick Karl, had been made a Field Marshal for his dull and costly victories. His gracious words as he accepted his baton were: 'At last!' The Crown Prince could not even say that. His exploits were being consigned to oblivion. He must steal no glory from the Chancellor or the Emperor, and must wait until the Victory Parade in June to be given his marshal's baton, covered with sky-blue satin and studded with crowns and eagles.

The award had come too late and was barely noticed in the Triumph. The Crown Prince's son William, riding behind him on his dappled pony, was more fascinated by his grandfather the Emperor, as he halted beneath the Brandenburg Gate to receive the keys of Berlin from a group of maidens in white. The Emperor recognized his grandson's devotion and stopped to put a hand on the boy's shoulder, amid the ranks of the Guards and the massed bands and the cheering crowds.

'This is a day you will not forget,' the Emperor said.

The boy never did.

CHAPTER NINE

How Long, O Lord, How Long?

BISMARCK WAS CREATED a Prince and was given an enormous estate. He seemed, now, to be the embodiment of the whole German Empire. He controlled the Reichstag through the National Liberals, and national communications through his agents and with the aid of the 'Reptile Fund'. The new Emperor was little more than the ceremonial head of state, while Bismarck ran all the business of the country. After a long visit to England to recover from the hardships of the war, the Crown Prince found himself again excluded from the Council of State and the War Cabinet. The only formidable opposition to Bismarck came from the General Staff, always jealous of its military powers and privileges, from the Junker reactionaries he was deserting, and from the Catholic aristocrats clustering round the implacable Empress Augusta. As for the German princes, most had been reduced to pensioned figureheads. 'They no longer want to govern,' Bismarck told Busch, 'and are glad when some one relieves them of the trouble.'[1]

Even the liberals and the middle classes, who once had looked to the ideals of the Crown Prince and his wife, now made Bismarck their idol because he was enriching them. France managed to pay off her war indemnity of five billion francs within three years. The flow of money into Berlin provoked a speculative boom there, which spread throughout the Empire. Money was so abundant, the British representative reported from Leipzig in 1871, that people did not know what to do with it.[2] In Berlin itself, the excessive liquidity led to enormous stock and property speculation, as great as that of London's South Sea Bubble or the Panama Scheme of Paris. 'The market had bullish orgies,' a contemporary wrote.

'Millions, coined right out of the ground, were won. National prosperity rose to apparently unimagined heights. A shower of gold rained down on the drunken city.'[3]

Much of the risk capital went into the railway schemes of Baron Strousberg, who was set on creating a railway empire in eastern Europe, as large as that of a Vanderbilt or a Gould – and by the same method: the watering of stocks until they were drowned under the inevitable deluge. Industry flourished with the orders for rolling-stock and track, building materials and luxuries. A new word was coined, the *Gründerjahre*, to describe the post-war boom years of ostentation and speculation, greed and display.

Bismarck had performed a miracle of balance and compromise between the new and the old. The Liberals were placated with a Reichstag, and prosperity and free trade within the German Empire. For these benefits, they gave up their demands for a bill of rights, and control over the Cabinet and the Chancellor. Although the Junkers lost their feudal privileges, many were pleased by the confirmation of their power and position in Prussia and at court. The social system remained a caste system, where appointments were the preserve of aristocrats and their sons. Even the generals were tolerably pleased when Bismarck arranged a deal between them and the Reichstag, by which military budgets would have to be agreed every seven years instead of every three. Through victory and German unity, Bismarck seemed to have found a synthesis for the irreconcilable conflicts of Prussian society. Giving every group something, he had reconciled the nation in the pride of unity. Only the masses stood outside the settlement – powerless, but patriotic and fairly prosperous. Their time was not yet, so Bismarck did not need to deal with them.

The forces that opposed Bismarck's plans for a united Germany seemed to him threefold: the Church, the unadaptable Junkers, and the Crown, which still had the power to dismiss him. The Church was attacked through an erroneous policy of extending state control over parochial schools, both Catholic and Protestant. This policy pleased the liberals and the anti-clericals, but alienated the southern German Catholic states. Hundreds of bishops and priests were imprisoned or expelled; within five years, a third of Prussian parishes had no pastors. This *Kulturkampf* was destroying the hard-won unity of Germany in the names of reason and state power.

The new British Ambassador, Odo Russell, managed the impossible.

He was on good terms with the Chancellor as well as with the Crown Prince. He analysed Bismarck's policy at home. The *Kulturkampf* would make the State supreme over all foreign influences, particularly papal, perhaps divine. The recent defining of the doctrine of papal infallibility was anathema to Bismarck: 'thinking himself more infallible than the Pope, he cannot tolerate two infallibles in Europe.' The abolition of feudal rights and the increase of court ceremonial weakened the aristocracy by putting it in costume. Most clever of all, Bismarck had persuaded the old German Emperor to distrust his family and the minor princes. The Chancellor alone appeared to hold the ring between liberals and aristocrats, the Emperor and the court. He had made himself indispensable to the German system he had created. The future sovereign, the British Ambassador concluded glumly, would be obliged to secure Bismarck's services.[4]

The future sovereign was being reduced, as former German sovereigns had been, to exercises in etiquette. The ceremonies of the Empire were even more exhausting than those of the Kingdom of Prussia. 'Party succeeds party – dinner after dinner . . .' the Crown Princess complained to her mother. 'It is really too much for one's nerves. Fritz says this last week has tried him more than the whole campaign.'[5]

The German Emperor seemed to have taken over the tricks of Versailles, where *Le Roi Soleil* had used ceremony as a form of rule. Endless protocol and public displays of obedience made all the rival princes impotent and subservient. The Emperor and Empress kept their son and daughter-in-law firmly in their place. Their role was to wait meekly behind the throne. In fact, the Emperor's haughtiness to his heir caused the Crown Prince to pass on the same ill-treatment to lesser princes, in order to salvage some pride.

In an interesting aside to her Foreign Secretary, Queen Victoria criticized her son-in-law for his behaviour on occasions of ceremony. 'The Crown Prince hates intrigue,' she declared, 'and is very straightforward and honest and kind-hearted but rather weak and to a certain extent obstinate, not conceited, but absurdly proud, as all his family are, thinking no family higher or greater than the Hohenzollerns; not proud to those below him, that is to the people, but proud and overbearing to other Princes.'[6]

Attendance at all major ceremonies was absolutely *de rigueur*; absence was an insult, if not actually treasonable. When the former British Ambassador stayed away on holiday from the Victory Parade in June 1871, it was taken as a political affront and contributed to his replacement by Odo Russell – very much *persona grata* at court. At other special state occasions, such as the funeral of the Queen Dowager in 1873, Queen Victoria insisted that a distinguished British representative be sent from England. These royal princes or noble lords were invariably struck by the profusion of orders and decorations worn by the imperial guests, even at a funeral. Although in mourning, most of the men glittered with the jewelled stars and embroidered sashes of their particular rank and distinction. An English aristocrat had to be present. To show respect was all. The court sought 'with the greatest avidity any small marks of favour from the Court of England'.[7]

Especially important was the confirmation service of Prince William, the Emperor's grandson. Queen Victoria sent to her 'Dearest Willie' a portrait of the Prince Consort, a large inscribed English Bible, and a small ivory bust of herself. She did not want him to forget his English and Coburg connections. She exhorted him to stick to his Protestant faith during an age of religious strife. Disbelief was now trying to raise its poisonous head and, under the form of science and intellect, progress and liberty, to shake the simple belief in the Heavenly Father and His blessed Son.[8] She also sent the Prince of Wales to the ceremony, feeling it important that her successor should be present at such a solemn step for an heir to the German Crown.

The confirmation service was a demonstration of how the Hohenzollerns still saw themselves as the sword in the hand of God. Prince William, himself, wore the uniform of the 1st Foot Guards and the riband and star of the Black Eagle. His father, who led him to the altar to make his responses, also wore his Guards uniform. Even the Prince of Wales was dressed in the finery of a British general, topped by the Black Eagle. The Emperor, too, was splendid in military dress and decorations, as were the invited princes of the blood and field marshals. Against this glorious array, only the ministers and the royal women looked drab, the Crown Princess in a black dress with a white bonnet, the Empress in a cream-coloured gown. Like peacocks or Mayan warriors, the imperial family put the finest feathers on the males.

The Emperor's love of tradition and form made him quarrel over the education of his grandchildren. The Crown Princess and her husband wanted to send Prince William and his brother Henry to the Gymnasium at Kassel so that they could meet German boys from ordinary families and experience the national system of education. The Emperor wanted to limit his eldest grandson to more military training and keep him ready to appear in the world on all occasions. That, the Crown Princess told her mother, would be an end of all study at once, and an end too of all hopes of his becoming a steady and serious man.[9] So the parents fought the Emperor on the subject through many unpleasant and violent scenes – and won their point. William and his brother were sent to Kassel for more than two years, but did not seem to profit much from the experiment. Their tutor Hinzpeter went with them and supervised them privately, ensuring that they made no friends with their class-mates. Hinzpeter thought the effect of the school on Prince William was only skin-deep, while the Prince complained to his imperial grandfather that he was humiliated by scoring fewer marks than mere commoners.

The autocracy of the Emperor towards his son was galling. The war hero of Wörth found himself treated like a child, given little to do, but forbidden to go away. He was not allowed to leave Potsdam or Berlin without his father's permission, which was often refused. 'Just think of Fritz at forty being treated like a boy of six ...' the Crown Princess wrote in indignation. 'It is a tyranny which I consider quite insupportable. A General is put above our children against our will with orders from the Emperor and our Home turned topsy-turvy – I own I feel in a perfect rage.' It was enough to make a saint swear.[10]

Yet the Crown Princess kept quiet, except when the continual attacks on England reached her ears. Then she could become spiteful and savage in defending her homeland, finding it ridiculous that it should be thought a sin to be a stranger in the Prussian Court. Her sin became greater when she made friends with the cultivated Hanoverian, Ludwig Windthorst, leader of the Catholic opposition party in the Reichstag. Like the Emperor, Bismarck thought that princes were tainted by the company they kept. If the Crown Prince's household were entertaining the chief opponent of the *Kulturkampf*, he might be considering Windthorst as Bismarck's replacement when the old Emperor died.

Bismarck was indispensable to his own system. His fear of a plot against him, was chiefly directed at the Crown Prince's mother. As the Emperor aged, the Empress gained more influence over him. In Bismarck's view, she had abandoned her support of the liberals because he had swung so many of them to his side. Now she was with Bismarck's old supporters, the reactionary Protestants, and the devout Catholics opposed to the *Kulturkampf*. It was a way of undermining the Chancellor's power. 'If she is not already a Catholic,' Bismarck claimed to Busch, 'she will be so very soon.'

Above all, Bismarck hated the Empress for indulging in direct diplomacy. 'She also interferes in foreign policy,' he confided to Busch, 'having taken it into her head that it is her vocation to plead everywhere in favour of peace – to be an Angel of Peace. She therefore writes letters to foreign Sovereigns, to the Queen of England for instance, which she afterwards mentions to her consort, who, however, says nothing about them to me.'[11] This brake on Bismarck's provocative diplomacy was especially disconcerting during the war scare with France in 1875, when royal intervention did much to scotch Bismarck's plans.

To protect himself, Bismarck visited the Emperor daily in Berlin and Potsdam. But when they were separated during the long summer recess, the Chancellor could not prevent the Empress from playing on her husband's fear that a revolution might result from the radical changes of the *Kulturkampf*. Then Bismarck had to go back and rebuild the morale of the old Emperor. Once during the religious crisis, he had to travel as far as Jueterbogk to join his royal master in his carriage. The Emperor was depressed, thinking of the scaffold once more and ready to abdicate. Acting as he had when he first became the chief minister of Prussia, Bismarck caught at the Emperor's sword-knot and appealed to his sense of duty as an army officer. By the evening, the King was cheerful and refused to accept Bismarck's threat to resign if he did not get his own way.

The Emperor still had the final say, but the Chancellor dominated him – as long as he lived. Interest in the state of the Emperor's health was almost ghoulish and provoked many secret messages in cipher. By the end of the war, in 1871, he appeared feeble and wandering in his wits. He seemed to recover, but in June 1873 he began to suffer from sick headaches, giddiness and fainting fits. These were the symptoms which had heralded his brother's madness. Bismarck took the matter seriously, and Odo Russell reported back to London that the Crown Prince might soon have to assume power.

That was Bismarck's nightmare, and his reason for hating the Crown Princess second only to the Empress. The Chancellor felt that he might be able to work round the Crown Prince despite his liberal convictions, if only his strong-minded wife were not his conscience and guide in times of peace. Bismarck told the British Ambassador's wife that he thought he could agree with the Crown Prince, but he feared never with the Crown Princess. As a result, he would be forced to persecute her through his control of the press, making her position with the public a very difficult one, in order to have his own way about the administration of Germany.[12]

He knew where she was vulnerable. First, as a foreigner who could always be accused of being an English agent. Second, as the malign influence behind the Crown Prince. Third, as a dangerous reformer, with her new hospital systems and girls' schools, so tainted with English innovations. Fourth, as a woman who disliked Prussian ceremonial and tradition, while favouring the artistic and the unconventional. Fifth, as a supporter of toleration for Catholics and even Jews. To all these exploitable weaknesses, the Crown Princess added candour and sensitivity. She was almost too easy a mark.

A reconciliation between the Chancellor and the Crown Prince, still lingering at the threshold of the throne, seemed probable; the one must inherit what the other had created for himself. There were attempts by mutual friends to bring this about, but they came to nothing. War could tolerate such a strange alliance, but not peace. While Bismarck could control the old Emperor, he did not want the bother of dealing with the heir apparent and his difficult wife. He would rather ignore the problem until it was real, reducing the Crown Prince's political role to insignificance, because he still had his head stuffed full with English notions about parliamentary government. 'The Crown Prince wants me to obey the majority,' Bismarck once exploded. 'That demands a suppleness of character and conviction that I do not possess.'[13]

Anyway, the English alliance desired by the Crown Prince and the Empress did not suit the Chancellor's book. The armies of Russia and France were the real threat to German security, while a naval power could be treated with suspicion and contempt. It was a favourite saying of Bismarck's, his *bête noire* Morier reported, that he lost five years of his political life by the foolish belief that England was still a great power.[14] Morier had been the first to accuse Bismarck of fomenting the war against France, by arranging the second Spanish offer to the Hohenzollern candidate. Now, Morier's confidential meetings with diplomats at spas, and his dining with the German Emperor and Empress at Baden, persuaded Bismarck that English intrigues against him never stopped. Morier was his sworn enemy, sent from southern Germany to spy on him and to concoct his fall. England might not be able to fight, but she could still plot against him through her agents abroad and in the imperial family itself.

Although Bismarck did not actually threaten England, Moltke did at one of the Chancellor's dinner parties. He was sitting next to the British Ambassador, and told him that the invasion of England was strategically easy. The people had no discipline and were unprepared to resist. As for a war of revenge with France, that had to happen. It was the main reason Germany kept such a large standing army. War, anyway, would last as long as humanity. God himself favoured it as the Bible proved.[15] When the Crown Prince visited Queen Victoria in 1871, he told her that they were living on a volcano. Some day, he said, Bismarck might try to make war on England.[16]

The Crown Princess knew that she offended Prussian society by her intelligence and independence, but she had been trained to be what she was, and she insisted on trying to provide an equal opportunity for suppressed Prussian girls. She worked actively to found three schools which would give higher education. Two of them were called after her, the *Victoria Schule* and the *Victoria Lyceum*, which even had an English headmistress. If the court were shocked by the alien princess's efforts to improve young women's minds, it was horrified by her insistence on sports and physical training which seemed unfeminine and improper as well as foreign and pernicious.

Her efforts to reform German hospitals and nurses' training provoked a similar reaction, but she had not listened to Florence Nightingale in vain. At the time of the war against France, Prussian care for the wounded was on a level with British neglect before the Crimean War. The hospital which the Crown Princess had struggled to start at Homburg, was run on the new English model. It was scrubbed and hygienic, open windows let in the air and let out the carbolic. The wounded soldiers recovered faster there. They were grateful and came to value the Crown Princess almost as highly as they did her military husband, but the German doctors thought her reforms dangerous and foreign. It was reported in Berlin that her methods were killing off the wounded rather than curing them. Her attempts during the years of peace to carry on her hospital work were blocked by her mother-in-law, who was suspicious of her innovations and jealous of her success. Only in the training of nurses were some of her reforms adopted.

The price the Crown Princess paid for insisting on better education for women, was that she appeared to be interfering and radical. She seemed to be acting like a Victorian missionary in a backward and savage country, which offended not only the court, but also most of the teaching and medical profession. She particularly offended the fundamentalist Protestant clergy, who were becoming increasingly powerful at court. To them, church and home and children should be the only concerns of Prussian women. What the Crown Princess called reform, they called subversion.

Her three elder children were learning to rebel against her teaching. They did not like the quiet life at Bornstadt, where their mother fled to escape from the stifling rooms and long ceremonies of Potsdam. William did not enjoy being made to groom horses and look after dogs. He preferred the mess and the parade-ground, the court and the glitter of life in the capital, where his grandparents encouraged him to resist his mother's foreign ways.

In point of fact, his mother's insistence on a Spartan English education had benefited her crippled child. He was becoming self-reliant and learning to suppress his self-pity. He worked all the time at developing his good right arm until he had a mighty grip, strong enough to make one hand do the job of two. His left arm was six inches shorter than the other and unable to lift a thing, but he learned to balance it unobtrusively on a belt or a sword-hilt. He did use it to hold the reins of his horse, but he could only direct his mount with his knees and his right hand.

His mastery over his infirmity gave him increasing self-confidence. He became the ringleader of his brother, Henry, and sister, Charlotte, in rebellion against their parents. Charlotte was the first to defy her mother openly. A capricious and frivolous princess, she wanted to get away from home as soon as she could. Since marriage was the only way out, she chose the shy, retiring and studious Prince Bernhard of Saxe-Meiningen, who tried to teach her Greek archaeology instead of listening to her chatter. As the prince was a suitable husband and as her daughter was making trouble in the house, the Crown Princess agreed to Charlotte's marriage when she reached the age of seventeen.

This caused a strong reaction from Queen Victoria, who accused her daughter of making a victim out of Charlotte because the young girl was unhappy at home. The Crown Princess found such an accusation unfair. Her mother had never visited her home in Germany and had never seen how they lived. How could she judge whether Charlotte was happy or not? The family circle was usually all simplicity and harmony when the Emperor and Empress left them alone, and when she and the Crown Prince were not forced to go about and entertain too much.[17]

The Crown Princess was living in a state of self-delusion about her three elder children, who were forming a little cabal against their parents. They doted on the Emperor and Empress, loving the splendour and importance of the old Prussian traditions. Always careful to show great honour to those who cared so much, Queen Victoria sent in 1878 two of her sons, the Prince of Wales and the Duke of Connaught, to the double wedding ceremony of Princess Charlotte and another Prussian princess. The Crown Princess suffered the tears and the sense of loss that her mother had suffered twenty years before, on losing her own daughter – and Queen Victoria did not mince her words about it, declaring: 'I think a daughter's marriage dreadful, repulsive.'[18]

The long and elaborate wedding ceremonies caused comments in *The Times*. Its editorial stated that royal marriages no longer had any important effect on the conduct of nations, which was a senseless thing to say in view of the recent royal efforts at keeping the peace, and a war caused by a Hohenzollern candidate. But *The Times* did praise the resolution of those who went through the observances, including an interminable torchlight procession of the Prussian ministers. The thoroughness of the national character was seen in its etiquette, *The Times* noted. The aged Emperor might have the satisfaction of thinking, as he watched the twenty-two repetitions of the same ceremony, that the spirit of discipline and the instinct of obedience presided over the court as well as the camp.[19]

One of the Prince of Wales's aides wrote to Queen Victoria about the strange marriage customs; she was always avid for such details. Apparently the *Grande Maîtresse* of Princess Charlotte's household distributed *Strumpfbänder* for the princes to wear in their buttonholes. These were pieces of embroidered ribbon which looked like bookmarkers. They were the remnants of an old custom, in which the youngest Hohenzollern prince had helped to disrobe the bride and had cut up her garters to give to the male guests. The aide also noticed what other Englishmen had noticed before him: the military splendour of the court, with its many magnificent uniforms bespattered with orders and medals was equalled only by the exceeding plainness of the women.[20]

The Crown Princess was not one of them. Although her figure had thickened with the bearing of her eighth and last child, Margaret or

'Mossy', her face was young and alive with the intelligence she could not hide. She remained in love with her husband, who treated her with trust as well as devotion. As the long years passed and the throne seemed no nearer, he learned to admire his wife's commitment to her ideals, and constancy in withstanding the pressures and pinpricks inflicted on them.

For Bismarck had become enraged again by Queen Victoria's marriage game. Her son, Prince Alfred, was engaged to the Tsar's only daughter, the Grand Duchess Marie; her children seemed to be trying to surround Germany with their blood alliances. Even the Crown Prince accused the Prince of Wales of working to populate northern Europe with anti-German marriages.[21] Ever since the defeat of the French and the founding of the German Empire, Bismarck had been aiming to preserve the peace of Europe, and consolidate the new nation. His greatest fear was a conflict on two or three fronts. France might combine with Austria or Russia in a war of revenge. In five years, the Third Republic had paid off its reparations, achieved national prosperity and equipped new armies. The German general staff feared French rearmament and wanted a quick preventative strike against the revived enemy across the Rhine.

This was not Bismarck's desire. Just as royal alliances prejudiced his diplomatic efforts to keep rival powers isolated or friendly with Germany, so the dominance of the general staff in time of war threatened the delicate balance of forces within Germany which he manipulated in order to give the new nation time to develop and grow together. A powerful army was essential for national security, but Bismarck never forgot his own loss of control during the wars against Austria and France. The war scare of 1875 had shown just how dangerous the military high command could be. Although Bismarck had allowed a Press campaign to be run, alleging that France would soon attack Germany at the head of a combination of Catholic powers, he had meant to intimidate the Third Republic, not to open hostilities. His problem was that, once Moltke and the general staff scented the possibility of war, they would not be put off. They urged on the Emperor the need to attack France in order to prevent an invasion of Germany. And the Emperor had listened to them rather than to his Chancellor.[22]

The French Government, however, had not repeated the mistakes of 1870. It did not wish to fight, and mounted a diplomatic campaign in order to threaten Germany with Bismarck's nightmare, the coalition of all the European powers against the new Empire. The Austrian Emperor warned his German cousin not to fight France again. The Tsar travelled to Prussia to repeat the same message. Queen Victoria sent a special messenger to Berlin carrying a letter to the Tsar. She reminded him of the recent joining of their two families and begged him to use his influence with his uncle, the German Emperor. As all the monarchs of Europe said they wanted peace, why should Germany have to fight?[23]

Faced with a possible war on three fronts, Bismarck had regained control over the General Staff without admitting that he had lost it. He was humiliated and on the edge of a nervous collapse. He declared that he would have to resign or retire to the country. If he continued to overwork, his doctor had told him, he would be dead in a few months.[24] He denied responsibility for the war scare, telling the British Ambassador that it had been caused by the irresponsible Press and various stock-jobbers. Military men had the right to desire a preventative war, but not to make one. In fact, he did not suscribe to the 'up and at 'em' principle; his slogan was 'Let them come on!'[25]

The Emperor would not accept Bismarck's resignation, but sent him away on sick leave to the country for five months. Before the Chancellor left, he took care to see the Crown Prince and maintain his innocence in the matter of the scare. He said he regretted England's unfriendly attitude. Queen Victoria herself had come out against Germany – something which she did not deny. 'It was I ALONE,' she informed the Crown Princess, 'who on hearing from ALL sides from our Ministers abroad of the danger of war, told My Ministers that every thing MUST be done to prevent it, that it was too intolerable that a war should be got up.' No one wished more than she did that England and Germany might go well together, but Bismarck was so overbearing, violent, grasping and unprincipled that no one could stand it. All agreed that he was becoming like the first Napoleon whom Europe had to join together in putting down.[26]

Queen Victoria had not known that Bismarck had briefly lost control to the military machine and had taken the blame for a war scare that he had initiated, but regretted. In fact, the combination of great powers against Germany had proved to the general staff and the Emperor that Bismarck was essential. His diplomacy had never allowed such a coalition to form against Germany. He had only permitted wars to break out when Austria or France stood alone. He was indispensable in preserving the new German Empire. Even the Crown Princess had to admit that. Although she thought him a very doubtful blessing, 'the idea that Bismarck has made us great—has made us feared, and therefore is perfectly

INFALLIBLE – is the presiding one!'[27] The Emperor himself found it useful to put all responsibility on to Bismarck by implication. When he wrote personally to Queen Victoria, he declared that the war scare of 1875 had been entirely a fabrication by the newspapers, especially *The Times*. He and Moltke had never even considered a preventative war.[28]

On reading the letter, Queen Victoria's Prime Minister had commented drily that the Emperor was not allowed to know what was said and done in his name.[29] The truth was that it suited the Emperor to make Bismarck seem responsible for all policy – and it suited Bismarck to appear so. The Emperor could do no wrong. The Chancellor was all-powerful. He stood between the throne and the German people. His domestic policies during the first seven years of the Empire were based on a series of checks and balances between various social groups and classes, that allowed for national prosperity and a bourgeois economic revolution. Bismarck saw himself as the architect of the new Germany, and any attack on his authority appeared to be an attack on national security. In a real sense, he was the state he was making.

To protect his power and to make his countervailing policies work at home and abroad, Bismarck had to fragment his opposition. His persecution of any potential rival could approach paranoia. The ambitious Count Harry von Arnim was thought to be forming a Catholic opposition group with himself as the prospective Chancellor. As a consequence, Bismarck had him prosecuted as a traitor who had betrayed government secrets. The Count was eventually sentenced to five years' penal servitude.

Bismarck was also determined to destroy the influence of the Empress Augusta, who attracted those elements who could not be reconciled to Bismarck's immense authority. The Crown Princess remained his lesser target in the attack on the integrity of the Empress, whom Bismarck's agents suggested should be banished or imprisoned. The Emperor did not come to his wife's defence, and the more she was abused and accused, the more civil, subservient and devoted did everyone in Berlin become to the Chancellor.[30] No one seemed to have the courage to counter-attack his press and spy network. 'It is an abominable system of his,' the Crown Princess protested, 'trying to pull down the royal family in the eyes of the public to appear a martyr! It is wicked, disloyal and ungenerous especially to women who cannot defend themselves; and the German public are so blind in their adoration of Bismarck that they would believe anything bad of us, if it came from him or was sanctioned by him.'[31]

She would not see the rationale behind Bismarck's assaults on any possible leader of an opposition. In the founding years of a new nation, a show of unity is essential, patriotism is especially a virtue. An alternative method of ruling a state appears a subversion. Bismarck believed that his policies were the best for the new Germany, and most were proving successful. The Crown Prince and Princess thought that other liberal policies would be more successful, but they had no power and resented their exclusion from it.

They particularly misunderstood Bismarck's constant supervision of them and efforts to keep them isolated. They felt themselves at the centre of a conspiracy by the Chancellor to make them impotent. In fact, they were only a small element in his grand designs, only two of several potential leaders of an opposition. Even Queen Victoria thought that her daughter had reacted too strongly against the Chancellor's surveillance when she had asked her mother's permission to burn all her letters. 'Every scrap that you have ever written – I have hoarded up, but the idea is dreadful to me that anyone else should read them or meddle with them in the event of my death. Will you not burn all mine? I should feel so much relieved .... I am sure that keeping much is a bad plan.'[32]

Queen Victoria had told her daughter to keep the correspondence. So survived perhaps the most valuable evidence of the power of royal kinship and diplomacy in the nineteenth century, which was dedicated to keeping the peace between England and Germany and in all of Europe. The apparent opponent of this policy, Bismarck, was now working towards much the same end. After the nightmare of the coalition against Germany in 1875, he had realized that his country must not appear too powerful. He wished to preserve the *status quo* between England, Austria and Russia, while keeping France too isolated to attack Germany. The most likely conflict was between the British Empire and the Russian one, particularly on the Black Sea, where England used Turkey as a bastion to keep the Russians from the Mediterranean. Germany's interest were not to take the side of either Russia or England, but to act as the honest broker between them and keep them as friendly nations.[33]

Unfortunately for Bismarck's policy of holding the balance of power in Europe, the Tsar in 1877 was going to war against Turkey on behalf of the persecuted Serbs. The German Emperor wanted to support Russia, although Bismarck insisted on remaining neutral. This displeased the Emperor, who retaliated by making Bismarck keep as head of the admiralty General Albrecht von Stosch, who was close to the Crown Prince

Crown Princess Frederick in 1883.

Crown Prince Frederick
in 1884.

Queen Victoria's Jubilee procession in Trafalgar Square, 1887. Crown Prince Frederick is the mounted figure in white uniform. Charlton.

Queen Victoria and her family at the time of her Jubilee. The Crown Prince, in white uniform, is standing on the right, while the Crown Princess is seated on her mother's left. Tuxen.

Group in San Remo including (*descending steps, from left to right*) Prince Henry (*light jacket*), Princesses Victoria, Sophie and Margaret of Prussia, Crown Prince Frederick (*bottom of steps*) and the Crown Princess behind him.

The funeral of Emperor Frederick III, 18 June 1888.

Emperor William II visiting Bismarck.

Empress Frederick in mourning surrounded by (*left to right*) Princess Victoria of Prussia, Princess Sophie with her husband Constantine, Duke of Sparta, and Princess Margaret of Prussia, September 1888.

Two widows: the Empress
Frederick with her mother,
Queen Victoria, in February
1889.

The south front of Schloss
Friedrichshof.

Group at Coburg, April 1894.

1 Prince Louis of Battenberg 2 Grand Duke Paul of Russia 3 Prince Philip of Saxe-Coburg 4 Count Mensdorff 5 Marie, Crown Princess of Roumania 6 Elizabeth, Grand Duchess Serge of Russia 7 Alfred, Duke of Saxe-Coburg-Gotha 8 Prince Henry of Battenberg 9 Louise, Princess Philip of Saxe-Coburg 10 Grand Duke Serge of Russia 11 Ferdinand, Crown Prince of Roumania 12 Grand Duke Vladimir of Russia 13 Arthur, Duke of Connaught 14 Albert Edward, Prince of Wales 15 Beatrice, Princess Henry of Battenberg 16 Princess Alexandra of Saxe-Coburg-Gotha 17 Charlotte, Princess Bernhard of Saxe-Meiningen 18 Louise Margaret, Duchess of Connaught 19 Prince Alfred of Saxe-Coburg-Gotha 20 Tsarevitch Nicholas of Russia 21 Princess Alix of Hesse 22 Victoria, Princess Louis of Battenberg 23 Irene, Princess Henry of Prussia 24 Marie, Grand Duchess Vladimir of Russia 25 Marie, Duchess of Saxe-Coburg-Gotha 26 Emperor William II of Germany 27 Queen Victoria 28 Victoria, Empress Frederick of Germany 29 Princess Beatrice of Saxe-Coburg-Gotha 30 Princess Feodore of Saxe-Meiningen.

The widowed Empress Frederick talking to Bismarck.

At Friedrichshof, May 1900: (*left to right*) Crown Princess Sophie of Greece; Victoria, Princess Adolf of Schaumburg-Lippe; Emperor William II; Empress Frederick; Charlotte, Princess Bernhard of Saxe-Meiningen; Prince Henry of Prussia; and Margaret, Princess Frederick Charles of Hesse.

Empress Frederick of Prussia in 1900, the year before her death.

and seemed to Bismarck another rival as Chancellor. Bismarck threatened to resign if Stosch were not dismissed, but the Emperor insisted on retaining him and sent Bismarck away on a long leave of absence. But Bismarck still knew only too well how to get his way, even with his opponents. He succeeded in priming the Crown Princess to write to her mother in defence of an emerging plan: England was to take Egypt from Turkey and leave Russia and Austria to pick up other choice pieces from the carcass of the 'Sick Man of Europe'. Queen Victoria was outraged. She and Lord Beaconsfield were both fanatics about supporting Turkey and keeping the Russians from Constantinople. When she showed her Prime Minister the Crown Princess's letter, he declared that it must have been dictated by Bismarck.

So the Crown Princess's worst fears had been realized. Bismarck had been so clever that she was saying his words without knowing it. When her mother told her that England would do what it intended without Bismarck's permission, she knew she had been duped. When British warships were sent to the Bosphorus, her old patriotism was re-kindled. 'How I do long for one good roar of the British Lion from the housetops,' she wrote, 'and for the thunder of a British broadside!'[34]

The thunder was not heard, nor was it needed. A combined threat from Austria and England was enough to halt the Russian armies just short of Constantinople. The peace imposed by the Treaty of San Stefano was made subject to a Congress of the great powers in Berlin. Bismarck was to be the arbiter. His policy and his country's armies had made Germany the centre of European diplomacy. Now he could let other nations fight, and call the end game.

For the Crown Prince the long wait seemed to be over. On 11 May 1878, a plumber named Max Hödel came from between two carts and fired two shots at the Emperor's open victoria carriage as it was passing down the Unter den Linden. The Emperor was with his daughter Louise, the Grand Duchess of Baden. She saw the would-be assassin; his complexion was sallow and grey, his expression one of calm despair.[35] He had fired too high. The Emperor's *Jäger* jumped down from the box to pursue the man, while the carriage drove on. Hödel was captured and nobody was hurt, except the socialists. He claimed to be one of them, and Bismarck introduced a bill to muzzle them and their newspapers. The National Liberals in the Reichstag, fearing that the new law might be used against them, opposed it, much to Bismarck's fury.

After 2 June, there was less opposition to repressive measures. On that day, Dr Karl Nobiling, a left-wing journalist, fired a double-barrelled shotgun at the Emperor's open carriage from the upper window of a house in Berlin. Twenty-seven pellets lodged in the Emperor's arms, five in his neck, and six in his left cheek and brow. One lead slug penetrated his jaw, another nicked an artery in his wrist. Torrents of blood flowed over the upholstery of the carriage, which was driven at snail's pace back to the palace. The old man insisted on walking unaided inside before fainting from loss of blood.

The Crown Prince and Princess were on a visit to England. There had been a disaster in the Channel on the day before, when the German flagship, *König Wilhelm*, had collided with the ironclad, *Grosser Kurfürst*, which sank with the loss of 250 lives. The British Navy had been ordered to give all assistance, and the Crown Prince had hurried to Dover to see what could be done. But the news of his father's wounding in Berlin sent the Crown Prince and his wife dashing back to Germany. Both thought that the old man of eighty-two would not recover from such serious injuries. Special trains brought them to Berlin in less than two days. The Emperor's palace was crowded with generals, ministers, servants, officers and attendants of all sorts. 'Most uncomfortable,' the Crown Princess thought. Every one showed the utmost concern and horror and alarm. The Emperor, himself, seemed calm and far more reasonable than all the others, who appeared to have lost their heads.

He did seem to be on the point of death. His face was swollen, and he was without his false teeth, which changed him, the Crown Princess noted. His head and arms were bandaged, and he was unable to move at all. He was lying on a horrible old bed with only relatives to nurse him. The Crown Princess soon changed that, bringing in a good English bed and arranging for proper medical care. 'Poor dear – my heart felt I cannot say what – ' she wrote, ' – to see him a venerable man of 82 struck down by the hand of lawless violence if not murder, lying so patient and helpless in his bed – a most pitiable object!'

Politically, of course, all was in a great muddle. The question was whether the Crown Prince would become the formal Regent during the Emperor's illness. Strong repressive measures would have to be taken and, since they were bound to be unpopular, the Crown Princess thought they should not be her husband's responsibility. Bismarck's mistakes had led to social strife; it was the Chancellor's duty to put things straight.[36]

A Regency Bill was brought to the Emperor to sign. Bismarck was at the bedside, as were the Crown Prince and Princess. His son was only to represent him, the Emperor said; the government was to be as before. Bismarck was to have unchecked power to halt subversion and to run the imminent Congress of Berlin. The Crown Prince was to remain a ceremonial figure-head, until the day when the old Emperor might pass away.

At his first State Council, the Crown Prince had to watch Bismarck deciding whether to dissolve the Reichstag with its Liberal majority against repressive measures, or to proclaim martial law.[37] Anti-radical feeling was running high; new elections were likely to bring in a majority in the centre and on the right. If this happened, Bismarck could secure the passage of an 'Exceptional Measure' giving the State the power to proceed against any subversives or trouble-makers in society. It put a big stick in the hand of the Chancellor's elaborate system of spying and denunciation. He could threaten his enemies legally whenever they dared to show their heads.

The Crown Prince could do nothing about Bismarck's swing back to the right. He had only the responsibility and agony of deciding on the execution of Hödel, who was probably mad. For weeks he would not sign the death warrant, but did so finally because of the need to deter future assasins. The Emperor thanked his son for sparing him the ordeal of taking another man's life; the Crown Prince had done right and God was pleased with him. Hödel refused all religious help and shouted 'Bravo for the Commune!' before his head was struck off.[38]

Like Cohen-Blind before him, Dr Nobiling died of self-inflicted wounds before he could stand trial. He was reported as having said that his reasons for trying to kill the Emperor were political and that he had had accomplices. This alleged evidence was enough to secure public support for the 'Exceptional Measure'. Nobiling's bloody work was also a piece of good luck, as Bismarck told Busch. If the pro-Russian Emperor had not been removed from the scene, Bismarck would not have had his way at the Congress of Berlin.[39]

As it was, Bismarck and Lord Beaconsfield got on splendidly. They seemed to recognize in each other a cunning and a candour as well as a certain reckless, romantic imagination. Beaconsfield thought Bismarck behaved like a sweet-voiced ogre. Bismarck loudly praised the old Jew for being so straightforward, for never stopping at small things, but going for the important things at once.[40] He rammed through the business in his normal hectoring way. The Russians were outsmarted and outgunned. The German Emperor always blamed the Crown Prince for the Russian losses at the Congress. As Regent, his son should have stood up for them against Bismarck, who had declared that the Eastern question was not worth the bones of a single Pomeranian grenadier. When the Crown Prince pointed out to his father that the Chancellor had not consulted him, the Emperor replied: 'I was ill and not expected to recover.'

Perhaps Bismarck had tried to please the next Emperor by favouring England's position at the Congress. He certainly told his intimates that he found it easier to deal with the Crown Prince and Princess than with the Emperor and Empress, who were becoming opinionated in their old age. While the Emperor liked the appearance of authority, the Crown Prince was modest and unassuming. He did not say, 'I have won the battle, I have conducted the campaign.' He said that his Chief of Staff had done it, and deserved the rewards. The Crown Princess was also preferable to the Empress, because she was unaffected and sincere. Family considerations had once made her troublesome, but these were now less important.[41]

So Bismarck trimmed his sails while the aged Emperor was ill, trying to make his peace with his next master. But when the Emperor was driven in triumph through the Brandenburg Gate at the end of the year, to take back the appearance of ruling from his son, it was the same performance as before. Incredibly, the peppering by lead slugs and pellets seemed to have improved the Emperor's health. His rheumatism and nervous attacks had been removed through acupuncture by attempted assassination. He looked as if he would live for ever. Dr Nobiling, he often used to say, was the best physician he had ever had.

CHAPTER TEN

Anguish and Omens

DIPHTHERIA STALKED GERMANY. It struck in the garret and the palace, in the back room and the nursery. In Hesse, Princess Alice watched three of her children stricken – and her husband, the new Grand Duke. Her daughter, 'May', died. When she told her sick son, he burst into tears. Trying to comfort him, she kissed him; it proved to be the kiss of death. She, herself, died of the disease on 14 December 1878, the anniversary of the death of her father, the Prince Consort.

The Crown Princess had been particularly close to Alice. 'Our darling!' she wrote to Queen Victoria. 'I can hardly bear to write her dear name: she was my particular sister, the nearest in age, the only one living in the same country with me! We had so many interests in common and all our children were so near of an age! ... Her last letter to me, a little pencil note, which, alas, I did not keep, was a cry of anguish for her sweet little flower, so rudely torn from its stem. I never heard from her again.'[1]

Three months later, her own little flower was torn from her. The ten-year-old Prince Waldemar also caught diphtheria. His tonsils swelled to the size of a walnut; he could scarcely swallow or shut his mouth. In spite of his sister's death, Waldemar's mother insisted on nursing him herself. She kept him isolated and was sprayed with carbolic before seeing her other children. After four days of choking with a rattle in his throat, Waldemar died. His mother thought him the dearest, nicest and most promising of her boys. It broke her heart to leave him lying so silent and so still, and see his pets in the next room; all his birds, his three dogs, the fishes in his aquarium and his little crocodiles. His mother could not bear the sight.[2]

179

The Crown Princess never recovered from the death of her youngest son. For months, she was in a state of shock and depression. Year after year, she would dwell on the memory of him. The pain and grief were like a hidden spring that would rise up and bubble with a force that could not be controlled. For twenty years she had always had a boy to put to bed; now all that was over. The two elder boys had gone away; the two beloved younger ones were gone for ever. The thought was terribly bitter.[3]

At the funeral, the Crown Prince threw himself on the little coffin, which was lined with white satin and full of camellias and white roses. Taking leave of his beloved son before he was laid to rest beside his dead brother, Sigismund, seemed a trial beyond endurance. The two elder sons had left home with their married sister, who was shortly to have her first child. Only the three younger girls remained – and the ceremonial duties of acting as the Crown Prince.

Despite the grief of the parents, the Emperor and the court did not wish to release them from their official duties. After Alice's death, Queen Victoria had to intervene personally to make the Emperor allow her daughter to wear public mourning and absent herself from most court occasions. 'Everyone in colours!' the Crown Princess complained. 'How they could think that I could go!'[4] With Waldemar's death, the Crown Princess's withdrawal into black and isolation was greater than ever. Such a display of grief and solitude antagonized the court. Although the Prussians had an official cult of the great dead, they found Queen Victoria and her daughter's private grief excessive.

The Crown Prince took his son's death so badly that he was ordered to take the cure at the baths in Kissingen. His wife was crippled with rheumatism and neuralgia. The birth in May of her daughter's first child, Feodore, lightened her mood, and made the Crown Princess a grandmother at the early age of thirty-nine. 'I should have far preferred a Baby of my own to a grandchild,' she confessed to her mother, '– but the happiness lasts too short a time ... A wee thing is really more to me than it is to many people.'

Thoughts of her daughter giving birth caused the Crown Princess to reflect: the process which she, herself, had undergone so often, seemed awful and terrifying. To her mother, she gave a revealing insight of the double vision with which so many Victorian women viewed their physical functions. 'This animal fabric of ours,' she wrote, 'has many aspects which are not so easy to get over – and which we should prefer to do without – still one must think as little as one can of this fact – and queer as nature is – look at that which is to be admired which ought to thrust the rest into the background!'⁵

Her dislike of Berlin society now became a revulsion. She bore up courageously through the christening of her granddaughter and the Golden Wedding of the Emperor and the Empress, even wearing white. for these occasions, but she found intolerable the spirit of espionage, malevolence, jealousy and malice that was rampant in the German capital. Home life, as in her dear England, was unknown. It might be possible for her to have it, if she were left alone, but habit and tradition ruled all at the retrograde court. The people there were frigid and bitter, stiff and dull; things and people grated harshly on her feelings. She felt herself in isolation.⁶

She must go away. She begged the Emperor to allow her to go with her husband and three daughters to Italy for the winter. After a struggle, the imperial consent was reluctantly given. They went first to Venice, then to Pegli, an enchanting place of old villas, magnolias, palms, cypresses, laurels, cedars, and orange and lemon groves. The Crown Princess thought it a 'faeryland' after the cold, dank north. She lingered there, glad to be missing the Berlin Season. When her husband was called away on official duties, she stayed behind with her daughters in her own warm world.

The price she was paying was the surrender of her two elder sons to their professions, and to other influences. Prince Henry had entered the navy at the age of ten; a gunboat, the *Blitz*, had fired a salute to honour the occasion. This was the famous gunboat which had fired a shot across the bows of a negligent British trawler in German waters, forcing her to dip her Red Ensign as a sign of respect. 'Mark this gun well!' Hinzpeter had told his two pupils. 'It is a historic gun, from which a historic shot was fired!'⁷

Prince William was not yet in a position to apply the historical lesson. He had always taken a great interest in the British Navy whenever he visited his grandmother in England. He had clambered all over Nelson's *Victory*, inspected ironclads at Plymouth and had even been down in a diving-bell. At Osborne, he could stand by the old cannon in the model redoubt where his British uncles had played. He felt more loved by Queen Victoria than by his own mother and was treated as if he were her youngest boy, a relationship which he liked to feel never changed during his grandmother's life.⁸

The one particular favour he craved, the Queen wisely granted: the Order of the Garter. She had given it to his grandfather and to his father. Now her grandson wanted it to prove that he had come of age. The Crown Princess pointed out to her mother that the Emperors of Russia and Austria had sent him their highest decorations; could England do less? Queen Victoria consulted Lord Beaconsfield, who thought there was every reason for conferring the honour; the young prince would never forget that he had received from Her Majesty the most illustrious Order in Christendom.[9]

The Crown Prince was almost as delighted as his son; not only because the Hohenzollerns cared so much for honours and orders, but also because it would link Prince William to England. The Emperor was also grateful, because it was the first time that the Garter had been bestowed upon three generations of a royal house. And when Prince William paid his next summer visit to Osborne and declared on his return that he would like to live always 'with Grandmamma of England', it seemed that Queen Victoria's diplomacy could do no more to help future relations with Germany.

Prince William also revered his grandfather, the Emperor, who took special pains to see him. They would often dine alone together, at a small green, rickety card-table in the palace on the Unter den Linden. A bottle of champagne would be served; the Emperor would pour one glass for each of them, then cork it again for the morrow, marking the level on the label. He would tell stories of the glorious past, of the battles he had won, the marching and the conquests. He impressed in Prince William's adolescent mind the grandeur and the power of the imperial state.

The Empress Augusta made her grandson literally her support; his strong right arm was a crutch whenever she held her court. He learned to endure boredom and small talk during the interminable *levées*, standing stiffly beside her, listening to her kind words to the endless queues of courtiers and diplomats.

Following his father's footsteps, he had attended Bonn University for four terms and had joined the same student corps, *Borussia*. But his studies were cut short. His grandfather insisted that he return to serve with his regiment: war training was the first duty of a Prussian prince. He was happiest when with the Sixth Company of the 1st Regiment of Footguards. His father had served in the Company and was proud of his son's quick grasp of military manœuvres.

At this time, England's military attaché in Berlin was the extraordinary Colonel Leopold Swaine. He had the great gift of inspiring trust in those he was sent to observe. All things to all soldiers, he was more especially the agent of certain English masters. Valued by both the German Emperor and Prince William because of his genuine admiration for their country's military machine, he reported directly to Queen Victoria and to the Prince of Wales, as well as to the War Office and to the Foreign Office. He particularly cultivated the difficult Prince William, who was becoming increasingly estranged from his parents. Swaine's private account to Lord Salisbury of the young man's character, particularly his love and hatred of England, was most revealing.

It had been continually instilled in him from his early youth, Swaine reported, that everything English was better than everything else. This had had an unfortunate effect, not only on the Prince himself, by increasing his natural obstinacy, but also on his entourage, who became so embittered by this forcing of England upon them that their advice was not always the best or the wisest. Falling, as it did, on strong Prussian soil, it frequently made the Prince appear to be anti-English, which he was not.

The Prince was intrinsically German; he insisted on being considered a German Prince before anything else. He looked upon other countries only from the standpoint of their usefulness to Germany. Brought up, as he had been, to regard the military strength of a country as the test by which everything else must be gauged, he saw England as comparatively weak and possessing a system of government which he could not understand.[10]

Swaine's character analysis was interesting, because it accused the Crown Princess of forcing the example of her homeland down her eldest son's throat until he gagged on it. There was some truth in the charge, particularly after his marriage, when he became independent and could react more positively against his upbringing. Unexpectedly, he had fallen in love with an Augustenburg princess, the daughter of the ignored claimant to Schleswig and Holstein. Both of his parents approved of his choice of Augusta Victoria, or 'Dona', but they feared that the Emperor and Bismarck would never allow such a match. In point of fact, both William's grandfather and the Chancellor did not wish to thwart the opinionated young man. They wanted to wean him from English influences and make him of their persuasion – something he was only too willing to become. 'I shall with the greatest pleasure enter my beloved

Regiment, as the Emperor wishes it,' he informed his mother as early as 1879, 'because I long for the dear Potsdam and the life there is so pleasant and nice. And the stern and regular duty will do me good.'[11]

Initially, the Crown Prince had to attend on Bismarck, with a personal plea for his eldest son's choice of a wife. 'We all have to dance attendance whenever it pleases him,' the Crown Princess complained.[12] Bismarck was surprisingly ready to agree. He had humbled the Augustenburg family too thoroughly to see a threat in one of their princesses, especially as she seemed to have all the German female domestic virtues. The Berlin people might not consider her grand enough, the Crown Princess thought, but 'they dislike everything foreign so much, that I fancy they will be better pleased with a Princess bred and born and educated in Germany – and more spite, ill-will, backbiting and criticism of the unkindest sort, she never can have to endure – than I have gone through for twenty-two years.'[13]

In fact, Bismarck intended to use Prince William as a counterweight to his father. He and his wife even came to the engagement party, which surprised the Crown Princess. It was something that the Chancellor never did. She had not yet recognized Bismarck's policy of turning her son against his parents. This was easy enough, for William was opposing them more and more. 'Willy is chauvinistic and ultra Prussian to a degree and with a violence which is often very painful to me. . . . Prussian Princes have a certain *genre* and it runs in the blood! With my children I often feel like a hen – that has hatched Ducklings.'[14] Queen Victoria attached great importance to Prince William's marriage. The Prince of Wales and his brother, the Duke of Edinburgh, were sent along, together with that ultimate in courtiers, Lord Torrington, who admired the magnificence of the troops, so fine and healthy and strong, in contrast to the youths of the reformed British Army. While the bride was driven like Cinderella in a glass coach pulled by eight white horses, Prince William commanded the Guard of Honour in front of the royal palace, which was lighted by thousands of large wax candles. For five hours no one was allowed to sit, and many of the ladies fainted. All the same, Lord Torrington found it a fairy scene and a miracle of complicated splendour.[15] Not so the Crown Princess, who hated ceremony. To her it was, like all Berlin State Weddings, exhausting, suffocating and interminable. She had to wear her diadem for seven-and-a-half hours. Standing for so long made her feel as if her legs were going to come off.[16]

Prince William's marriage came at a time when the Crown Prince again seemed to be gathering an opposition party around him. Bismarck had abandoned his alliance with the National Liberals in the Reichstag. He now relied on a loose coalition of the centre and the right, sometimes supported by the few socialists. But in the elections of 1881, the Liberals won enough seats to threaten Bismarck's majority against them. The Crown Princess thought that he did not care one bit. She wondered why he did not say straight out, 'As long as I live – both the Constitution and the Crown are suspended.'[17]

Bismarck's reaction to the Liberals' victory was to become more reactionary; his power depended on pulling the teeth of an opposition. Early in the following year, the Emperor issued an imperial rescript, countersigned by Bismarck, which stressed his royal authority. The English Press thought the rescript resembled one of King Charles I's messages to the Long Parliament.[18] The Crown Prince had not been consulted, and privately disapproved; his public silence was considered a form of acquiescence. On the other hand, his two sons thought that Bismarck's policies were sublime. It was rumoured that the Crown Prince would approve of anything the government did, were it not for his English wife. She felt quite worn out. 'If you hear I have the typhus or am off my head,' she told her mother, 'pray do not be astonished.'[19]

Things were not so bad as the Crown Princess made out. The Liberals had been successful. The extreme age of the Emperor made them look to the Crown Prince as the guarantor of the fall of Bismarck. Their leader, Eugen Richter, was invited by the Crown Prince to a secret consultation. The go-between was young Stockmar's successor, Karl von Normann, who was now the Prince's Court Marshal. A trusted and devoted aide, he arranged the meeting in his rooms beside the Neue Palais. One of Bismarck's spies informed the Chancellor, who told the Emperor that there was a conspiracy by the opposition. Normann was summarily banished to the tiny Duchy of Oldenburg. As he left, the Crown Prince embraced him and said: 'When I am Emperor, you will be the first whom I will recall.'

The new Court Marshal, Count Radolinski, was one of Bismarck's creatures. An intriguer, he was not suspected by the Crown Prince or his wife. His orders were to report on everything to Bismarck, and to get rid of the faithful Count Seckendorff, who was still running the household. Radolinski failed to incriminate Seckendorff, whose brother was dismissed by the enraged Bismarck after twenty years' service in the Foreign Office. The Crown Princess's friend, Lady Ponsonby, told Queen

Victoria that she would not be able to believe all the espionage and intrigue in Germany. Radolinski had been brought in because Bismarck wanted a man of his own near the Crown Princess in order to control the Crown Prince when he became Emperor. The new Court Marshal's mission was to betray her and to detach her family from her.[20]

Until his son's marriage, the Crown Prince had been sent on ceremonial missions abroad: to Italy to attend the funeral of King Victor Emmanuel; to Russia for two imperial funerals. The Tsarina Marie had died in 1880, and the Crown Prince was sent to St Petersburg to represent his father who was the Tsar's uncle. A gale was blowing and the Neva was rising. The bridge over the rushing river was so buffeted that it almost collapsed as the funeral procession was passing over it.

With indecent haste, the Tsar married his mistress, a Russian countess who had been kept by him in the Winter Palace and who was the mother of four of his children. He did not live long to enjoy the marriage, being assassinated by a bomb in the following March. Bismarck seemed to take pleasure in sending the Crown Prince back to this dangerous city. The heir to the throne received threatening letters before he left Berlin, but police protection was so stringent in St Petersburg that the funeral passed without incident. 'I felt sure it would,' the Crown Princess told her mother, 'as there could be no object in attempting the life of so many Foreigners at once.'[21]

Murder remained the terror of all royal persons. Voltaire had called Russia a despotism tempered by assassination, which it was. The Crown Prince returned from St Petersburg convinced that all sovereigns would be murdered by nihilists and socialists. The Crown Princess did not agree. She hoped that the days of Guy Fawkes and the Gunpowder Plot were firmly in the past. She even read the whole of Karl Marx's *Das Kapital* and was so interested that she asked a member of parliament in London to send her a report on the author. Marx spoke of her and the Crown Prince with due respect and propriety. It would not be Marx, the report concluded, who would turn the world upside down.[22]

The Crown Princess distrusted communists and socialists, but because of her liberal faith, she could not accept persecution of them. Another rift between her and the Government was her refusal to accept a new wave of anti-Semitism and social discrimination. 'In the royal family we stand quite alone with our opinion,' she informed Queen Victoria, 'and in what is called society.'²³ The Crown Prince made a point of condemning such discrimination to Baron Magnus, the president of the Jewish community in Berlin, and in so doing, made plain his opposition to the Government.

Bismarck noted the heir apparent's flickers of rebellion, and promoted the son in his place. Prince William was shown confidential Foreign Office dispatches and was given hours of briefing in diplomacy by the Chancellor himself. When the Crown Prince wrote to protest that it was unsafe to give an indiscreet young man secret information, Bismarck threw the letter on the fire and did not reply. By stressing his version of foreign policy to Prince William, Bismarck widened the split between the son and his pro-English parents. He even went so far as to accept a whole new campaign concerning colonies in order to have bargaining counters with England in his efforts to hold the balance of power in Europe.

Prince William always sought to emulate England, more than he would admit. He wanted a large navy, and possessions overseas. 'The sole aim of German colonial policy,' Bismarck told the new Tsar, 'was to drive a wedge between the Crown Prince and England.'²⁴ It would also drive a wedge between Prince William and his parents. Bismarck's sudden claims to South-west Africa and the Cameroons, Togoland, Fiji and New Guinea were not simply a question of the flag following trade; they were domestic sugarplums for Prince William and the German people. Diplomatically, the policy was of small value; as Bismarck said, his map of Africa lay in Europe. He needed to revive the League of the Three Emperors and protect Germany's eastern and southern frontiers. The push overseas was only a matter of forcing the colonial powers, England and France, to deal with him. If he needed help in Europe, he could always make either of them concessions abroad. Yet colonies implied confrontations. As the Crown Princess prophesied, 'This colonial sugar-plum might easily turn into a bitter-almond.'²⁵

After fulfilling delicate missions to Madrid and to Rome, the Crown Prince found himself abruptly replaced as Prussia's royal representative abroad. Bismarck knew that Prince William was a devoted supporter of the revived League of the Three Emperors. The Crown Prince was not in favour of such a reactionary alliance. So in 1884, Prince William was ordered to St Petersburg in place of his father, to attend the wedding of the Tsar's brother to Princess Elizabeth of Hesse. The Crown Prince was completely dumbfounded at being replaced; he had never dreamed that such a thing could happen.

In St Petersburg, Prince William believed that he had struck up a friendship with Tsar Alexander III. He made no bones about his belief that a foreign conspiracy was being carried on by his mother and his British relatives. 'On no account trust my English uncles,' he wrote to the Tsar. 'Do not be alarmed by anything you may hear from my father. You know him, he loves being contrary and is under my mother's thumb, and she, in turn, is guided by the Queen of England, and makes him see everything through English eyes. I assure you, the Emperor, Prince Bismarck and I are of one mind, and I shall not cease to regard it as my highest duty to consolidate and support the Three Emperors' Alliance.'[26]

So Prince William had betrayed his parents and accused them of being foreign-born wife. As if performing a state duty, Prince William and his and Chancellor were making pariahs of the heir to the throne and his foreign-born wife. As if performing a State duty, Prince William and his wife, 'Dona', produced son after son to secure the succession to the throne. They quite ignored and forgot their parents' existence, the Crown Princess complained. They always asked the Emperor and Empress about everything and took all their orders direct from them. She was not even informed of what they meant to do. 'Willy goes daily to his Grandpapa for all he wants and cuts his Papa – of course it is a great deal more convenient for them, but for us it is most painful and disagreeable.'[27]

Inexorably, the rift between the Crown Princess and her eldest son was becoming an abyss of misunderstanding. They were so similar that they could not recognize themselves in each other. As the young diplomatist, James Rennell Rodd, noted on his frequent summer visits to the Neue Palais, Prince William and his mother were temperamentally too alike ever to get on. Both were idealistic, indiscreet, impetuous and impatient of opposition. And both had the unconscious habit of royalty, the prerogative of always being right.[28]

From their own points of view, both were in the right over the next falling out. The Crown Princess's daughter Victoria, 'Moretta', fell in love with 'Sandro', Prince Alexander of Battenberg. He had accepted the throne of Bulgaria, and was seeking to make his new country independent of the Russians. This royal mismatch could become a time-bomb, given the explosive situation in the Balkans, and in the complex diplomacy between Germany, Russia and England. To make matters worse, Queen Victoria's youngest daughter, Beatrice, was becoming engaged to 'Sandro's' younger brother 'Liko', Prince Henry of Battenberg. The Queen of England and the Crown Princess seemed determined to cause international complications by marrying their daughters to minor German princelings, who might be charming and good-looking, but who were unsuitable by rank and politics. Prince William was outraged, and even the Crown Prince was annoyed. Nothing angered the Hohenzollerns more than Queen Victoria's preference for a love-match to any arranged mingling of the correct blood royal.

Bismarck might discount the importance of royal marriages in his brave new world of great power diplomacy, but he knew their relevance. The old Tsar had been pro-German because he was the nephew of the German Emperor. Alexander III was anti-German because of his Danish wife. Marriages implied alliances. The Chancellor could not accept that there were no political considerations behind the two love-matches with the Battenberg brothers. He thought that England was using 'Sandro', Prince of Bulgaria, as a weapon against Russian expansion. His engagement to Queen Victoria's granddaughter, a princess of the German imperial family, killed two birds with one precious stone. It gave the impression of Anglo-German support against the Tsar.

'The old Queen is fond of match-making, like all old women,' Bismarck said to Busch, '. . . but obviously her main objects are political – a permanent estrangement between ourselves and Russia.'[29] What he did not know was that the Crown Princess had already brought up diplomatic reasons to make her mother back 'Moretta's' choice of a husband. Queen Victoria was set on the Russians never reaching Constantinople. What could be better than Anglo-German backing of a strong buffer state on the border zone of Turkey?[30]

Bismarck's political objection to the marriage was cogent; it might break up the League of the Three Emperors. The German Emperor recognized this and vetoed the match, which was very unpleasant for the Crown Princess.[31] But the veto, and the unpleasantness, would last only so long as the Emperor lasted. The Crown Prince might be against the marriage because he was touchy on the subject of inferior Battenberg breeding, but if he assumed the Crown, he would not withstand the pressure of his wife and her mother. In family matters, Bismarck knew that Queen Victoria was not accustomed to contradiction. She would bring with her, he joked, the parson in her travelling-bag and the bridegroom in her trunk. And the marriage would come off at once.[32]

Bismarck used the 'Sandro' affair to set Prince William even more against his English mother. William spoke so badly of his younger sister's suitor that his father found it difficult to keep his temper. His mother spent sleepless nights worrying over the rift in the family. Worse than angering his parents by his insolence, William had taken to staying away altogether.

'How can you justify your behaviour towards us?' the Crown Prince asked his son.

'I thought I would not be welcome,' William replied, 'because you, dear father, have for a long time shown me quite openly that you cannot bear me.'[33]

His father and mother might adopt a policy of perfect passive patience, but Queen Victoria would not be thwarted by a grandson, or allow a child to insult his royal mother. She told her daughter that William was a very foolish, undutiful and unfeeling boy, who needed a good 'skelping' as the Scots would say and, seriously, a good setting down.[34] She offended him by refusing to see him when he wanted to come to England in 1885. Unable to understand the effect of his candour and rudeness on other people, he could not fathom the reason for his rejection by his favourite grandmother. 'He never sees his own behaviour in the right light,' his mother wrote of him 'and fancies his opinion quite infallible – and that his conduct is always perfect – and cannot stand the smallest rebuke – though he criticizes and abuses his elders and his relations, as though he knew far better than they did.'[35]

The Tsar had already been moving against the Prince of Bulgaria without prompting from Germany. Russian connivance led to an invasion by the Serbian Army. Unexpectedly, 'Sandro' led the Bulgarians to victory at Slivnitza. Only an Austrian threat to intervene stopped him from annihilating the Serbian Army. A pro-Russian faction in Sofia, however, kidnapped him in a coup, and he was sent up the Danube into exile. Forced to abdicate, he returned briefly to power, but was made to abdicate finally. Eventually, another ruler was chosen for Bulgaria, the Coburg Prince Ferdinand, who now seemed an enemy of his own relatives; he was putting a foreign throne before his own family.

Queen Victoria sent off dozens of letters to her Foreign Secretary demanding support for 'Sandro' in Bulgaria. But the British had no warships in the Black Sea and no troops nearby. They could not repeat the bluff which, at the Congress of Berlin, had made 'Sandro' the Prince of an independent Bulgaria. Morier, now ambassador at St Petersburg, was trying to maintain some British influence there, and threw 'Sandro's' cause to the wolves, which incurred Queen Victoria's displeasure. On her instructions, he received a severe reprimand from the Foreign Office, but he was not replaced. The Crown Princess thought her mother very kind to their fat friend.[36]

Bismarck continued stalking the Prince of Bulgaria even in exile, telling the Emperor that the young prince wanted to become leader of the opposition in Germany as a tool of English influence. He persecuted 'Sandro' as he had persecuted Harry von Arnim, and made the Emperor refuse him a place at court or a commission in the German Army. Hounded, broken and penniless, 'Sandro' retired to Darmstadt. Despairing of marrying 'Moretta' because of the Emperor's veto, he began a liaison with a blonde Austrian singer called Johanna Loisinger.

Bismarck was so successful at plaguing those who crossed him that the Crown Princess became increasingly afraid of him. Although she would not give up the idea of her 'Moretta' marrying 'Sandro', she had to stay silent because of the Emperor's implacable opposition to the match. Her unwavering support of 'Sandro', and her constant use of royal messengers and private ciphers convinced Bismarck that she was still her mother's agent in Germany. Now she was betrayed by an old member of the 'Coburg' group, who had wisely backed Prussia in its war against Austria: Duke Ernest wrote an anonymous pamphlet, *Co-Regents and Foreign Influence in Germany*, which might have been dictated by Bismarck himself.

The Duke knew of the liberal political ideas once shared betwen his dead brother, Queen Victoria, the Princess Royal, King Leopold and the Stockmars. He used his inside knowledge to confirm Bismarck's suspicion of a working partnership between Queen Victoria and her eldest daughter. In England they did not tolerate any foreign influence, Bismarck declared. Lord Palmerston had opposed and persecuted the Prince Consort for his alleged or real influence over the Queen. Germans were expected to submit to that sort of thing and regard it as a matter of course. 'We are an inferior race,' Bismarck said ironically, 'ordained to serve them.'[37]

Bismarck's hatred of English assumptions of superiority exaggerated his suspicions, but these had an element of truth. The Crown Princess remained half-English in Germany, half-German in England. Divided between the two nations, she could seem disloyal to both of them. It was the snare in a successful royal marriage, which had now lasted until its Silver Wedding – the snare which *The Times* had foreseen on first learning of the engagement. The Crown Princess was an educated woman with an inquiring mind, who wanted to know what was happening in Europe, and this was her right and duty because she would soon be the German Empress. The result was that Queen Victoria asked every visiting dignitary to call on the Crown Princess, brief her thoroughly and act as a personal courier for confidential messages between Berlin and Windsor.

These constant clandestine communications with England seemed proof to Bismarck of his worst fears about the Crown Princess, but in her firm conviction that England and Germany must achieve accord, she could see herself only as an agent of mutual understanding. Her royal duty was to bridge the gap between the two countries. She believed in a linked group of royalty and aristocrats, ruling Europe and preventing wars by personal contacts.

The aged Emperor was failing at last. As he approached his ninetieth birthday, he had to take morphine for kidney and bladder trouble. When he walked, he shuffled his feet so that people felt that the least crease in the carpet would trip him up and he might tumble at any moment.[38] His birthday celebrations in March 1887, were curtailed so as to spare him undue fatigue, but he was flattered that all Europe had come to honour him – perhaps for the last time. Every royal house sent a major prince or grand duke. Queen Victoria sent the Prince of Wales, who took the opportunity to play the peacemaker with Prince William. He suggested that the military-minded young man come to England in the summer to attend the army review, and that there be an exchange of officers between the British and German Armies – an idea which found favour with the old Emperor.

As the first Kaiser was sinking, the Crown Prince fell ill. Just before the birthday celebrations, his throat swelled up. He found it difficult to swallow or to speak. Cancer was a possibility; his life might be in question. He had waited too long. He might never be Emperor after all.

CHAPTER ELEVEN

At The Throat

'HOARSENESS, GENTLEMEN,' THE Crown Prince joked to a deputation from the Reichstag, 'prevents me from singing to you.'[1] Throughout that winter of 1887, his throat had been irritated, and early in March, his doctor, Wegner, called in a specialist, Professor Gerhardt, who discovered a nodule at the bottom of the left vocal cord. Instead of leaving it alone, the professor decided to remove it. Daily he tortured the Crown Prince, first with a snare, then with a ring-knife, and, finally, with a red-hot electric wire to burn out the growth. The voice, the Crown Princess told her mother on Gerhardt's advice, would return completely.[2]

It did not. The Crown Prince was often unable to complete a sentence. Another specialist was summoned, Professor Ernest von Bergmann, a surgeon and a liberal supporter of the Crown Prince. The swelling on the vocal cord had not healed. Bergmann thought that it was deeply rooted and should be removed surgically by splitting the larynx from the outside. This appalling diagnosis reached the ears of the Crown Princess. 'I was more dead than alive with horror and distress when I heard this,' she wrote to Queen Victoria. 'The idea of a knife touching his dear throat is terrible to me.' The Crown Prince was very depressed; he now often thought his father would survive him.[3]

When the news of the proposed surgery came to Bismarck, he was distressed and annoyed. He had not been informed officially of a danger-ous operation to the heir to the throne, and he intended to stop it. Through the Emperor, a further consultation was ordered, this time to include another three eminent doctors. After a careful examination of the growth, four of the six doctors decided that they had detected cancer and that the diseased area should be cut out at once.

Gerhardt and another doctor disagreed. They reported to Bismarck that the operation would be at the risk of the Crown Prince's life. Although Bergmann assured the Crown Prince that the operation was suitable for old people and children, he told Prince William privately that the Crown Prince would lose his voice altogether and might die.[4] Certainly, when Bergmann performed the same operation years later, to prove to medical students that he could have saved the Crown Prince, his patient died under the knife.[5]

At this point, Bismarck intervened again. He forbade the operation without the consent of the Crown Prince and the Emperor. According to Rennell Rodd, he visited the British Embassy to determine the best available throat specialist for a further opinion. The choice lay between three authorities: one French, one Austrian and one English. Political considerations favoured the London specialist, Morell Mackenzie. He spoke fluent German, his textbook on throat diseases was known in Germany, and he was socially prominent at home. As an outside adviser, he seemed the best choice to Bismarck and to the six German doctors, who told the Crown Prince of their wish to bring in the London man.

Up to this point, the Crown Princess was not responsible for summoning Morell Mackenzie. She knew perfectly well the risk of asking for an English consultant. If the Crown Prince's condition became worse or if he died under treatment, the alien doctor would be held responsible. She told her mother that many were so benighted they would blame her for suggesting a foreigner. If Queen Victoria would have the goodness to help them out of the difficulty, and say that she was sending Mackenzie to report to her on the state of the patient's throat, no one would take offence.[6]

Later, the Crown Princess was widely blamed for sending for Morell Mackenzie. The evidence is that she did not even know his name until he was recommended by the German specialists and the British Embassy. Her preference for a London doctor was undoubted, as was the German doctors'; a foreigner would take all the blame if the Crown Prince were to die under the knife. Bismarck's wish to have Mackenzie was not prompted by a desire to implicate the Crown Princess in yet another English conspiracy. He appears to have been having second thoughts about the young Prince William succeeding his grandfather as Emperor.

The ill and weak Crown Prince would depend more surely on the Chancellor than would his ambitious and vainglorious heir.

In the Neue Palais, the Crown Princess prepared two rooms for the operation. A hard sofa was scrubbed with carbolic acid for the patient, who was to be given chloroform. When Mackenzie arrived on the eve of the operation, his coolness and deftness reassured the Crown Princess. Tactfully, he postponed making any decision, but, using forceps, removed a fragment of the growth for microscopic examination by Doctor Virchow, a leading German expert. Bismarck, himself, came to visit the Crown Princess and was very nice to her. He said his wife advised her not to allow such an operation. The Crown Princess replied that she had nothing to allow. What the responsible authorities decided was best, would have to be accepted.[7]

Queen Victoria was not so confident of Morell Mackenzie as her daughter was. Her own doctor reported to her that Mackenzie was very clever in the throat line, but that he was greedy about money and was disliked for that.[8] However, money was of no consequence when the Crown Prince's life was in question. Virchow's analysis showed no signs of cancerous tissue, but he wanted to examine a larger fragment from the affected area. In removing that, Morell Mackenzie apparently injured the Crown Prince's other vocal cord, or so Gerhardt claimed. Mackenzie was even suspected of deliberately cutting out tissue from the healthy vocal cord for Virchow's microscope, which again showed no evidence of cancer. The war between the rival doctors was on.

The Crown Princess began to hope. She listened to Mackenzie, who promised that he would cure the Crown Prince without an operation, if the patient would come to England. With her instinctive trust for the kind of doctor who had treated her childhood ailments in her homeland, the Crown Princess was only too ready to listen to what she wanted to hear. The German doctors were still stressing the need of an immediate operation to remove the probably cancerous growth. 'The Doctors will not allow that Dr Mackenzie's view is right and theirs is wrong,' the Crown Princess wrote to her mother. 'But I am convinced of it! Fritz ought to be under his care, and we must see how.'[9]

Even the temporizing Professor Gerhardt thought Mackenzie too sanguine. The Crown Prince's friends saw in the London expert a shrewd self-advertiser who wanted the Crown Prince as an exclusive patient. There was a struggle about the treatment of the illness, all along the line, with the Crown Princess trusting blindly in Mackenzie's optimism, and the German specialists priming Prince William's belief that the postponed throat operation could prove to be his father's death-warrant. Bismarck sat on the sidelines, wanting to preserve the Crown Prince's life for as long as possible.

A quarrel flared up as to who was to go to Queen Victoria's Jubilee. While his father was scheduled to have the operation, Prince William had presumed that he should represent the German imperial family for the occasion. He had bombarded Queen Victoria with telegrams, telling her that at the Emperor's command, he was coming in his father's place. But with the prospect of Mackenzie's treatment in England, the Crown Prince more than ever wanted to represent his country at the great Jubilee of his mother-in-law. She had bidden him to come and ride in front of her coach as he had done before in the state ceremonies after the Prince Consort's death. 'You both must not be absent on this day which will move me deeply,' she wrote to her daughter. 'You must take care of yourself, so as to be well for it. It would not be wise to speak much, but the procession to Westminster Abbey will not be too bad.'[10]

The Crown Princess replied that her husband's one hope was to attend the Jubilee. The Emperor had given his consent, if the German doctors allowed his son to go. If he had been a few years younger, he would have gone himself. As it was, the Crown Prince was terribly annoyed at William coming forward so much to take his place. People did not like him to leave the country because of the Emperor's age. Yet he clearly ought to come to England and get himself cured by the only man who had offered him any hope.[11]

Bergmann, himself, approached the Emperor and tried to get the old man to stop his son leaving for England in June. But the Emperor told him that the Crown Prince was not a child and should go for treatment where he thought best. When another analysis by Virchow found no cancerous tissue in two more fragments from the growth, the Emperor allowed the visit to England to proceed. Even the German specialists suspended their judgement. They were, the Crown Princess thought, like the doubting apostle Thomas, and would at last believe that the growth was harmless.[12]

Although she appeared optimistic, the Crown Princess was terrified that her husband might die. She knew that her protection in Germany would die with him. If she were widowed, his father or his eldest son might demand the right to go through his papers. Most of these were confidential and many showed his dealings with the Liberal opposition in Germany and with Queen Victoria. Already, he and the Crown Princess had begun to destroy papers, burning them with their own hands. The trip to England was a heaven-sent opportunity to store the more compromising ones in a secure place. Queen Victoria was asked a favour. Under the present circumstances and for the moment, her daughter wished to bring over all the private papers to England. Could they be locked up in the iron room leading from the Prince Consort's Library at Buckingham Palace? 'We should feel much happier,' the Crown Princess wrote. 'I can explain more when we meet.'[13]

Surveillance on the journey to England was being increased. Count Radolinski was one of many reporting constantly to Bismarck, and to the supporters of Prince William, who thought that the Crown Prince might die before reaching the throne. At Balmoral, Radolinski engineered a quarrel with the Crown Princess's most trusted servant, Count Seckendorff, in an effort to get rid of him. But the Crown Princess gave Radolinski a piece of her mind, defending her man, although she could not stop such insane endeavours to destroy Seckendorff. She could not dismiss Radolinski, even though she knew he was a tool of Bismarck's intrigues.

There was worse for her to fear, if the Crown Prince should die. Her persistence in the 'Sandro' affair had turned the Empress Augusta against her and against her daughter, Princess Victoria. The Empress despised the Battenberg family. She wanted the Emperor completely to disinherit the Crown Princess and her daughter if they disobeyed the imperial command and allowed the Battenberg marriage to take place. Bismarck had to plead with the Emperor not to give offence to his son by changing his will, but the threat remained. It was all a question of whether the father or the son would die first. For the Crown Prince had little to leave to his wife if he did not inherit his father's private fortune.

Fearing the worst, the Crown Princess had to raise a delicate matter. When her father, the Prince Consort, had died, she had begged Queen Victoria to exclude her from his legacy because so many of her sisters were still unmarried. Now she must consider the possibility of being left with an unmarried and disinherited daughter on her hands. 'Perhaps you could find a small portion for me,' she asked Queen Victoria, 'which would go to that child.' It was particularly important, because her eldest son William was dead set against the Battenberg marriage. The Crown

Prince feared that, if he died, his son would not deal kindly with his mother and 'Moretta'.[14]

Queen Victoria rallied to her daughter's support. There was a small amount of money which would go to the Crown Princess and 'Moretta', if the Crown Prince died or if they were cut out of the Emperor's will or maltreated by Prince William because of their disobedience. To the Crown Princess, the situation seemed intolerably like the Middle Ages, but she was still determined that the deposed Prince of Bulgaria marry her daughter, even if a fortune were lost because of it.

The peace in Europe, however, meant more than a royal wedding. Bismarck took another step to block the marriage and render 'Sandro's' return to the Bulgarian throne impossible: a Re-insurance Treaty was signed with Russia. Germany accepted that Bulgaria and its Prince should be completely within the Tsar's sphere of influence, and would not interfere if the Tsar wished to take Constantinople. This, Bismarck reflected, had neutralized Germany's eastern flank against attack, which left only the possibility of a French war of revenge in the west.

So, during the Crown Princess's absence, Bismarck had driven the final nail into the coffin of her prospective son-in-law's hopes of being recalled to his Balkan throne. The Chancellor was determined to defeat her and Queen Victoria in their championship of the Battenbergs. Bismarck threatened to resign if the Battenberg marriage ever took place, even if the Crown Prince lived to be Emperor. A European war might threaten, if Germany seemed to be joining England in a Balkan conspiracy against Russia.

Riding a white charger in the Jubilee procession, the Crown Prince looked like a spectre at this feast of Empire. He was wearing the white uniform of the Pomeranian Cuirassiers. His helmet, with its eagle crest, and his silvered breastplate glittered in the sun, setting off the sash of the Order of the Garter and the sky-blue of his Marshal's baton. Bearded and erect, silent and drawn, he was the white knight of his own glory, riding out to honour the fifty years' reign of the Queen of England. Around him rode the princes of Europe and the world, the Hussars and the Horse Guards, all escorting the open gilt landau in which Queen Victoria, her white bonnet spangled with diamonds, sat with the Princess of Wales and the Crown Princess. After the service in Westminster Abbey, the Queen kissed the Crown Prince on the cheek – and then embraced him again on her way from the coronation chair, as if she knew this was the last time she might see him well again.

He visited Mackenzie in Harley Street nearly every day. The swelling in the throat diminished, and at the end of June, Mackenzie succeeded in snipping off the last of the growth on the vocal cord. Virchow's analysis of the tissue showed that it was a hard, compressed, warty growth, which showed no sign of spreading. Mackenzie seemed to have completed the cure that he had promised. The Crown Princess took the Crown Prince off to Balmoral to recuperate. With them was a young doctor, Mark Hovell from the Throat Hospital, who was charged to watch over the Crown Prince's recovery. The Prince was soon able to speak in his natural voice again, to the delight of Queen Victoria, who knighted Mackenzie for his skill and service.

Although there was strong pressure to return to Berlin, the Crown Princess insisted that her husband complete his cure in the pinewoods of the Tyrol. At Tolbach, he caught a severe cold and his larynx again became inflamed. Mackenzie was summoned to Tolbach and was dissatisfied at the state of his patient, the more so because he had assured the Crown Princess in August that everything was entirely favourable and that a complete cure was only a question of time.[15] He recommended Italy as the best place to recover. So the royal couple moved through Venice and the flowering gardens of Baveno to the Villa Zirio at San Remo on the Italian Riviera. Although the Crown Prince's presence in Berlin was continually demanded, his wife would not let him go.

She was right, in view of his health, but wrong so far as her standing in Germany was concerned. She was putting his life before her position. The fact was that if the Crown Prince were to die, the British Ambassador informed Queen Victoria and Lord Salisbury, it would hardly be possible for the Crown Princess to return to Germany, because she had kept her husband abroad. The newspapers were demanding that German doctors be consulted, though Bismarck himself made no move; the ground was too delicate for him to tread.[16] The situation was made worse when the German Emperor caught a severe cold, which gave him abdominal pains and necessitated treatment with morphine. How could the heir to the throne remain absent when he might become Emperor any day?

But on arriving at San Remo, the Crown Prince's own condition deteriorated. Dr Hovell examined his larynx and detected a new tumour beneath each vocal cord; both tumours seemed to have a malignant aspect. Mackenzie was summoned by telegram and made another examination. The Crown Prince asked him if it were cancer.

'I am sorry to say, Sir,' Mackenzie said, 'it looks very much like it, but it is impossible to be certain.'

The Crown Prince was silent for a moment, then managed a smile.

'I have lately been fearing something of this sort,' he said, before thanking Mackenzie for being so frank with him.[17]

Oddly enough, his knowing the worst caused the Crown Prince briefly to feel cheerful and to speak freely. It was the uncertainty that had made him melancholy. Recognizing the probability of cancer, Mackenzie immediately summoned for consultation two specialists from Vienna and Berlin, Schrötter and Krause. As the only foreign doctor, Mackenzie realized that he would be held responsible if the Crown Prince died. He had to protect himself with other eminent opinions. Had his treatment been successful in England, he would, of course, have taken the sole credit.

Now that Mackenzie had confirmed the original diagnosis of the Berlin doctors, the storm broke on him and the Crown Princess. In Vienna, a professor told his audience that the Berlin doctors had always been right; an operation should have been carried out on the Crown Prince long ago; he should not have been sent travelling; cancer grew anywhere, whether in London, Berlin, Baveno or San Remo. Thirty reporters were dispatched by various European newspapers to waylay Mackenzie at the Hôtel Méditeranée. Daily reports on the state of the Crown Prince's throat publicized the doctors' disagreements.

Prince William now intervened. Acting on the old Emperor's orders, he arrived at San Remo with Dr Moritz Schmidt, a bigoted laryngologist from Frankfurt. He called a medical conference in his hotel room and listened to the various opinions of the English and German doctors. Although there was general agreement that the throat was cancerous, none of them wanted the larynx to be completely removed unless the patient consented. After such an operation the Crown Prince, if he lived, would never speak again.

Prince William now angered his mother, who was nursing her husband night and day, putting icebags on his throat and trying to keep him from despair. Her son told her to have the Crown Prince dressed and made ready to return with him to Berlin for an operation. She refused, barring the way into the Crown Prince's bedroom and rebuking her son with considerable violence. He was present, however, when the doctors confirmed to the Crown Prince that he had cancer.

'He received the news like a Hohenzollern and a soldier,' Prince William wrote to his grandmother Queen Victoria, 'upright, looking the doctors straight in the face. He knows that he is irretrievably lost and doomed! And yet he did not move an inch or a muscle.... It is quite horrible this confounded word "hopeless"! Poor Mama is doing wonders, she is perpetually on the verge of completely breaking down, and yet she keeps on that gigantic struggle against her feelings only not to distress Papa, and not to let the household see her grief.... I could not telegraph *en clair* as the French tap all telegrams going to England.'[18]

Prince William did not mention his intervention to Queen Victoria, only his anxiety. His mother, however, complained bitterly about him to her mother, claiming that he had been misled. His advisers, including Dr Schmidt, were telling him that the Crown Prince was so ill that he should not accept the succession if the Emperor died – 'but pass it on to William!!' This would be more than a death-blow to the Crown Princess. If her husband did not succeed to the throne, he would not be able to provide for her and her daughters nor be of any use to his country even for a limited time.[19]

Worse than Prince William's blundering was the behaviour of Dr Schmidt. Both he and Dr Krause advocated a course of potassium iodide, because they thought that the growth might be syphilitic in origin. Schrötter considered this to be an old wives' tale.[20] Schmidt's nose for scandal was matched by his indiscretion. In the course of a lecture at Frankfurt, he insinuated that the Crown Prince was suffering from something of contagious origins – an assertion which the French press immediately linked to false scandals about the Prussian Prince who defeated them eighteen years before. In the Berlin *State Gazette*, Schmidt also accused the Crown Princess and Mackenzie of allowing the throat cancer to spread, when it could have been checked by an operation in the early stages. An anti-Semite, Schmidt even claimed that Morell Mackenzie's real name was Moritz Markovitz, which explained why he was such a bad and cunning doctor.

Dreadfully hurt by these insinuations against the Crown Prince and those devoted to his case, the Crown Princess continued her fight to keep him alive. 'As to a certain plot –' she informed her mother on 29 November, 'it has not succeeded. They have not been able to tear Fritz out of the hands of Sir Morell, Dr Krause and Dr Hovell – nor to drag

Fritz to Berlin, put him under incompetent Doctors, and force the operation on him, which would either kill him or reduce him to the most AWFUL existence you can imagine. They cannot therefore force Fritz to resign as they would, nor get rid of me!'[21]

More than the Crown Prince's life was at stake; peace in Europe depended on his throat. Lord Salisbury was extremely worried, mainly because Prince William's attacks against Mackenzie, and against his mother's treatment of the Crown Prince seemed to show great prejudices against England. Such prejudices would be fatal to the policy which both governments wished the two countries to follow, Salisbury wrote to the British Ambassador in Berlin. 'Between us and Prince William's perhaps unchecked rule there only stand now three lives.' The Emperor was ninety and failing, Bismarck was seventy-three, and the Crown Prince was menaced by a disease that did not pardon.[22] If William succeeded, he would probably back Russia against England on the Eastern Question and plunge Europe into war. Only Bismarck could stop him.

Yet all that winter, the Crown Prince hung on in San Remo, and the Emperor hung on in Berlin. Both seemed determined to see each other out. The Emperor was plagued by the intrigues of the reactionaries around him, who hoped to make him accept Prince William as his immediate successor. But he would not put aside the rights of his son, despite the courtiers' spurious claim that an ancient law decreed that no Hohenzollern could succeed who was not sound of body. The Crown Prince and Princess were also beset by spying and intrigue in their villa which was packed with doctors and informants. The trusted Lady Ponsonby reported to Queen Victoria that all letters were stringently checked before posting in case they had been tampered with.[23]

Queen Victoria, herself, communicated with the Crown Prince and her daughter by cipher telegram; only her son-in-law and his wife knew the code numbers. They personally decoded the messages and replied by the same cipher, reporting daily on the state of the Crown Prince's throat. One important paper had to be copied out by the Crown Princess herself before it was returned to Queen Victoria by royal messenger. Nobody could be completely trusted in the whole household. 'I can not now get rid of people, who cabal and intrigue against me,' the Crown Princess wrote to her mother, 'but when I have the power and liberty to do so, it must be done ... At Potsdam and Berlin it will be FIFTY times worse!!'[24]

The illness of the Crown Prince, however, was a matter of desperate concern. The future of Germany and of Bismarck depended on whether the heir to the throne lived a little longer. Not everyone was a spy in the household, only those who considered it patriotic to resist the English influence and the forced optimism of the Crown Princess and Mackenzie. These two looked incredulous if any hopeful sentence were uttered. They were in touch with the calumniators in Berlin who were determined to present everything the Crown Princess said or did in a bad light. They made no secret of the fact that in their eyes, patriotism consisted in devotion to Germany, to the Emperor and to Bismarck. To him, they sent every detail of gossip, often consisting of pure invention.[25]

The Crown Princess may have hoped to rid herself of disloyal members of her household, but she could do nothing about the reporters who swarmed outside the Villa Zirio and whose indiscretions drove her mad. 'We cannot move or sneeze without telegrams being sent right and left,' she complained. 'It is really TOO odious, complicates our existence and makes so much mischief, creates such confusion. They have printed two harmless letters of a perfectly private nature Fritz and I wrote a little while ago, and now they begin to comment on them!'[26]

The Crown Princess continued to sort through her husband's essential papers. She wanted them stored in a safe place and preserved from prying eyes. She meant to keep everything that demonstrated his past importance. The three volumes of the Crown Prince's *War Diary*, which showed how much Bismarck had had to depend on his support in order to make his father Emperor in 1871, were smuggled out by Dr Hovell. Despite orders that he be intercepted by police or Customs officials, he managed to reach the British Embassy in Berlin, and the volumes were sent to Queen Victoria by royal messenger. This escapade confirmed Bismarck's opinion that the English doctors around the Crown Prince were also agents.

It had been an excess of caution on the part of the Crown Princess. Nothing in the *War Diary* was incriminating, merely unflattering to Bismarck's claim that he had been the sole creator of the German Empire. Yet she was right to fear that, if her husband were to die, she would come under attack. She was being blamed for everything because of her supposed prejudices against all things German, particularly German medicine. Her elder children were her harshest and most outspoken critics; they believed that they had been deliberately alienated from good old Prussian values. Every discussion ended with their conclusion: 'You are wrong – you must be wrong because you are English.'[27]

'So they already look upon me as dead,' the Crown Prince wrote bitterly in his diary.[28] His second son, Henry, brought a letter which stated curtly that the Emperor had authorized William to sign State papers if his father were too ill to do so himself. The Crown Prince had not been consulted or informed. Bismarck's letter to him arrived after his son's presumptuous message. Replying to the Chancellor, the Crown Prince stood on his rights. He was in sound mind and in full possession of his physical strength, he wrote to Bismarck. 'In view of the confidence I have in you, I beg you both urgently and frankly to have consideration for me in future, in spite of my absence, and to get in touch with me before taking any decisive steps.'[29]

The weakening Crown Prince now relied on the Chancellor who had, after all, opposed the larynx operation. 'It is better to fall into the hands of God than of men,' Bismarck answered the Crown Prince. He, personally would rather expose himself to the dangers of disease than of surgery. The experiences of the past six months tended to prove him right. With God's help, the Crown Prince's strong constitution would withstand the onset of the disease for a long time to come.[30]

So Bismarck seemed to be taking the side of those few who believed that the Crown Princess was preserving her husband's life by refusing the throat operation. He did not even support the old Emperor in having the Crown Prince recalled to Berlin. He had much more of a free hand when the heir to the throne was absent. His expressed wish to prolong the Crown Prince's life was the truth. He could manage better under an Emperor Frederick than under the impetuous William.

On 17 January 1888, the Crown Prince had a violent fit of coughing and spat out a large fragment of his larynx. Virchow again found no evidence of cancer in the expelled tissue. Mackenzie went so far as to tell the Crown Prince that the throat malady might only be perichondritis. But on 8 February his windpipe became blocked and he could hardly breathe. 'Oh God!' he complained at last, 'I can't bear it any longer.' A tracheotomy was performed by Bergmann's assistant, Dr Bramann, who inserted a metal cannula (tube) in the windpipe below the blockage, which enabled the sick man to breathe more easily. His wife was still hopeful that his life would be spared.

Soon after the successful operation, Bergmann arrived. He soon picked a quarrel about the type of cannula being used. He wanted a large one of lead, while Mackenzie preferred smaller ones, made to his design by the local silversmith. Bergmann's cannulae irritated the Crown Prince's throat until he began bringing up bloody matter, which another analyst diagnosed as definitely cancerous. Mackenzie himself accepted this diagnosis, while Bergmann remarked that he was doing his best 'to keep this abominable colleague within the bounds of medical decency.'[31]

The Crown Prince could not speak for himself, and the Crown Princess had to struggle to keep her mouth shut. 'Of course, I am tongue-tied,' she wrote to her mother. 'I dare say nothing against the infallible wisdom of the German medical authorities, or I should be torn to pieces.' For three weeks, the Berlin doctors took charge of the treatment of the Crown Prince, whose condition deteriorated rapidly. He looked dreadfully ill and altered – thin, sunken and pale.[32] The Crown Princess was sure that he would recover only if Mackenzie and Hovell were allowed to treat him again. Evidently, Bergmann had lost her and her husband's confidence, and he was soon forced to withdraw from the case, leaving it to the English doctors to do their best and their worst.

Prince William came again to San Remo with the Emperor's request that his son come back to Berlin, if humanly possible, because he felt his own death was near. Bergmann told Prince William that his father had only six months to live, and that the journey to Berlin would be his last. The Crown Princess refused to move her husband from San Remo; at this moment it would be utter madness. So Prince William returned to Germany alone, to find that his grandfather was dying. On 7 March he sent a telegram that the Emperor was very weak after a bad night; the Crown Prince should return.

The Prince of Wales was visiting San Remo. His mother wanted a direct report on the Crown Prince's condition from her eldest son, who could also bring back all the important information and messages from her daughter. He gave his sister the strength and comfort she needed to grasp the nettle and accept the return to Berlin. The Crown Prince must be present at his father's death-bed, even if it proved to be also his own. She sent a cipher telegram to Queen Victoria, telling her that she had made the decision.

ABSOLUTELY IMPOSSIBLE TO REFUSE TO GO TO BERLIN UNDER THE CIRCUMSTANCES, AT ANY RATE FOR A SHORT STAY. SIR MORELL THINKS THAT THERE IS A RISK BUT HE TRUSTS HE WILL BE ABLE TO AVERT REAL DANGER.

The Emperor lay on his camp-bed, his red neckband, shabby from his many campaigns, wound round his neck. His wife, Augusta, sat beside him, herself crippled by rheumatism and a blood disease, scarcely able to move. She sent for the miniature of her husband's first love, Elise Radziwill, so that he could look at it as he died. It might have been an act of charity or of revenge. He could see the face of young beauty in his weak hand, and the face of aged majesty sitting in judgement over his death-bed.

Towards evening on 8 March, the Emperor died, before the son who had made him Emperor could return. As the bells sounded his knell, a telegram was sent to San Remo, which arrived at eleven o'clock the next morning. The old Emperor was dead. The new Emperor was condemned to die. In spite of his weakness, and the tube in his windpipe, he put on his general's uniform, with the orange sash and star of the Black Eagle, and presented himself to his wife, now the German Empress, and his awed household. Then he took off the star of the Order and pinned it to his wife's dress. She burst into tears at last and clung to him. It was her medal for her devotion in keeping him alive, for her endurance and her concern. He scribbled a message for Mackenzie on a pad: 'I thank you for having made me live long enough to be able to reward the valiant courage of my wife'.

That was the truth of the matter. Medical knowledge was so limited in the nineteenth century that many, like Lord Byron, died of the doctors' attention. Half the battle of keeping a patient alive was the bolstering of his confidence and morale. Throughout the new Emperor's long illness, his wife and Mackenzie had encouraged him, day after day, to get through another month. Her hope and care gave him the will to live on. Brave soldier as he was, he could not have stood it without the sustaining faith of his wife and the soothing treatment of the English doctor.

If the German specialists were right in saying that Mackenzie should have diagnosed cancer earlier, they were wrong to insist on a brutal operation which might have killed the patient immediately, and certainly would have mutilated him and lessened his will to live. Bismarck, himself, felt that the best strategy was a delaying action for as long as possible. God should be trusted more than the knife. The new Empress and the English doctors agreed. Although their optimism was false, it did support the sick man throughout his long sufferings. If, as *The Times* said, his father's longevity resulted from the stimulus of implacable routine, his own survival was sustained by certain love and by unlikely hope.

Whatever the risks of travelling to Berlin, the new Emperor had to go, or appoint Prince William as Regent in his place. And this, after his eldest son's presumptuous behaviour, he would not have. In the time left to him, he intended to do all he could to secure the future of his family and of Germany. His son would have to stand by, waiting to take over as he, himself, had waited for so long. Prince William would also oppose all that his father tried to do. As he told Count Eulenburg, his father's reign, or rather his mother's through her husband, would mean the ruin of Germany.[33]

She was sure that it would be the salvation of Germany, so often delayed, so precarious now. She must make her husband live. She and Mackenzie set off with the new Emperor by special train to Berlin, although Bismarck had warned the British Ambassador that public feeling was so incensed against the London doctor that he would hardly be safe.[34] The new Empress ignored these warnings as she ignored her own unpopularity at court. Mackenzie was the only specialist she trusted. He would stay with her to prolong her husband's life.

They travelled through the cold and snow towards the north. At Leipzig, Bismarck met the imperial train. As he tried to kneel to kiss his new master's hand, the Emperor raised him in a silent embrace. The journey ended at Charlottenburg, where there was both palace and royal mausoleum. In that resting-place, the light fell from azure windows on the Carrara marble sarcophagi of the dead Kings and Queens of Prussia, while niches awaited the Emperors and Empresses soon to follow them.

CHAPTER TWELVE

The Short Reign

THE EMBALMED BODY of the Emperor, in its sable-covered coffin, was borne to the ancient Dom Church on the shoulders of sixteen gigantic sergeants of the Foot Guards. The Life Guards rode in escort, their horses' hoof-beats muffled in the snow. Flaring torches were held by the soldiers who lined the route. Inside the church, thousands of wreaths had been strewn on the flagstones; the princes and dignitaries crushed the laurel and bay leaves underfoot as they moved in line towards the coffin beneath the candelabra. Dressed in his Foot-Guards uniform and wrapped in his grey campaign-cloak, the Emperor lay, his head resting on white satin pillows. The line of mourners bowed before the monarch lying in state and paid their last respects.

The Prince of Wales had come from San Remo to Berlin for the funeral. His mother had wanted at least one representative in British uniform, but he had left it behind, and had to appear in the uniform of a Colonel of German Hussars, carrying his honorary Marshal's baton. Afterwards, at luncheon with his sister and her husband at the Charlottenburg palace, he was surprised to find the new Emperor looking quite like his former self, with a flushed face and an animated expression – but mute. To communicate, he wrote rapidly on a block of paper and waited for a reply. He ate well and swallowed easily and did not look like a dying man.

Everyone thought him doomed except his wife and Count Seckendorff. The general mood was matched by the weather, gloom within and without. Morell Mackenzie told the Prince of Wales that the new Emperor's condition was very grave. He had a rending cough and was being weakened by all the business of state. 'The patient is worse – ' an aide of the Prince of Wales wrote to Queen Victoria, ' – steadily going down hill – walking now along a precipice – overhanging the valley of the shadow of Death!'[1]

The new Emperor could not take the risk of attending his father's funeral procession, and watched from a palace room. He forbade the aged Bismarck and Moltke to appear because the bitter cold would also be a threat to them. Huge arches, crowned with the Prussian eagle and draped in black crêpe, were erected along the Unter den Linden. Between them, ropes of twined evergreens linked square black pillars which supported great cauldrons of flaming pitch. All the people of Berlin seemed to have taken to the streets. Mobs fought with the police, and invaded the large houses on the avenues, seeking to watch the cortège from the upper windows.

At eleven o'clock in the morning, the bells of the Dom began to toll, and were answered by the bells of every church in Berlin. The funeral service commenced in the presence of the new Empress and her son, Crown Prince William, who stood in the middle of the nave behind the Imperial Standard. 'The Dom presented at this moment an extraordinary display of martial splendour,' an observer wrote, 'surpassing, perhaps, any previous spectacle of a similar kind that has been seen in Europe in modern times. The high officers, civil and military, arrayed in brilliant uniforms, surrounded the coffin; the Imperial and Royal Princes in the nave, notwithstanding the mourning emblems which they wore, presented an equally dazzling appearance; and the general effect was enhanced by the attendant guard of honour, with their drawn swords. The royal ladies in the left gallery and the clergy before the altar offered the only contrast to the blaze of bright and varied colour which glowed within the walls of the national Cathedral.'[2]

After the service, the body of the Emperor was placed on a plain black hearse drawn by eight black horses. The coffin was shrouded in a purple velvet pall, on which his plumed helmet gleamed. Picked squadrons of cavalry led the way, their red and white plumes dancing above their dark cloaks, the black and white guidons flickering on their lances, while the 1st Foot Guards looked like armed Capuchins under the white mitres of their helmets. Behind the hearse marched most of the kings and princes and grand dukes of Europe, in honour of the Emperor who had ruled over the making of the greatest military power in the world.

Yet to the new monarchs, the funeral procession was a reminder of their own mortality. At his palace window, the Emperor Frederick broke down when he saw the hearse. 'People in general consider us a mere passing shadow,' the new Empress wrote to Queen Victoria, 'soon to be replaced by reality in the shape of William!! I may be wrong, but it seems to me as if the party that opposed and ill-treated us so long, hardly think it worth while to change their attitude, except very slightly – as they count on a different future! It is an inestimable blessing to be relieved from a thraldom and tyranny which was exercised over us in the poor Emperor's name, as now the right thing can be done for Fritz's health! But oh – if it is not too late! too late! This agonizing thought haunts me! Yes, we are our own masters now, but shall we not have to leave all the work undone which we have so long and so carefully been preparing?'[3]

She would have to leave all her prepared work unfinished. Her husband's case was terminal. Already she was being accused of wanting to rule, through a sick man, as a woman Emperor. Even Queen Victoria's Prime Minister, Lord Salisbury, was perturbed that she might try to make her English views a matter of German policy. He wrote to the British Ambassador in Berlin, telling him to keep his distance from the Empress. He hoped she would not ask for advice. If she did, it would be reported to Bismarck and would be taken for foreign interference. If she did not, it would show that she understood the pitfalls surrounding her and knew where the line of safety lay. She must not be detected trying to shape Germany to an English pattern, otherwise she would incur a most serious risk. Her role must be mildly Bismarckian and intensely German.[4]

Treading delicately, she did not fail in that role. Her husband's first proclamation, and his open letter to Bismarck, showed a wish to rule in a more liberal and constitutional way, but not at the price of offending the Chancellor. He wanted to appoint Liberals as Ministers, but he did not yet dare to proceed for fear of forcing Bismarck to resign. The Chancellor himself treated the new Emperor and Empress with caution and courtesy, so long as he was allowed to do what he was doing already.

But the Empress soon felt his claws. Bismarck wanted to prolong the period between Reichstag elections, but the Emperor delayed signing the bill. Bismarck demanded to see the Empress, who stood between him and her husband's sick-room. He told her angrily that the Emperor was exceeding his prerogative, and that his Chancellor would resign, if the bill were not signed. The Empress soothed Bismarck and said that her husband would sign it, once he understood that he was bound by the

Constitution. So Bismarck quietened down 'and drew in his claws like a tiger that had changed its mind and decided not to hurl itself at its victim'.

The Emperor did insist, however, on an amnesty, particularly for the political offenders who had been arrested and imprisoned by Stieber and other agents of Bismarck. This had been the fate of some of his own liberal supporters. The Chancellor protested that such an amnesty would loose subversives all across Germany, but the Emperor had his own way. And when the reactionary Minister of the Interior, Robert von Puttkamer, used his agents to interfere in the Reichstag elections, the Emperor summarily dismissed him, an act of political courage which Bismarck had to accept.

Bismarck continued his campaign of surveillance, spying, innuendo and quarantine against the new rulers. Count Radolinski's place as his chief agent was taken over by the Adjutant-General Winterfeld. The Emperor had trusted Winterfeld as a staff officer, but the man was ambitious and determined to be on the right side of the coming régime. They always had an eye on William, the Empress wrote bitterly concerning the double-dealers in the imperial entourage, as if he already had one foot on the Throne whilst his father had one foot in the grave.[5]

She had her own puny Intelligence system inside and outside Germany. She used her confidante, Ernest von Stockmar's widow, to liaise with the Liberal Deputy, Dr Ludwig Bamberger. He was an honest and principled man and a long-time admirer of the new Emperor; he was also politically astute and well-informed. Through Baroness Stockmar, he was consulted about political problems. She brought back his answers verbally – only occasionally by letter. During her husband's illness, the Empress confided more and more in her most trusted German adviser, revealing the depths of her isolation and bitterness. 'Give me three words spoken by the Empress, the official world says,' she wrote to Bamberger, 'and we shall turn her into a foreigner, into a traitor, into an enemy of the Reich.'[6]

Officially in power with her husband, she could get nothing done, no reforms made. Her resentment and frustration were expressed in long letters to Bamberger. She declared to him that the ministers were not the Emperor's servants, but his enemies. They violently opposed everything he wanted, and he was too ill to force a change of administration. He did not have one devoted political friend near him; all had been deterred or sent away. She was the only one who could tell the Emperor the plain truth. How few at court were willing to support her! Without her and her few friends like Baroness Stockmar and Bamberger, the Emperor would be a total prisoner.[7]

After thirty years of waiting and planning, the Empress found her reign brief and illusory. Time was too short to change anything, the Emperor too ill to do much. Clutching at straws, she even believed that Bismarck was on her side because he treated her decently. She claimed that he could not do what the Emperor wanted because he was prevented by the other ministers. This was another illusion; secretly, the Chancellor was thwarting any change, because he knew the Emperor would not reign long.

The Empress still had to fight Bismarck on one thing. She had not given up the idea of marrying her 'Moretta' to Sandro Battenberg. Her husband still disapproved of the match, but he was too weak to resist her determination, although privately he let Bismarck know that he opposed it. The Battenberg Prince had been replaced by Ferdinand of Coburg as the ruler of Bulgaria, but Bismarck still asserted that the marriage would lead to a rift with Russia and with England, and told the British Ambassador that he would leave office if the wedding took place. He claimed that the Empress was aware of his intention to resign and had said there were other Chancellors in Germany.[8] He managed to stop the Empress from asking Sandro to visit Charlottenburg, and provoked Crown Prince William into sending Sandro a message: 'If you marry my sister, I shall consider you the enemy of my family and my country.'

Bismarck presumed that Queen Victoria was still supporting her daughter and granddaughter in the Battenberg match. This was English interference in German diplomacy. So he loosed a virulent attack in the bought Press against the Queen and the Empress, accusing them of plotting against Germany for foreign interests. The smear campaign was so poisonous that Queen Victoria, who intended to pay a first and last visit to her son-in-law and daughter in Berlin, was advised by her Prime Minister that it was unsafe to go there. There might be hostile demonstrations, and a certain confrontation with the angry Crown Prince William, who would soon inherit the throne.

Queen Victoria had a sceptre of steel. She was determined to go to Berlin to see her son-in-law the Emperor before he died. Actually, she was already cooling on the Battenberg marriage. She had heard of Sandro's long love affair with Johanna Loisinger. He was no longer in love with Moretta, who had not seen him for four years. The Queen was also a realist, and had no intention of causing a crisis in Germany which would lead to Bismarck resigning while his royal master was slowly sinking. Although she resented losing to Bismarck on her own ground, she was not as stubborn as her daughter about it. The royal marriage game was not worth the candle, if it could light so many fires abroad. All the same, she was not amused, and complained: 'How Bismarck and still more William can play such a double game it is impossible for us honest, straightforward English to understand. Thank God! we are English.'[9]

Before she arrived in Berlin, the Emperor was nearly killed by his doctors. After a severe coughing fit one night, he found it difficult to breathe through the cannula. Mackenzie had a new lead cannula made. Aware of his precarious position in Germany, he asked Dr Bergmann to insert it. Bergmann fetched a cannula of his own, one without the rounded end which avoided damaging the tissues of the throat. He pulled out the old breathing-tube and thrust in his new one, missed the incision in the windpipe and forced the cannula inside the flesh of the neck. The Emperor began to splutter and bleed copiously. Again Bergmann tried to thrust his cannula into the wrong place and had to pull it out again. The Emperor coughed and coughed. Streams of blood flowed from his throat. The agitated Bergmann pushed his forefinger into the wound to enlarge it, then failed again to insert his cannula. He gave up, and ordered his assistant, Dr Bramann, to insert a smaller tube, which Bramann did with ease.

After Bergmann had left and the bleeding had subsided after two hours, Mackenzie was summoned, according to his account. 'Why did Bergmann put his finger into my throat?' the Emperor whispered. 'I do not know, Sir,' Mackenzie replied. 'I hope you will not allow Professor von Bergmann to do any further operations on me.'

'After what I have seen today, Sir,' Mackenzie answered, 'I beg most respectfully to say that I can no longer have the honour of continuing in attendance on Your Majesty if Professor von Bergmann is to be permitted to touch your throat again.'[10]

Bergmann's random stabbing with an unguarded tube resulted in an abscess in the patient's neck. Pus flowed out and made the Emperor's condition more serious. It was the fatal blow, according to Mackenzie. Bergmann's account was completely different, although he was forced to withdraw from the case. He claimed that he had saved the Emperor's life. He had found the Emperor suffocating from maltreatment by the British doctors and had brought him round by putting a finger in his throat and using his assistant's cannula. Mackenzie's assistant thought that Bergmann had been drinking and that his roughness was the result of alcohol rather than nerves. Certainly, the Emperor never allowed Bergmann to attend him again and wrote on his pad 'Bergmann ill-treated me'.[11]

It was his life, and he had to be the best judge of who was helping or harming him. Undoubtedly, he supported Mackenzie, who now designed an aluminium cannula which allowed his patient to breathe easily for the remainder of his short days. Sadly, politics interfered with medical judgements. Mackenzie came from England and was presumed guilty no matter what he did; Bergmann came from Germany and was presumed credible no matter what he said. The Emperor did, however, decorate Dr Krause and Dr Virchow for their part in his treatment. A dying man does not mind where his medical advisers come from, only what they do to him.

When Queen Victoria arrived at Charlottenburg station, the Empress with her children was waiting to greet her. The Queen kissed her daughter and found her looking careworn and thinner, but not ill. She was led by Crown Prince William to a four-horse barouche, which took her to the palace. She passed between a guard of honour and beneath the drawn swords of two gigantic sentries to the old rooms of Frederick the Great. These had not been used since the last King of Prussia's death, but had been redecorated by the Empress to receive her mother. The Queen of England then went to see her son-in-law, who was lying in bed, his face unaltered. He raised both hands in pleasure to see his mother-in-law and gave her a nosegay.

Later at breakfast, the Empress told her mother that she and her husband had never had a quarrel with Bismarck over the Battenberg marriage. 'The whole dreadful bother,' she said, 'had been purposely got up.' It was intended to prove to the new monarchs how powerful the Chancellor was and how insubstantial was their rule. Lord Salisbury was less charitable, writing to the British Ambassador in Berlin that alcohol by day and narcotics at night must have affected Bismarck's brain.[12] Queen Victoria, however, decided to put an end to all misunderstanding between Germany and England over the Battenbergs by receiving the Chancellor in a private audience. He was brought to her by the Empress at noon the next day.

The Queen was agreeably surprised to find Bismarck so amiable and gentle. He referred to their meeting at Versailles thirty-three years before, but did not add that their failure to meet for so many decades had caused him to underestimate her powers in diplomacy. He talked a great deal about the German Army which, he said, could deploy millions of men in defence of the fatherland against Russia or France. He hoped that the British Navy would help, if Germany were attacked. He only wanted to defend the borders of the present Empire, which was large enough for its role in Europe.

After hearing what Bismarck wanted, Queen Victoria told him what she wanted. She said that she was glad there was not to be a Regency under Crown Prince William. She did not say that she knew of a plot by William's supporters to have him act for his sick father in order to stop the Empress acting for him, on the principle that the Hohenzollerns, Prussia and the German Empire would not permit a woman to rule them.[13] Bismarck promised the Queen that there would not be a Regency. 'Even if he though it necessary, which he did not,' the Queen's journal recorded, 'he would not have the heart to propose it. I appealed to Prince Bismarck to stand by poor Vicky, and he assured me he would, that hers was a hard fate. I spoke of William's inexperience and his not having travelled at all.'

Bismarck replied that Crown Prince William knew nothing about civil affairs at all, but he was certainly clever. 'Should he be thrown into the water,' the Chancellor declared, 'he would be able to swim.' The half-hour interview ended with Queen Victoria discussing other personal affairs.[14] She was very probably telling Bismarck that she had persuaded her daughter not to proceed with the Battenberg marriage because of the political complications. At all events, Bismarck came from the interview, smiling and wiping the sweat from his forehead. 'What a woman!' he is reported to have said. 'One could do business with her!'

This was the long-delayed meeting between the leaders of the two rival systems of diplomacy, which kept the peace and the balance of power in Europe. Queen Victoria had shown that she would throw away her trump card, royal marriage, if necessary for the good of her country. 'Grandmamma behaved quite sensibly at Charlottenburg,' Bismarck told Busch. The Queen needed German friendship for Britain against Russia, and she was prepared to make a sacrifice for it. She even brought about a reconciliation between Crown Prince William and the Empress, who was now considered by the Bismarckians as more of a supporter than her own mother of English interests in Germany.[15]

That night at the British Embassy, Bismarck showed how much good-will had resulted from the meeting. He had already told Crown Prince William that the Queen of England's visit was like an officer going round the outposts and seeing that the pickets were all doing their duty. Now that he was sitting opposite her at dinner, he was ebullient. Noticing a bon-bon which was topped by a likeness of the Empress, he grabbed it, unbuttoned the top of his coat and placed it against his heart.[16]

The Chancellor had heard that the people of Berlin had turned out in their tens of thousands to cheer and throw flowers at the coach bearing the Empress and her mother to the embassy dinner. His warnings of hostile demonstrations had been proved excessive, the vicious Press attacks were proving redundant. They stopped, except for one which slipped through the net, as soon as they had started. The Empress's influence would expire with her husband, and he – Mackenzie told Queen Victoria – would not live above a few weeks, possibly two months, but hardly three.[17]

The next day in a bitter wind, Queen Victoria took the salute at a march past commanded by her grandson William. She then bade farewell to her son-in-law, who kissed her photograph, but coughed so much that she had to leave. At the station, her daughter broke down. 'It was terrible to see her standing there in tears, while the train moved slowly off, and to think of all she was suffering and might have to go through. My poor poor child, what would I not do to help her in her hard lot!'[18]

She could not help her daughter now, but she could have helped before. Bismarck's deep suspicion of her manipulation of her daughter in England's interests did not survive his meeting with her. As the Crown Prince whispered to the British Ambassador, he wished she had come to Berlin years sooner. How useful it might have been, judging by the good will the visit had engendered.[19] It had briefly stopped the intrigues against the dying Emperor and the slanders against his wife. 'It had been of the highest value in freely brushing away industriously woven cobwebs,' Lord Salisbury was informed. The many spiders had to return to their holes.[20]

After Queen Victoria's visit, the spring came. The Emperor's health remained stable, although he could not swallow much more than milk. He could be taken out for a drive and show himself to the crowds. When the Crown Prince pressed him, he agreed to review a march-past led by his son, a ghost Emperor watching his successor usurp his command and his glory. The pressure of business was so great that he had to allow William to sign minor State documents for him. But his wife did all she could, often fanning him for most of the night before spending the day without rest at letters, telegrams, audiences and keeping herself *au courant* with everything.[21]

Although little could be changed in politics, precautions could be taken for the future. The Emperor used his inheritance to provide for his wife and daughters. The Empress sent her mother a copy of a letter which the Emperor had written to be given after his death to his eldest son. She feared that the original might be destroyed. 'Please consider it most secret!' she begged Queen Victoria.

On 2 May, she also dispatched by royal messenger a box containing her husband's journals and some more papers which she did not think safe in Germany. They were to be kept in her mother's strong-room, with the other boxes of confidential documents, brought to London at the time of the Jubilee or sent from San Remo. Her reason for storing the papers abroad was, according to her, because of invasion of privacy. All the dead Emperor William I's most secret and intimate papers were being plundered by utter strangers and agents, sent by Bismarck to see whether there were documents that might compromise his official version of German history.[22]

The precautions taken by the Empress may have seemed excessive, but she knew how vulnerable she was, how exposed and powerless in all but name. She was pretending to rule on borrowed time at a court which only pretended to obey her condemned husband. 'Whatever Fritz wishes done meets with the most systematic and persistent though silent opposition, plainly showing that these people only submit to the present reign as a form, but resist it as a reality! A few months of health or comparative health would enable Fritz to put an end to this.'[23]

The Emperor made a valiant effort and attended the wedding of his second son, Prince Henry, to Princess Irene of Hesse, herself a grandchild of Queen Victoria. Stick in hand, he appeared before the assembled guests in the blue damask room of the palace, dressed in full uniform with all his orders. His wife felt her heart turn over. Handsome and dignified, but thin and pale, he welcomed everyone and embraced Irene and Henry. His wife kept back her tears with difficulty and felt with bitter sorrow that they would never again see him attending such a gathering as Emperor. The wedding was very beautiful but very sad. The Emperor stood it well, and did not have a fit of coughing during the service. The chapel was filled with roses and other flowers. Irene was very moved. Her delicate little figure seemed almost bowed down by the weight of the bridal jewels, particularly the crown. Full mourning had been put aside for that day, but the ladies wore grey or white.[24]

Throughout that last May in Berlin, the Empress carried on, her nerves occasionally giving way from bad bouts of neuralgia. She was becoming more popular, especially after she had insisted on visiting the victims of heavy floods in East Prussia. The people might admire her devotion in trying to keep her husband alive, but she had few friends in the government or at court. As Colonel Swaine reported to the Prince of Wales, these were sad times in Berlin. The approaching death of the Emperor made all trim their sails. It seemed as if a curse had come over the country, leaving but one bright spot. That was where a solitary woman stood doing her duty faithfully and tenderly by her sick husband against all odds. It was one of the most, if not the most tragic episode in a country and a life ever recorded in history.[25]

On 1 June the Empress decided to move, so that her husband might die in his favourite home, the Neue Palais. He had rechristened it the Friedrichskron, officially after Frederick the Great, whose name he himself bore as Emperor and defender of his country. The River Spree bordered the park of Charlottenburg, so the Emperor could be taken to Potsdam by boat. The royal steam yacht, *Alexandra*, brought the imperial family, past cheering crowds on the banks and past the fortress of Spandau, through the Havel lakes to the Glienicke Bridge, where they disembarked for Friedrichskron. Before leaving, the Emperor had paid a visit to the mausoleum at Charlottenburg, to see where his father lay. He did not choose to lie there.

'How glad I am to be here at last,' the Emperor told his wife softly and continuously at the Friedrichskron. The weather soon turned warm and fine. The sick man lay out on the palace balcony, or drove in a pony-chaise to view the trees and flowers which he had planted with his wife. Their own creations never looked more beautiful to them, the Empress noted – the sun was said to shine more beautifully just before setting. The nights were not good, his appetite was poor and meals were a torment. Nevertheless, though he was growing physically weaker and more tired, he retained the liveliest interest in everything. He signed documents, wrote letters and made entries in his diary, gave instructions and occupied himself with trivia, read all his newspapers through from beginning to end.[26]

He could not hold out for long. It was the triumph of will over body. His last official act was to insist on receiving the King of Sweden. With great difficulty he put on his uniform, but his wasted face and shining eyes signalled his approaching end. The British Ambassador noticed the smell of death on him, and feared the last stage of the tragedy. To his wife, the Emperor seemed like Admiral Keppel aboard his sinking British man-of-war, saluting the French admiral with a broadside, although the water was rising higher and higher.

A fistula had appeared in his throat so that even his milk now passed out through the cannula. Mackenzie had to feed him with milk through a rubber tube, but some of it seemed to reach the lungs, causing an inflammation. Now he could take no more nourishment and became a fevered skeleton. He struggled for breath throughout the night of 14 June and the next morning it was clear that he was dying. His wife gave him some white wine on a sponge to suck. When she asked him if he were tired, his last words to her were a croak, 'Oh, very, very ...'

The imperial family gathered round the unconscious man. They could hear only the slight rattle of breath through the cannula. In the hour before noon, he woke and started to write on his pad: 'Victoria, I and the Chil –.' His hand dropped, a gasp came from the tube in his throat and he fell back dead. Mackenzie closed the eyelids with a practised hand.

'Oh, the look of his dear eyes,' his widow wrote to her mother, 'the mournful expression when he closed them for ever, the coldness and the silence that follow when the soul has fled. Oh! my husband, my darling, my Fritz!! So good, so kind, so tender, brave, patient and noble, so cruelly tried, taken from the nation, the wife and daughters that did so need him. His mild just rule was not to be.'[27]

The Empress had enough strength for a last farewell, no more, or she would have gone mad. She returned to her room to find herself a prisoner. 'What undignified and abominable things took place on this disastrous day!' she wrote in her diary. 'William's first act as Ruler was to have our house, our sanctuary, our quiet house of mourning where death had set up his throne, cordoned off by a regiment of Hussars who appeared unmounted with rifles in their hands from behind every tree and every statue!' He wanted to have Mackenzie arrested immediately, but was stopped by the Minister of Justice. Soldiers were stationed between the kitchen and the telegraph office, so that the servants could not even telegraph to Berlin for crêpe and mourning. Winterfeld immediately flung himself on the Emperor's private writing-table and desk, tore everything open, and rummaged as if he expected to find traces of State documents, possibly Liberal plots. The Empress Frederick turned away from the miserable spectacle with pride and disgust.[28]

This indecent and paranoiac behaviour of the new Emperor had been provoked. On the eve of her husband's death, the Empress had sent Dr Hovell to the British Embassy with a portmanteau and a hatbox filled with confidential papers. The Ambassador knew nothing of their contents, but packed them himself in diplomatic bags and sent Colonel Swaine off with them that night to Queen Victoria in Balmoral. The spy in the British Embassy had reported Dr Hovell's mission to Bismarck and to Crown Prince William, whose impetuosity matched his mother's fear. The Crown Prince had reacted by having the Friedrichskron surrounded by a cordon of dismounted Hussars while his father was still alive. As soon as he had become German Emperor, a regiment of infantry was ordered at the double to seal the palace.

The Empress could find no one to defend her except the British Ambassador and the Minister of Justice, Friedberg, who had been honoured by her dead husband. When her son demanded that she surrender all State papers immediately to him, she faced him down. All State papers had been returned by the late Emperor after reading or signing them, she said. The rest were private papers. 'Those the Emperor has given to me,' she claimed. 'And I do not suppose that you wish to take them from me.'

He did not quite dare to seize them or to continue the search for them. Nor did he have the baggage of the suspect British doctors ripped apart. 'You have the power,' the Minister of Justice told him, 'but you have not the right. If you exercise the power, you will begin your reign badly.' Had the full search been ordered, the British Ambassador would have felt bound to intervene, and it would have led to a serious diplomatic incident. As it was, the intrusion ended without scandal, a kind of black farce.[29] 'There is something medieval in the incident of Dr Hovell's portmanteau,' Lord Salisbury observed drily. 'No doubt there was plenty of matter in it to have sent all the Empress Victoria's friends to Spandau.'[30]

That was her reason for sending her private papers to safety abroad. She was protecting her liberal friends and Coburg advisers from inevitable persecution by Bismarck. Their advice to her and her dead husband would be seen as a conspiracy against the Chancellor's authority. Her correspondence with her English relatives would also be misinterpreted. The Prince of Wales was immediately sent to Berlin for three reasons: his official duty, to represent the British Crown at the Emperor Frederick's funeral; to support his sister through her time of trial and persecution; to bring back in his baggage the last of her confidental documents.

Against the wishes of the dead Emperor and his wife, the new Emperor William II allowed a port-mortem. He was under pressure from Bergmann, who had to establish that the death had not been caused by his drunken clumsiness in May. It was found that the whole larynx was a gangrenous ulcer, and there were traces of septic broncho-pneumonia in the lungs. No mention was made of the abscess caused by Bergmann; this had spread so much that it was diffused all over the throat. The German doctor's reputation was saved, while the Empress grieved that the specialists had dared touch her husband's dear face, his sacred mortal remains.

For a day and a night, the late Emperor lay on his deathbed in Friedrichskron. Swathed in white to the chin, his head bound, his hands crossed on his sabre, he looked like the figure of a Teutonic Knight on a tomb. After the post-mortem, his remains were shrouded in his military cloak and decorated with his Orders and medals before being laid to rest in a coffin in the Jasper Hall of the palace. His wife put in the coffin his favourite miniature of her, with a lock of her hair and his wedding ring. 'I, his wife,' she said, 'lie there too!'

The imperial family held a service in the Jasper Hall. The next day, thousands of people came out from Berlin to stand in line and bow to the dead figure. There was no formal lying in state or state funeral, merely a simple ceremony at the Friedenskirche in the park of Sans Souci, where he was buried by the side of his dead son Waldemar. The Emperor Frederick had not wanted any pomp and was given none by his son. Life Guards in black uniforms escorted his coffin, muffled drums signalled his end. His old chestnut charger, 'Wörth', followed the coffin, neighing continually. It was said later that no one mourned so much at the funeral as his horse.

The Empress did not attend the final ceremony. She fled with her daughters to the little country house at Bornstädt. She could not stand the memories, the false condolences, the soldiers and the intruders. Bismarck did not even come to call on her, he could not bring himself to say that he regretted her husband's death. His creature, Busch, expressed his satisfaction that they were relieved of that incubus, and that his place was now to be taken by a disciple and admirer of the Chief.[31]

In her grief, the Empress depended on the support of her brother, the Prince of Wales. She had always been devoted to him. He would be her defender in place of her husband, just as her husband had served after the death of Prince Albert as Queen Victoria's support and ceremonial representative. On 23 June, the Prince of Wales telegraphed to Queen Victoria that he had arranged to return to England the next day. It would be inadvisable to linger longer with his sister, and he did not wish to hear the new Emperor's speech to the Reichstag, which praised the policies of his grandfather and hardly mentioned his father at all.

During the Prince of Wales's stay in Germany, Bismarck and his son, Herbert, had done all they could to alienate the heir to the English throne. The brief era of good feelings inaugurated by Queen Victoria's visit was abruptly terminated. The Chancellor spoke of the late reign in a manner which was most offensive to the Prince of Wales, the British Ambassador reported. He said that, in fact, the Emperor had never been competent to reign because of his illness. The country had been governed by the Empress despite the German Law.[32] The Ambassador was glad that the Prince of Wales was leaving because he looked at things from a very personal point of view. He had spent most of his time with his sister the Empress, and she was embittered against the Bismarcks and against her son. This could have increased his antagonism towards the rulers of Germany.

Queen Victoria did all she could from a distance, writing to her grandson, the new Emperor, that he should help his mother at this terrible time of dreadful trial and grief. But even if he would, he could not. He had a nature as impetuous and wilful as hers, and a pride more easily pricked. He was, too, surrounded by advisers who insisted that she had always kept far too close to England and could not be trusted. She must now be totally isolated, her contacts scattered and broken. Only then would the Reich be protected from her alien influence.

The Kaiser's mother knew what her fate would be for the rest of her life. She lamented in her diary: 'Why does such pain not kill immediately?'[33]

CHAPTER THIRTEEN

Old Scores, New Places

'I MUST HAVE a nook of my own, something to arrange and care for – and look after, as all other occupation is gone. For thirty years what an interest I have taken in public affairs and politics ... now that is all over!!!'[1] The widowed Empress Frederick knew that her influence, however small, was now at an end. Her circle of friends and advisers would be broken and scattered. Even the memory of her husband's short reign of ninety-nine days would be denied and wiped out. She could only retire and try to record what she thought was the truth.

Her first concern was for the safety of the evidence she needed to collect material for a life of her husband; she had little save her correspondence with her mother and with him. Her letters to the Stockmars and to her confidante, Countess Blücher, had all been burned. So had most of the other documents which, because of their dealing with the German Liberal opposition, might have proved compromising. In a letter written on 20 June 1888, she implored her mother never to surrender the boxes of papers in the strong-room at Windsor Castle. 'FRITZ wished you to take care of them and keep them,' his widow declared. No matter how much pressure was applied by the new Kaiser and the Bismarcks for their return, Queen Victoria must resist. 'They cannot and do not KNOW what is there or where it is now! Fritz tore up and burned heaps, both at Charlottenburg, here, Baveno, San Remo – and before we left for England last year, so I can give quite satisfactory explanations.'[2]

The Empress Frederick's explanations were quite satisfactory. She wanted to preserve those documents necessary to ensure her husband's place in history. She also wanted to protect her liberal advisers. Bismarck wanted only one version of recent German history to survive, the one he would present in his memoirs. In them, he would appear as the sole architect of the German Empire, and the Crown Prince would play an insignificant part in it. As for the liberals who had opposed him, Bismarck had long waited to scatter the remnants of the Coburg group and had taught the new Kaiser to see them as conspirators around the Empress Frederick. The documents which the Empress thought to be private papers were seen by the Chancellor and the Kaiser as the property of the State.

There is still a legal debate in the United States and in England about the ownership of copies of official papers, once a president or a prime minister leaves office. The security of the State is in conflict with the needs of memorialists and historians. Bismarck was certainly not prepared to wait for a legal ruling in his attempts to have all the papers of the dead Emperor seized. When the Kaiser sent Winterfeld, who had ransacked the imperial desk and writing table at Friedrichskron, to announce his accession to Queen Victoria, the General was cold-shouldered by the court. The Queen heard that he had complained of it, but was unrepentant. He had been a traitor to his old master, and never mentioned his name or spoke a word of regret. He had spoken only of his pleasure in being chosen to announce that his new master had succeeded to the throne.[3]

Naturally, Queen Victoria did not tell Winterfeld of the papers in her possession. She was most surprised to hear on 14 July that her daughter wanted the three large boxes of papers, which had been brought over at the time of the Jubilee, returned to Germany. A compromise had been reached with Bismarck's agents. The contents of the boxes would be examined only by her and the Minister of Justice, Friedberg, whom she trusted. Papers judged official would be handed over; she would keep the remainder. Lord Salisbury did not like the idea, suspecting the unknown contents of the boxes as much as Bismarck did. When the boxes were on German soil, Bismarck might have them all seized. Surely it would be safer, Salisbury advised Queen Victoria, to have them examined, and to send only those that were to be given up.[4]

The three boxes were, however, returned without having been examined in England; the other packets of documents were retained. The Empress sorted the contents with Friedberg, and allowed three of Bismarck's men to go through her husband's safe and desk. All papers of an official or political nature were given up. She kept the ones that she thought were private; she would store these in a safe place where nobody could get at them. Their having been in England at the time of her husband's death had been a godsend; now all the foolish and false people who had been prowling the palace, like Harpies, ready to seize every-thing, had dispersed.[5]

By this time, her defence of her husband's reputation was developing into a war. The first shot was fired by Bergmann on behalf of the German doctors. He published a report on the late Emperor's illness. A biased attack on Morell Mackenzie, it accused the English doctor of false optimism and actual malpractice, asserting that an early operation for throat cancer would have saved the Emperor's life.[6] The report stung Mackenzie into replying with equal bias and self-justification, in a book entitled *The Fatal Illness of Frederick the Noble*. Charge was met with counter-charge, innuendo with smear. In Germany, Mackenzie's book was confiscated by the police. The Empress Frederick called this action a perfectly despotic proceeding worthy of St Petersburg.[7]

The doctors' war was inflated out of proportion by the political campaign to eradicate the memory of the short reign of the Emperor Frederick. The same people, his widow said, who had wanted to kill him by an early throat operation were now hounding Mackenzie for having helped her to keep him alive. Her son, the Kaiser, was a tool in their hands. He was prejudiced against all doctors from her homeland. 'An English doctor killed my father,' he told his entourage, 'and an English doctor crippled my arm – and this we owe to my mother who would not have Germans about her!'[8]

Believing this, the Kaiser supported Bismarck's vindictiveness in smashing the last of the Empress Frederick's 'Coburg' friends. The thought of pro-English conspirators close to the German throne had tormented the Chancellor for more than thirty years. His opportunity to strike was furnished by the indiscretion of one of them, Professor Geffcken. He had made a copy of the Emperor Frederick's *War Diary* for 1870 and 1871, and had extracts published in the German press, which made clear how much the Crown Prince then had influenced the creation of the German Empire, in the teeth of his father's hesitations and Bismarck's objections.

Having always claimed infallibility and omnipotence, Bismarck was furious. Officially, he declared the extracts from the diaries to be for-geries; privately, he accused the Empress Frederick of leaking State secrets to the 'Coburg' conspirators. Geffcken was arrested in Hamburg and put on trial, while she was forced to leave Friedrichskron, her husband's last resting-place. 'I feel I must cling to every table, every footstool in his room!' she wrote in her journal.' Everyone thought that the publication of the *War Diary* was her way of avenging herself by attacking Bismarck's reputation.

Her son, the Kaiser, was exasperated by her. He bitterly attacked his father in front of her, asking how he could write such imprudent things. He also resented the fact that his father did not take him into his confidence for fear that he would run off and reveal all to Bismarck. The Empress Frederick had accidentally surrendered the original of the *War Diary* with the rest of the official papers in the boxes returned from England. There could have been no better proof for her enemies that she had had nothing to do with the publication.[10] And no better proof of the fact that Bismarck knew perfectly well that the extracts from the *War Diary* were not forgeries.

The Empress Frederick thought that Geffcken was bound to be convicted of high treason, just as Count Harry von Arnim had been. 'Justice is a mere farce here!' she wrote to her mother. 'Tribunals, Police, Post and Telegraph Office, are the tools of Prince Bismarck, and the greater part of the press too, as he has 16 millions of marks "secret funds". The desire to incriminate me must be very strong in Berlin.' Baron Roggenbach's house had been searched and private papers taken, while her go-between, Baroness Stockmar, had been interrogated. All this police activity was an indirect attack on her. 'I was Fritz's wife. I am English – and love Germany and its people too well. I know too much. I can see – and read and hear – therefore I must be ... calumniated and attacked – it is so easy – as I am defenceless and a lady.'[11]

When the case came to trial, Bismarck's prosecutor had to concede that the *War Diary* was genuine, and Geffcken went free. The professor had committed an indiscretion, but not treason. In revenge, Bismarck had Geffcken's indictment widely publicized. It named all the 'Coburg' survivors as conspirators against the welfare and safety of Germany. These were said to include most of Bismarck's known political enemies: Stosch, Roggenbach, Windthorst, Freytag and the dead Normann.

Sir Robert Morier, the prime contact between England, the Empress Frederick and the German Liberal opposition, was also mentioned in the Geffcken indictment. An especial target for Bismarck's hatred, he was thought to be the head of British Intelligence in northern Europe, although, unknown to Bismarck, the Kaiser's friend, Colonel Swaine, was now playing this role. Morier was a friend of the Empress Frederick's and a direct contact with Queen Victoria. If there were an English conspiracy in Germany, it was most vulnerable in the person of this fat diplomat at St Petersburg.

Through articles planted in the German Press, Morier was accused of having betrayed German troop movements to Marshal Bazaine in 1870, and this, it was said, had resulted in a French victory at Vionville, where Prince Frederick Karl lost 16,000 men. The disclosure came from the German Military Attaché in Madrid, one of whose duties was to see that the exiled Bazaine received a pension. Bismarck's son, Herbert, garbled the information, asserting that Bazaine had defeated the Crown Prince. The implication was that the Crown Prince had endangered his own men by passing military information to his wife, who had passed it on to her sister Princess Alice in Hesse-Darmstadt – and so to Morier.

The truth was that Morier had sent only two telegrams containing military information from Darmstadt before the battle, detailing the probable positions of the headquarters of the three German armies that were advancing on France. The information had been passed to the British Ambassador in Paris and may have been intercepted, decoded and interpreted. Bazaine himself, in a letter to Morier, categorically denied that he had received any military information from Darmstadt. The telegraph authorities confirmed that Morier had sent only the two coded telegrams to London. The accusation was a deliberate smear by Bismarck's propaganda machine. Its aim, as a letter to *The Times* pointed out, was to show that the Emperor Frederick was in the habit of blabbing to the English, who turned his confidences to a treacherous and malevolent use.[12]

It was also intended to hit at the pro-French Prince of Wales, who was close to Morier and who had quarrelled with the Bismarcks and with his nephew, the Kaiser. Angry at his uncle's championship of his English mother, the Kaiser deliberately snubbed him by refusing to meet him during a State visit to Vienna. In vain, the Prince of Wales insisted to Queen Victoria that the Kaiser apologize for the snub, and that the Bismarcks retract their allegations against Morier. Anglo-German relationships reached a low ebb, and Lord Salisbury wanted a reconciliation. Morier demanded vindication and used *The Times* to clear his name, starting a Press war in Germany between the remaining liberal papers and those of the right wing. He had the best of the controversy in print, but no apology came from the Bismarcks.

To the British Ambassador in Berlin, Bismarck confessed how seriously he took Morier's role as a spymaster and intriguer. He said that Morier had been in constant communication with a group, which included Geffcken, Roggenbach and Stosch, who were trying to overthrow the Government. 'It is a habit with me to stand by my friends,' Bismarck said, 'and to be hostile to my enemies without counting the cost.' Morier was nothing to him except in Germany, where he wished to destroy the man's influence for ever. He ended the discussion by including the Empress Frederick in the group working against him.[13]

Bismarck extended his accusations of spying to a former foe, the Dowager Empress Augusta. Although she was old and dying, he could never forget an injury. The deceased Dr Brandis, who had been her counsellor, was accused of having passed secret information about the war to Morier for transmission to England.[14] In a spreading stain of insinuation and indictment, he blackened the names of both the Empresses, their groups of advisers and friends, the leading members of the Liberal opposition, the British Ambassador at St Petersburg, and the British Crown. It was the death-blow to the survivors of the 'Coburg' group. Their last hopes had died with the Emperor Frederick, and they were now being scattered to the far corners of Germany and of Europe.

Not satisfied with this, Bismarck hounded Prince Alexander of Battenberg out of the country. During the short reign of the Emperor Frederick, the Chancellor had deterred him from giving the Battenberg Prince command of a German regiment and a position at court. Now he incited the new Kaiser against 'Sandro', whom he accused of being a British agent. The Kaiser made it clear to the Prince that he would never receive a post at court or in the German Army, or be allowed to marry the Kaiser's younger sister. This ill-treatment provoked Prince Alexander into marrying his mistress, Johanna Loisinger. He renounced his royal title for that of Count Hartenau and went to Austria, where he was given the rank of Lieutenant-Colonel. He died two years later, a broken man.

In November, the Empress Frederick left for England to spend the winter with her mother. She took her three younger daughters with her, also the private papers she had preserved from the three large boxes that had been returned to Germany. 'No one need know it,' she wrote to her mother, 'and I have a perfect right to do with my own property what I like! They are not safe here!' She would write a complete life of her husband in secret. Their thirty years of struggle deserved to be recorded; she would not allow them to be wiped off the history of Germany by the

Bismarcks. The attack on their friends and the seizing of their letters and the lies in the Press would not be allowed to obliterate the truth. She thought that Richelieu's famous saying suited Bismarck, 'Give me but one WRITTEN LINE in a man's handwriting, and I will make it suffice to bring him to the gallows.' But Bismarck did not have the entire Spanish Inquisition at his disposal. In spite of his little reign of terror, the facts would out.[15]

The situation was so charged that the Kaiser had almost refused to allow his mother to go to England for the long winter stay with Queen Victoria, but he dared not provoke his mighty grandmother more than he already had. Soon after his accession, she had sent him a long letter of advice which he had ignored. He had felt he was being treated as a grandson and not as German Emperor.[16] Bolstered by Bismarck's fury at this further proof of interference from England, he had delayed answering the letter. When he did reply, it was to denigrate his father's reign. He claimed that he had had to spend months clearing up the paperwork after the complete stagnation he had inherited. He also insisted on setting aside a decent period of mourning, in order to meet the Emperors of Russia and Austria and the King of Italy, before coming to England. 'The fate which sometimes hangs over nations,' he grandly informed his grandmother, 'does not wait till the etiquette of court mournings has been fulfilled.'[17]

Queen Victoria was so piqued by his impertinence to her and his bad behaviour to her widowed daughter that she refused to invite him to England at all. She certainly would not postpone the Empress Frederick's visit, as Lord Salisbury suggested, just to mollify her grandson and the Bismarcks. 'You all seem frightened of them,' she scolded Lord Salisbury, 'which is not the way to make them better.'[18] Her bereaved daughter must come over, and the Queen of England would take the unprecedented step of meeting her at Port Victoria to do her honour.

In fact, the three months which the Empress Frederick spent in England did much to ease the tensions in Germany. Queen Victoria advised her daughter to try to put up with her son's thoughtlessness and the slanders of his advisers. Even he hoped that her absence might heal the breach between them. 'My mother and I have the same characters,' he admitted to the British Ambassador in Berlin. 'I have inherited hers. That good stubborn English blood which will not give way is in both our veins. The consequence is that if we do not happen to agree, the situation becomes difficult.'[19]

He urged Queen Victoria to allow him to visit her; he wanted to bring a naval squadron. She was still offended, but much wiser than her eldest daughter in recognizing political necessity. Lord Salisbury had pointed out that English public opinion would not tolerate a diplomatic rupture with Germany because of personal quarrels within royal families.[20] Queen Victoria replied that, while she could not forget the events of the past twelve months, she hoped that her manner to her grandson would not show her true feelings. If the peace of Europe depended upon an open show of friendship between Germany and England, the Kaiser could come to the Solent with his warships.[21] Even her daughter would finally approve. The relations of England and Germany should not suffer, the Empress Frederick told her mother, despite Prince Bismarck's wickedness and William's folly.[22]

The German Emperor still had to make his peace with his English uncle and his mother, whose ill-treatment had made Queen Victoria's blood boil. 'When a young man is in the wrong and he happens besides to be an Emperor – ' the Prince of Wales wrote to his elder sister, 'it is not palatable to admit it! But I have built him so many golden bridges that if he will not cross them – it is not my fault!'[23] Like his mother, the Prince of Wales was ultimately prepared to put his country before his pride, which was something the Kaiser still had to learn.

Lord Salisbury also insisted that diplomacy come first, and urged the Prince of Wales to pocket his dignity and eat humble pie in order to keep on good terms with the Bismarcks and the Kaiser. There were no apologies from Germany, only further insensitive actions. The worst of these was the removal of the name of Friedrichskron from the old Neue Palais, when the Kaiser took it for his own palace. This new effort to erase the memory of the Emperor Frederick hurt the Empress and her defender, the Prince of Wales. 'It is really too monstrous!' he wrote to his sister. 'Could you not have protested? There are certain things that almost surpass all comment! And it is almost best to be silent in words – though our thoughts are all the more intense!'[24]

Silence was golden, indeed, and a fresh uniform was very heaven to the new Kaiser. As a war-like peace-offering, he wanted to make Queen Victoria colonel of a German regiment of dragoon guards – an honour never before offered to a foreign sovereign. In return, the English Queen took advice from the Prince of Wales and gave the Kaiser his secret desire, the title and uniform of a British Admiral. 'Fancy wearing the same uniform as St Vincent and Nelson,' he wrote to the British Ambassador in Berlin, 'it is enough to make one quite giddy. I feel something like Macbeth must have felt, when he was suddenly received by the witches.'[25]

He and his sailor brother, Prince Henry, were greeted by the British Fleet at Spithead with a full naval review. It was followed by special army manœuvres at Aldershot. The Prince of Wales was present and discreet, while Queen Victoria was gracious and welcoming at Osborne. She seemed to be taking Colonel Swaine's advice: 'Treat the grandson as Emperor and he will remain grandson. Treat the Emperor as grandson and he is lost as such for ever.'[26] Immense care was taken to show him the respect that he felt was his due. In fact, he irritated the Prince of Wales immensely by making him stand aside, in his own domain, the Royal Yacht Club at Cowes, to allow his imperial visitor to go through the door first.

The effect of the visit to England was immediate: the Kaiser veered as emotionally and as violently as his mother often did. He no longer feared English influence, but desired it. Lord Salisbury complimented Queen Victoria for having wrought such a change. On his return to Germany, the Kaiser invited the Channel Fleet to visit the German Navy at Kiel. He went there to inspect the British ironclads and invited their officers to attend a reception at the Empress Frederick's. Having an English mother was an advantage at last, if he could inspect her country's fleet.

She felt a stab of jealousy at her son's success in England and with her mother. She did not want to hear about the visit, which seemed to her a change of loyalty by her own family. Queen Victoria had graciously to receive all the Kaiser's advisers who had behaved so disgracefully and abominably and treacherously to her and her husband. It was more difficult for her that her son was making the court and the Bismarcks do what she had always tried to do – achieve a good understanding between Germany and England. These new friends of her homeland were the same people who had denounced her as too friendly to England, and who had abused her husband unjustly and ungratefully for remaining true to his principles. It was ironic and sad.

She was grateful to her mother for advising the Kaiser not to listen to lies against his mother, but it was too late. His mind had been thoroughly poisoned against his parents. She could not utter a word against him because almost every member of her entourage was his creature. Her old friends and advisers had been cut off from her, and everyone else would have her believe that the Kaiser was right.[27]

She did have a few loyal people near her in her household: Count Seckendorff and the Countess Perponcher had been with her for decades, while the Countess Brühl and the extremely able Baron Reischach had gained her confidence and remained with her. Her isolation was exacerbated because she had been excluded, even by her own mother, from the centres of diplomacy. Anglo-German relations were no longer affected by her hope of inheriting the throne; her personal suffering could not be allowed to disrupt them.

Queen Victoria and the Prince of Wales were now dealing with the Kaiser face to face; the Empress Frederick was unnecessary to that direct diplomacy. The Prince of Wales might come to Homburg to spend three weeks with her privately in September 1889, to mollify her about the Kaiser's visit to England, but he could not restore her position of importance. Her eldest son had not only inherited the German throne, but also replaced her special connection between the German and English Courts.

The Kaiser's preoccupation with the English relationship and the British Navy was in the national interest. As a young man, he had sent back to his German grandfather detailed reports and sketches of the forts, docks, armaments and ironclads at Portsmouth.[28] As an admiral of the British Navy, he would study it, he told his English grandmother, as if it were his own.[29] Although he claimed that he wanted the British Navy to remain the strongest in the world, he secretly wished to build up the German Navy to be superior. To do that, he needed to know about British marine technology and developments. Free from the slightest taint of espionage, he and his aides would be privileged observers who could report to the German Admiralty.

It was common ground that royal visitors did not demand to be shown anything that was militarily sensitive. When Prince Henry of Germany visited Gibraltar in 1889, he was not allowed to see the ridge of the Rock, where new fortifications were being constructed. He took it in good part, quite captivated, rather than repelled, by the firm, but well-mannered regrets, that even His Royal Highness could not be allowed to pass.[30]

The Kaiser's naval interests led him to visit Greece and Turkey later in 1889. He wished to attend the wedding of his sister Sophie to Prince Constantine, Duke of Sparta and heir to the throne. While he was at

Athens, he inspected the British Mediterranean Squadron which was lying offshore. He showed the greatest interest in and knowledge of the complex characteristics of ironclads.[31] In a speech on board, he admitted that the German Navy was dependent on the British for instruction and example. He took it upon himself to advise his grandmother to increase the size of the Mediterranean Squadron from five to twelve first-class battleships in order to counter the French Fleet at Toulon. Through his friend, Lord Charles Beresford, he even sent a strategical scheme to Lord Salisbury based on the tactics of the German Navy.

His British admiral's uniform did, as he admitted, take hold of him.[32] In point of fact, he had replaced his mother and father as Queen Victoria's royal Intelligence source on foreign armaments. While discreet about what Germany was manufacturing, he sent her information about American cruiser specifications, and Russian and French experiments in small arms. According to his sources, Britain should immediately begin building two dozen ironclads for her own security, while the French and the Russians would be unable to go to war for some four years because of their botched rearming.[33]

The Empress Frederick was also at her daughter Sophie's wedding in Greece, as was the Prince of Wales. She was reminded of her own wedding as her daughter and the Duke of Sparta stood at the altar wearing their golden crowns, before walking three times round it with their lighted tapers. Briefly, she felt at the centre again, but was soon reminded of the passing of the old order. She was summoned back to Germany from Italy for the funeral of the Dowager Empress Augusta. For once, she wrote to her mother, the sight of the dead woman was not unpleasant.

'You would have thought she was just going to a fête or a soirée! Her face was so calm and peaceful and had grown younger. There seemed not a wrinkle, and the eyes that used to stare so, and look one through and through were closed, which gave her a gentler expression than I ever saw in life. The false hair in ringlets on her brow, the line of the eyebrows and eyelashes carefully painted as in life – a golden myrtle wreath on her head, and an ample tulle veil, were well arranged, flowing and curling about her head and neck and shoulders – hiding her chin and her hands folded, her bracelets on and her wedding ring. The cloth of gold train, lined and trimmed with ermine which she wore for her Golden Wedding was very well folded and composed about her person and over her feet, and flowed far down on the steps in front! She looked wonder-

fully well, and really almost like a young person. I felt if she could have
seen herself she would have been pleased. She was the "Empress", even
in death, and surrounded with all the stiff pomp and ceremony she loved
so much.'[34]

Except for herself, the most formidable of the 'Coburg' group at court
had gone. The Dowager Empress had usually opposed Bismarck and
had usually lost to him. The Empress Frederick was now left even more
alone in her beliefs. As if to show how utterly her old supporters had
joined Bismarck, Gustav Freytag wrote a pamphlet called *The Crown
Prince and the German Imperial Crown*, which was even more malicious
than the turncoat Coburg Duke Ernest's second attack on his former
allies, *The 99 Days*. Freytag not only damned the Emperor and Empress
Frederick, but said also that Princess Alice of Hesse-Darmstadt had helped
her sister to pass German military information to the French during
the war of 1870. To show repentance for his past loyalty, Freytag
even sent the scurrilous pamphlet to Bismarck for approval before its
publication.

This was Bismarck's swan-song in revenge. What he had done to
others would soon be done to him. When the Kaiser wanted new labour
legislation, Bismarck unwisely opposed it. He spoke of the dangers of
socialism growing if appeased. He wanted the Reichstag to pass anti-
socialist measures and threatened to resign if he did not get them. The
Kaiser would have accepted his resignation, but he had no replacement
ready. He remained courteous, but inwardly he was seething. He was
not his aged grandfather or sick father, necessarily dependent on the
powers and infallibility of Bismarck. He wanted social reforms, a larger
army and navy, and more colonies. He was not prepared to be baulked
by an ageing Chancellor, however indispensable he was thought to be.

Matters reached a crisis when the Kaiser called for an international
labour conference in Berlin, and the Chancellor tried to stop it by his
usual underhand methods. He told the British Ambassador that he could
not agree to what the Kaiser was doing, and had decided to resign some
of his posts. His imperial master had no doubts. 'He thinks he can do all
things and he wishes to have the entire credit all to himself.'[35]

From the Kaiser's point of view, socialism had to be controlled and
led, not ignored or resisted. Bismarck's policy was to allow socialism to
progress until it was necessary to call out the troops and sweep the
streets with grapeshot. This might have been possible in the time of the
Kaiser's grandfather, but not now. For a young monarch, such a policy

would be a disaster. 'It would have been said,' the Kaiser told the British Ambassador, 'that my only idea of governing was by bayonets.'[36]

Unable to tolerate Bismarck's opposition, which seemed to be threatening the dynasty, the Kaiser made him resign on the pretext of bad health. He conjured up a diagnosis as dangerous as that which had threatened his father's life. He had been assured, he wrote to Queen Victoria, that if the Chancellor had kept on a few weeks longer, he would infallibly have died of apoplexy. With deep regret, therefore, the Kaiser had decided to part from Bismarck in order to keep him alive.[37]

Such splendid hypocrisy was worthy of Bismarck himself. It was, Lord Salisbury thought, a curious nemesis on the Chancellor. He had been overthrown by the despotism he had created. No German constitution could save him from dismissal by a young Emperor who wanted to be his own Chancellor, Chief of Staff and his own Minister in every department – a task beyond any human powers.[38]

So the Chancellor was retired as thoroughly as the Empress Frederick. He had visited her before his fall, perhaps hoping for her mediation, possibly trying to prove she was still plotting against him. He had told her then that the trouble was the Kaiser's habit of accepting advice from all sides instead of from him alone. The Empress Frederick kept her own counsel, but she thought Bismarck was necessary for Germany and for the peace of Europe. In fact, his removal caused no flutters. There seemed to be an utter absence of movement throughout Europe, Lord Salisbury wrote to Queen Victoria.[39] The Chancellor was no more irreplaceable than anyone else.

As if sorry for himself or for all his misdeeds, Bismarck paid another courtesy call on the Empress Frederick, the call which his ambition had stopped him from making after her husband's death. 'He did not exactly complain – ' she wrote to Queen Victoria, 'but I think he feels very deeply that he has not been treated with the consideration due to his age and position. We parted amicably and in peace, which I am glad of – as I should have been sorry – having suffered so much all these long years under the system – that it should appear as if I had any spirit of revenge.'[40]

His system, which had broken her, had broken him. The stage was now cleared for the Anglo-German diplomacy of the next two decades. It would be a traditional mixture of the royal and the ministerial. On the one side was Queen Victoria and the Prince of Wales, who would eventually become King, and their Foreign Secretaries. On the other was the Kaiser and a succession of imperial servants. To emphasize his policy of direct diplomacy, he hastened to meet Queen Victoria when she visited Darmstadt in April 1890. He wanted to reassure her that he would manage better without Bismarck. 'He said it would have been impossible to go on with him,' the Queen wrote in her journal, 'and that his violence in language and gesture had become such, that he had to put a stop to it. He was sorry to say that Bismarck was intriguing with Russia behind his back.'[41] This last was a sop to his grandmother, whose suspicion of Russia was a constant throughout her long diplomacy.

Although the Empress approved of Bismarck's replacement, General Leo von Caprivi, who had been a prospective Minister of War when her husband was alive, she did not approve of her son's autocracy. He seemed to be acting as a German Tsar and governing by ukase. The system had not changed. Bismarck was gone, but William had learned to play the despot from him.[42] Fortunately, two of the outstanding quarrels between mother and son were resolved. The ill-starred 'Moretta' was betrothed to Prince Adolf zu Schaumburg-Lippe and could put aside all memories of her 'Sandro'. And with her provision from her dead husband and the proceeds of a legacy, the Empress Frederick could afford to refuse the minor grace-and-favour residences offered by her son, and build herself a house at Kronberg near the Rhine in the forested Taunus hills. There, on an estate of 250 acres, she had a German architect design for her 'Friedrichshof', which would house the art treasures and papers she had been collecting for so long.

She wanted a home that would be no *schloss*, but more of a large English country house with a turret or two like Osborne. She instructed her architect that nothing about it should catch the eye, but that it should hold the gaze. She told her mother that 'Friedrichshof' was nothing extraordinary, but solid and in good taste. In style, it was a mixture of Tudor, Italian Renaissance and eighteenth-century classical, but comfortable without appearing too grand. The park was her pride. Reclaimed from the forest, it was already stocked with old chestnuts and cedars, larches and firs; and she had planted a rose garden, where she loved to walk.

Her retirement to a country estate so far from Berlin signalled her retreat from politics. Except for an occasional trip abroad, she would become the widow, the country lady which, in part, she had always wanted to be. She made a hurried journey to Greece for the birth of her daughter Sophie's first child, who was born prematurely after a difficult labour, amid the usual accusations concerning the incompetence of the doctors. Later, Sophie was received into the Greek Orthodox Church, which provoked an outburst from her brother, the Kaiser, who was unwilling to surrender a sister's allegiance to him as head of the German Church. 'Whether I go to hell or not is my own affair,' she told the Kaiser from the safe distance of Greece.[43]

After he had acquired Heligoland in exchange for minor claims in East Africa, relations became so good between the Kaiser and England that he agreed to allow his mother to pay a semi-official visit to Paris in 1891. It was intended that she arrange for the exchange of contemporary works of art between Paris and Berlin, but her nostalgia got the better of her discretion. Instead of confining herself to visiting studios and choosing pictures for the exhibition, she went on to visit the places her husband had occupied during the siege of the French capital. She had only thought to make pilgrimages to Versailles, where the German Empire had been proclaimed, and to Saint-Cloud, which had been destroyed by artillery, but she provoked such a storm of chauvinism in the national press that she was almost forced to flee to England. Her brother, the Prince of Wales, commiserated with her. The French, he wrote, were not to be depended upon and lacked the chivalrous feelings for which they had once been famous.[44]

She was never again employed in affairs of state, and was condemned to retirement until she died. The last decade of the century was a magnificat for Queen Victoria's long reign, and a demonstration of her expertise in helping to keep the peace of Europe. Her eldest daughter could have no part in it, because she was no longer privy to any Intelligence which might help her mother.

'We could have made the young Generation ours by bringing them in contact with the influences of another better, deeper, and higher intellectual and political atmosphere,' the Empress Frederick wrote to Queen Victoria about her elder children. 'The Chain was snapped in two – their beloved Father with his influence and authority is gone to join our beloved Papa – and I am only a powerless and useless relic of the past – a shadow – of what once might have been – and never came – and who is to gather up the broken threads of the slender web we had been YEARS weaving – only to see it torn up – and trampled under foot in the most ruthless manner – I know not!'[45]

CHAPTER FOURTEEN

Retirement and Requiem

THE WEB OF Anglo-German understanding had always been tenuous. Queen Victoria and her eldest daughter might have thought that the English and the Germans were natural allies because of linked dynasties and shared faiths and cultural affinities, but the differences between the two countries were fundamental. Economics, political structures, communications and the differing natures of their élites, pushed the two nations into competition and misunderstanding.[1] The individual efforts of the English queen and her daughter began to appear futile, as Germany, which had always refused to be England's pupil, now became her rival.

When the Empress Frederick retired to her Friedrichshof, the German economy was already outstripping the British one. Bismarck's game with overseas colonies became a matter of national prestige. Imperialism might seem irrelevant to the ousted Chancellor, but it was important to the Kaiser and his countrymen. The young Emperor was determined not to deny national feeling, but to put himself at the head of it. Half-English as he was, he could not seem to placate England. Fearing patronage by his mother's homeland, he wanted to be superior. He intended to unite his nation by outdoing hers.

By choosing to rule personally, the Kaiser found his personal choices governed largely by social and economic forces beyond his control. Queen Victoria could covertly influence politics and diplomacy; she could not decide them. The Kaiser could decide, but at the risk of public exposure. By taking power from Bismarck, he lost freedom of choice. He could not dissociate himself from his Government's demands as

Queen Victoria could. This was particularly true in his relationship with his grandmother's country. He may not have wanted personally to provoke Queen Victoria, but he felt that national interests dictated his assertions. Britain had her empire, her powerful navy and overseas trade. He could not deny his country these blessings merely because they might seem a threat to his mother's homeland.

The Empress Frederick was against Germans having colonies in Africa. In her opinion, they did not understand how to manage or govern them, only the British did. The campaign to acquire them excited false patriotism. And given her huge army, why did Germany also need a huge fleet? Her eldest son's one idea was to have a navy larger and stronger than the British Navy, although this was really pure madness and folly. She hoped she could make him see how impossible and needless it was.[2]

The Kaiser did not see how impossible and needless it was. He was always irritated by his mother's references to 'our fleet', when she was referring to the British Fleet. His royal yacht, *Hohenzollern*, was really a gunboat. On his yearly trips to the Cowes Regatta, he would inspect the ironclads which greeted him with broadsides and bunting. He insisted on visiting the dockyard at Portsmouth, and sent German admirals to report on the launching of new battleships. Although he protested that he wanted the British Navy to be powerful enough to defeat all other navies combined, his expanding warship programme worried his grandmother and her admirals, presenting, as it did, the prospect of an arms race. She was not fooled by his use of his British admiral's uniform to pry into naval secrets. She once had to warn Lord Salisbury against the commander of one of her own battleships: 'Lord Charles Beresford should be watched and not be told or shown anything,' the Queen instructed, 'as I know it for a fact (the Duke of York told me) that he writes every week to the German Emperor who is better informed about our navy than I am.'[3]

If the Kaiser could not assert himself too strongly against his grandmother, it was a different matter with his uncle, the Prince of Wales. Not only did he insist on taking precedence whenever they met, but he enjoyed racing his yacht *Meteor* against his uncle's *Britannia* for the Admiral's Cup. He won twice and crowed about his victories in telegrams to Queen Victoria. On one occasion, he was accompanied to the Regatta by two cruisers, *Weissenburg* and *Wörth*, which had been named after his father's victories against the French. This made his pro-

French uncle indignant, and led to criticisms of German tactlessness in the British press. The Prince of Wales and the Kaiser were so different in temperament and character that they continued to underestimate and dislike each other. The Prince of Wales thought the Kaiser a liar and a bully, while the Kaiser thought his uncle a banal courtier.[4]

Behind the scenes, the conciliatory Prince of Wales wanted to keep his imperious nephew favourably disposed towards England, and to grant him the marks of respect which he craved, but which Queen Victoria liked to withhold in order to show her power. In 1894 the Kaiser made it known through Colonel Swaine that he wanted a British army officer's uniform to add to his admiral's one. 'This would never do,' Queen Victoria declared. 'He is far too much spoiled already.'[5] Her ministers agreed with her, her son did not. The Prince of Wales understood the importance of rank and title in the Kaiser's mind; he, himself, was touchy over these matters. In the end, after mounting pressure from her son and grandson, Queen Victoria gave way with bad grace.

She granted the Kaiser his desire at an occasion which put herself at the head of the united family in her dead husband's homeland. She went to Coburg in April 1894, to attend the wedding of her only Hessian grandson, Grand Duke Ernest Louis, to her grand-daughter, Princess Victoria Melita of Saxe-Coburg-Gotha. She was surrounded by four generations of her royal relatives, including one great-grandchild. There were so many of them that there had to be two sittings for dinner at the schloss. In the family group portraits taken during her stay, she looked like an aged queen bee, with the Kaiser on her right and the Empress Frederick on her left and her three sons standing behind her among the serried ranks of the family. She condescended to make the Kaiser an Honorary Colonel of the Royals; after all, he had sent a squadron of her Prussian Dragoons all the way to Coburg to honour her. The Kaiser declared that he was quite overwhelmed to think that he could now wear besides the admiral's blue uniform, the traditional British redcoat.[6]

This display of family unity overemphasized the kinship and harmony between the thrones of Europe, particularly as the Tsarevitch Nicholas announced his engagement to the bridegroom's youngest sister, Princess Alix of Hesse. In fact, diplomacy and peace-keeping through royal marriages were declining factors in international affairs. The industrial powers of England and Germany were finding each other to be competitors for the markets of the world, and the growing industrialism of Russia was causing strains within the structure of that retrograde society which threatened the throne of the Tsar. The products of the machines and the rise of the working classes manning them were demanding new methods of dealing with internal and international affairs. Materialism menaced royalism, economics was the enemy of crowns.

There was a family and a political falling out after the Coburg gathering. Before then, the Kaiser had gone out of his way to conciliate his grandmother and his mother. He settled most of the outstanding family quarrels. The Guelph Fund, which Bismarck had used to finance his press manipulation, was restored in part to the Duke of Cumberland, the King of Hanover's heir. The Kaiser gave his mother in restoration the old castle of Kronberg in the Taunus Hills, which was near the grounds of her newly built Friedrichshof. As another mark of reconciliation he went to the wedding of his last unmarried sister, 'Mossy', to Prince Frederick Charles of Hesse. And he continued flattering his grandmother in England by calling her the Nestor or Sybil of Europe's sovereigns, revered by all, feared only by the bad.[7]

Yet from 1895 to 1898, the Kaiser's family pride and colonial ambitions prejudiced his relations with Queen Victoria and with England. He lent official recognition to national sentiment, in supporting the independence of the Boers in the Transvaal. This led to his imprudent telegram of congratulations to President Kruger for having forced the surrender of the Jameson raiders without having to ask for the help of friendly powers. He was so furious at the raid that he even thought of returning his British uniforms, saying that they were only fit to be worn by South African *banditti*.[8] Queen Victoria was even more incensed, and sent her grandson an angry telegram, accusing him of being very unfriendly towards England: 'It would have been far better to have said nothing'.

Indignation against the German Emperor was so great in England that he could not make his annual visit to Cowes. In fact, he did not visit England again for three years. Quite deliberately, Queen Victoria provoked his fears, inviting the new Tsar and Tsarina to Balmoral, where the Kaiser was not able to visit her. She began a private correspondence with the Tsar and made her distrust of the Kaiser clear to the Russian ruler. 'I am afraid that William may go and tell things against us to you,' she warned the Tsar, 'just as he does about you to us. If so, pray tell me openly and confidentially.'[9] She wished to prove that her Intelligence system was superior to the young Kaiser's, whom she did not even invite to her Diamond Jubilee.

In response, he did not try to alleviate colonial and international conflicts between the interests and industries of the two powers. Although he continued to correspond privately with Queen Victoria as her most dutiful and devoted grandson, he offended her by his violent hostility to his sister in Greece, over a Cretan crisis. She was also annoyed by his insistence that England join him in sharing out the Portuguese Empire and the Pacific islands. Colonial and commercial rivalries were playing their part in the bad feelings between Germany and England in the middle of the decade, but personal pride also counted. As Colonel Swaine commented, the principle culprit was the Emperor himself. He could not get over his annoyance that the Kruger telegram had had exactly the opposite result from what he had anticipated. He had been convinced that a country without any army corps would not stand up to him who had twenty corps on a peace footing. All the same, Swaine thought that war between the two countries was improbable. The Elephant could not fight the Whale.[10]

That the rifts between the two nations could be widened by the personal feelings between their two sovereigns was offensive to the Prime Minister, Lord Salisbury. Like Bismarck, he deplored the fact that the Kaiser would deal directly with Queen Victoria and allow personal feelings to influence his country's diplomacy. When he heard that the Kaiser had called him an enemy, he wrote to the British Ambassador in Berlin: 'It is a great nuisance that one of the main factors in the European calculation should be so ultra human. He is as jealous as a woman because he does not think the Queen pays him enough attention. I believe that in a true constitutional spirit he holds me responsible for all the personal decisions of my Sovereign. This is very unfair ... Yet Her Majesty, in dealing with her own personal movements and proceedings, is quite as despotic as the Emperor William is in dealing with foreign affairs.'[11]

The Kaiser was further infuriated by Queen Victoria's apparent interference in German affairs over the question of the succession to the Duchy of Coburg held by her second son, Alfred, whose heir had died. Without consulting the Kaiser, the Queen gave her consent to her third son, the Duke of Connaught, taking up his inheritance as heir presumptive. The Kaiser felt it necessary for the Duke to live in Germany and enter the German Army. If not, the Reichstag might pass a law declaring that foreign princes were incapable of succeeding to a German throne.[12]

'He has got it into His Imperial Head,' the British Ambassador reported back from Berlin, 'that He is neglected by the Royal Family, or rather to use his own expression, that they treat him as a *quantité négligeable*.'[13] All would be well if Queen Victoria invited him to come to England for her 80th birthday, or if that were impossible, to Cowes. He was invited to Cowes, and this smoothed his ruffled feathers to some extent.[14] At the Wartburg castle in Thuringia, he told the Dukes of Coburg and Connaught that any heir to the Duchy would have to be educated as a German prince if he wished to succeed. Faced with this ultimatum, the Duke of Connaught and Prince Arthur resigned their claim in favour of the young Duke of Albany, who immediately left Eton to be educated in the ways of his adopted country.

This placation was not enough. The Kaiser now declared that British warships had bombarded German property in Samoa. The action was a taint to the national honour and an attack on his self-respect. In the most astounding letter in this whole period of direct royal diplomacy, he denounced Lord Salisbury by name to Queen Victoria. If he did not get satisfaction from the British Government over Samoa, he threatened serious consequences. Neither he nor the German people would accept being treated as if they were from Portugal, Chile or Patagonia. He wanted redress or he could not visit England. Public opinion would not allow it.[15]

Instead, he received a reprimand from Queen Victoria. She had passed on his letter to Lord Salisbury, who agreed with her that it was quite new for a sovereign to attack in a private letter the minister of another sovereign. Queen Victoria declared herself greatly astonished. 'I never should do such a thing,' she asserted, 'and I never personally attacked, or complained of Prince Bismarck, though I knew well what a bitter enemy he was to England and all the harm he did.'[16] She had conveniently forgotten that she had attacked Bismarck to the Kaiser's grandfather, as the 'one person' who wanted to break the peace of Europe – yet it was true, she had not named him. She knew the correct form of international accusation.

An accident to the Kaiser's wife gave him a good reason for not appearing at Cowes. But in November, he did cross the Channel on a courtesy visit to Queen Victoria. The Queen found him sensible and kind, and a good understanding was re-established. It was just in time, because the Boer War was about to begin, and England needed every friend in Europe that she could muster. 'The German Emperor wants to be our friend –' the British Ambassador in Berlin was told, 'but he would like to be our only friend.'[17]

It was a curious reversal of the war of 1870. Then Germany had been condemned for its military superiority and atrocities against civilians. Now Britain was accused of worse behaviour, of raising vast armies to crush a few Boer commandos, and of herding Boer women and children into concentration camps to die. The Kaiser, however, remained Britain's only friend in Europe and refused offers from the Russians and the French to intervene and force her to make peace. The war, he declared, had set many stones rolling and no one could say where they would stop, but he would not forget that he was the devoted grandson of Queen Victoria. He would not join in any combination against her. He would be glad to think that he had in any way contributed to the last years of her reign being passed in peace.[18]

He did, however, listen to an appeal from the Boers, when they were losing the war. He was asked to act as a mediator in negotiating terms for peace. He said that he would, provided that both sides wanted it, but when Queen Victoria replied that her whole nation was with her in fixed determination to carry the war through without any intervention, he understood, and repeated his determination 'to see that you shall have fair play'.[19] There would be no intervention by Germany or anyone else. 'The Teutonic people,' he told Colonel Swaine, 'must stand shoulder to shoulder, or the Slavs will destroy us.'[20]

Undoubtedly, the special relationship which Queen Victoria had developed with her first grandson since his childhood, played an important part in preventing the great powers of Europe from coalescing to exploit England's weakness during the Boer War. Bismarck had died in 1898. With his death, the great promoter of the balance of power in Europe was gone. The new Chancellor, von Bülow, did little to check the Kaiser's temporary support of England until he should have a navy powerful enough to challenge her on the seas. The Empress Frederick was ill and had retired to Kronberg. A direct relationship between the Kaiser and his grandmother was possible, even though commercial and international rivalries led to bad blood between the two nations. The Prince of Wales aided and abetted in this burial of bad feelings, which was so necessary for England's security, so personal in Germany's strategy.

With the sudden failing of Queen Victoria's health in the middle of January 1901, the Kaiser's reaction showed that his devotion to his grandmother was no sham. Cancelling celebrations for the bicentenary of the Prussian Kingdom, he hurried by special train to Osborne to be present at her deathbed. 'NO notice whatever is to be taken of me in my capacity as Emperor,' he told the Prince of Wales. 'I came as grandson.'[21] For the last two and a half hours of Queen Victoria's life, he stood beside her left shoulder at the head of her bed. After her death, the new King had to go to London to attend the accession Council, leaving the Kaiser to make the arrangements for the lying in state. He ordered Union Jacks to be draped round the walls of the room where his grandmother's coffin lay, covered with flowered wreaths. He stayed away from public affairs in Berlin, remaining in England for the funeral. His uncle was so moved by his behaviour that the Kaiser found himself raised to the rank of Field Marshal. Even Lord Salisbury, so long the enemy, met him in amity.

Queen Victoria's death seemed to have brought about the understanding between England and Germany which had been the goal of her lifelong diplomacy, but it could only be a temporary understanding between the two industrial and commercial rivals, whose respective governments were so different. On his return to Berlin, the Kaiser stopped at Homburg to visit his mother, who was now also stricken with an incurable cancer. They had become reconciled over the past few years, but he could not stay with her long. He had to return to Berlin, where he found himself unpopular because of his show of devotion to the Queen of England. Public opinion in Germany allowed less and less to the personal feelings of sovereigns.

The Empress Frederick's cancer came to light after a bad riding accident she had suffered three years before. Her horse had reared, the Empress had fallen off the wrong side on to her head. Her riding habit had caught on the saddle, so that she was trapped between the horse's hoofs. The frightened animal had trampled on her right hand. The injuries did not seem to heal and cancer was diagnosed.

She had been active and happy in her retirement until then, making her country house into a museum of her taste, and a shrine to her husband's memory. 'One loves one's own things too much,' she used to say. 'One strokes them with one's eyes.' Portraits of the House of Hanover and her closer German relatives lined the walls. Busts of her husband and of her dead child, Waldemar, stood over the great Italianate fireplaces. Collections of books and coins, medals and photographs, silver and old oak engaged her interest and absorbed her time. She became the benefactress of Kronberg, building a hospital and an old people's home and a modern school, and restoring the ancient castle and church in the town. She made a memorial park for her husband and unveiled his statue there in 1889. If she could not help to run the affairs of a nation, she could organize her own estate and neighbourhood.

Her unwilling isolation from her country's affairs was revealed at the Villa Imperiale at Homburg, where she was visiting her brother, the Prince of Wales. An American journalist was granted an interview. She launched into a monologue on America and Anglo-German relations and internal problems in Germany. Hour after hour passed, while the Empress Frederick held forth. Never for a moment did the stream of talk stop. The journalist remembered Carlyle's words on Macaulay: 'Flow on, thou shining river.' He did not perceive the loneliness of a brilliant and powerful woman, who needed any outlet for her opinions, so carefully guarded at home, so needlessly neglected by her son, the Kaiser.[22]

She was not entirely alone. Count Seckendorff had remained with her to the end as head of her household. He travelled with her on painting expeditions to Italy, where she created landscapes and portraits for the walls of Friedrichshof. Her remaining attendants were loyal to her, especially her chamberlain, Baron Reischach, who was the first to know that she had cancer. She told her mother and daughters that it was only chronic lumbago.

As her symptoms became apparent and she began to waste away, the truth could no longer be concealed. Her three younger daughters left their husbands and came to nurse her. Her son, the Kaiser, now found time to pay her frequent visits, and her brother and defender, the King of England, came to visit her at the end of February 1901. His nephew received him with state honours at Frankfurt and, with unusual tact, withdrew to leave his uncle alone with the dying Empress. She and the King had much to say to each other and little time.

'You are so brave and good for the heavy trial and pain which it pleases God to inflict you with,' the King wrote to her. 'After dear Mama you are the one person in the world who ought not to suffer, for if anyone from her life and virtues is more prepared to go straight to heaven, it is yourself! It often seems to me that it is the bad people that prosper in this world – and not the good ones!'[23]

On 5 August, the Kaiser was standing beside his mother's bed when she breathed her last. A butterfly flew in through the open window and circled the face of the dead Empress and flew out over the rose garden she loved. She had lived long enough to see an Anglo-German understanding between her son and her brother. Although temporary and unsatisfactory and full of stress and misunderstanding, it was a truce that would allow the new century at least a decade of respite.

Her life may seem to have been wasted, a long preparation for a role that she would never play. She had been trained for a throne. Her marriage had been arranged to influence the creation of a liberal, constitutional and united Germany. She had been thwarted by the interminable reign of Emperor William I and the intolerable rule of Bismarck. She could have echoed her brother's lament to her when he was unable to move because of a torn ligament: 'I hardly like to ask them when I am likely to change my position – anyhow the French saying is applicable – *Qui sait attendre?*'[24]

She knew how to wait even less well than her brother did. She was always impetuous and forthright. Her many great qualities withered away during her long attendance at a foreign court, which gave her no more understanding than she gave to it. She was always a stranger in a strange land, except in time of war. Her heart remained in her homeland. Though she tried to be a good Prussian and a good German, she could not forego her essential Englishness for which she received so many wounding criticisms. She was a double patriot in an age that increasingly demanded commitment to a single nation.

Personal royal contacts across artificial frontiers were her birthright, because the kings and queens of the new nations were sometimes foreign-born. These personal contacts were still maintained by her brother in England and her son in Germany. The Emperor was told that, if there were any disagreements between the two governments, he should write to his uncle, the King, who would do his best to smooth matters down.[25] While these last exponents of the art of royal diplomacy were alive and were corresponding with the Tsar and the Austrian Emperor and the King of Italy, an alternative system of Intelligence and conciliation was helping to prevent the outbreak of the First World War. That war did not come until King Edward VII was dead. By its end, the international contacts of royalty and aristocracy would have been swept away together with their power.

The Empress Frederick was fortunate to live in an age when her life was still important to her two countries. She was a woman who was destined to act between her mother and her husband, to work for them both and to be suspected for that. She was loyal to a fault, but loyal to two people in two different nations. She was the heir to a tradition that was the victim of the rise of the modern state. Bismarck was the architect of the unity of Germany, and his commitment to his country made him resist anything he thought alien and persecute anyone he thought a threat to his authority. Both the pride and the misfortunate of the Empress Frederick was to be the eldest daughter of Queen Victoria. She could never forget it, nor could Bismarck.

For a Princess Royal trained in England and wedded to Prussia, it was a tale of two countries. It was the best of times, it was the worst of times, it was the spring of hope, it was the winter of despair; she had everything before her, she had nothing before her, until her time was done.

Source Notes

LIST OF ABBREVIATIONS

RA: The Royal Archives, Windsor Castle
PRO: Public Record Office
FO: Foreign Office

Letters: *The Letters of Queen Victoria, A Selection from Her Majesty's Correspondence*,
   First Series, 1837-61, ed. by A. C. Benson and Viscount Esher, 3 vols. (London,
   1907). Second Series, 1862-85, ed. by G. E. Buckle, 3 vols. (London 1926).
   Third Series, 1886-1901, ed. by G. E. Buckle, 3 vols. (London, 1930).
Further Letters: *Further Letters of Queen Victoria*, from the Archives of the House of
   Brandenburg-Prussia, ed. by Hector Bolitho (London 1938).
Queen Victoria's Journal is preserved in the Royal Archives.
English Empress: *The English Empress, A Study in the Relations between Queen Victoria
   and Her Eldest Daughter*, by Egon Caesar Conte Corti, with an Introduction by
   Wolfgang, Prince of Hesse (London, 1957).
Kronberg Archive: This consists of the Archives of the Princess Royal, later Empress
   Frederick of Germany. The letters and papers are kept at Friedrichshof, Kronberg.
NOTE: The confidential letters and papers sent by the Emperor and Empress Frederick
   to Windsor Castle were all returned to Germany. They are no longer in the Royal
   Archives.

CHAPTER ONE: MINUET BEFORE A WEDDING

1. *The Greville Memoirs, 1814-1860*, ed. L. Strachey and R. Fulford, 8 vols. (London
   1938), IV, p. 338
2. *Letters*, I, 1, p. 237, Queen Victoria to Leopold, King of the Belgians, 12 October
   1839
3. *Letters*, I, 1, p. 321, Queen Victoria to King of the Belgians, 5 January 1841

4. Princess Catherine Radziwill, *The Empress Frederick* (London 1934), p. 45
5. *Letters*, 1, 2, p. 126, Queen Victoria to King of the Belgians, 29 September 1846
6. Radziwill, *The Empress Frederick*, p. 29
7. *Denkwürdigkeiten aus den Papieren des Freihernn Christian Friedrich von Stockmar* (Braunschweig 1872), p. 358
8. RA, M 12/5
9. RA, M 12/39
10. *Denkwürdigkeiten*, p. 391; see also RA, M 12/14
11. RA, M 12/50, 55, 62
12. RA, M 13/68, Lady Lyttelton's Journal, 24 August 1845
13. RA, M 14/50, Queen Victoria for Miss Hildyard, 17 December 1846
14. RA, M 13/55, the Princess Royal to Queen Victoria, October 1844
15. RA, M 12/35
16. RA, M 13/75, 70, Lady Lyttelton's Journal, 27 August, 6 September 1845
17. Baron Ernest von Stockmar, *The Memoirs of Baron Stockmar*, trans. G. A. Mueller, 2 vols. (London 1872), II, p. 207, *note*
18. *Letters*, 1, 2, pp. 183-4, Queen Victoria to King of the Belgians, 1 March 1848
19. *Letters*, 1, 2, pp. 177-9, the King of Prussia to Queen Victoria, 27 February 1848
20. RA, M 15/98, 105
21. *Queen Victoria's Journal*, 1 May 1851
22. Sir Theodore Martin, *Life of the Prince Consort*, 5 vols. (London 1875-80), II, p. 385
23. *Further Letters*, p. 25, Queen Victoria to the Princess Augusta of Prussia, 19 June 1851
24. *Further Letters*, p. 44, 2 April 1854
25. For a fuller understanding of the role of the military attaché, see Alfred Vagts, *The Military Attaché* (Princeton, N.J. 1967)
26. Erich Marcks, *Bismarck, eine Biographie 1815-51* (Stuttgart 1951), p. 472
27. See *George, Duke of Cambridge*, ed. E. Sheppard, 2 vols. (London 1907), I, p. 197
28. RA, M 13/78, Lady Lyttelton to Queen Victoria, 9 December 1845
29. *Queen Victoria's Journal*, 29 and 30 September 1855
30. *Letters*, 1, 3, p. 187, Queen Victoria to King of the Belgians, 22 September 1855
31. RA, Z 61/9, Lord Clarendon to Queen Victoria, 22 September 1855
32. RA, Z 61/12, Queen Victoria to Lord Clarendon, 24 September 1855
33. *The Times*, 3 October 1855
34. RA, Z 61/22, Lord Clarendon to Queen Victoria, 3 October 1855
35. RA, Z 61/29, 36, Lord Augustus Loftus to Lord Clarendon, 9 and 10 October 1855
36. RA, Z 61/46, 47, see the King of Prussia to the Princess of Prussia, 3 January 1856, and her reply to him
37. RA, Z 61/69, Queen Victoria to Lord Palmerston, 26 March 1856
38. Quoted in Egon Corti, *The English Empress* (London 1957), p. 29
39. *Queen Victoria's Journal*, 16 July 1857
40. Anon, *The Empress Frederick: a Memoir* (London 1913), p. 44
41. RA, Z 67/92, Prince Albert to Lord Clarendon, 26 November 1857
42. Prince Albert to Prince Frederick William, 24 February 1857, Kronberg Archive
43. *Letters*, 1, 3, p. 321, Queen Victoria to Lord Clarendon, 25 October 1857

44. See *Correspondence between General Leopold von Gerlach and the Delegate to the Federal Diet, Otto von Bismarck* (Berlin 1893), p. 313, 8 April 1856
45. RA, T 1/136, 161, the Princess Royal to the Prince of Wales, 18 September 1856 and 10 July 1857
46. RA, M 17/31 and 33, the Prince of Wales to Prince Albert, 25 March 1856
47. Queen Victoria to the Princess Royal, 28 July 1858, Kronberg Archive
48. RA, T 2/107, the Princess Royal to the Prince of Wales, 21 December 1859
49. RA, Z 261, Queen Victoria, 'Remarks, Conversations & Reflections', Prince Albert's Birthday, 1857
50. RA, Z 291/20, Queen Victoria, 'Remarks', 20 December 1857
51. RA, Z 261, Queen Victoria, 'Remarks', 8 January 1858

CHAPTER TWO: ADIEU TO ENGLAND

1. RA, T 1/195, the Princess Royal to the Prince of Wales, 31 December 1857
2. Walburga Lady Paget, *Scenes and Memories* (London 1912), pp. 62-4
3. *Queen Victoria's Journal*, 25 January 1858; see also RA, Z 261/31 and 32
4. RA, Z 261/36
5. RA, Z 5/6, the Princess Royal to Queen Victoria, 2 February 1858
6. RA, Z 261
7. Sir Theodore Martin, *Life of the Prince Consort*, IV, p. 169
8. *Dearest Child: Letters between Queen Victoria and the Princess Royal, 1858-1861*, ed. R. Fulford (London 1964), pp. 31-2
9. RA, Z 70/4, Lady Howard de Walden to Lady Caroline Barrington, 4 February 1858
10. RA, Z 62/103, Lord Bloomfield to Lord Clarendon, 6 February 1858
11. RA, Z 70/9, Baron Ernest von Stockmar to Queen Victoria, 7 February 1858
12. For accounts of the ceremonial entry, see RA, Z 70/11 and 19, in which Lady Churchill and the Grand Duchess of Mecklenburg-Strelitz write to Queen Victoria about her daughter's reception in Potsdam and Berlin
13. RA, Z 70/17, Lady Bloomfield to Queen Victoria, 10 February 1858
14. RA, Z 70/26, the Grand Duchess of Mecklenburg-Strelitz to Queen Victoria, 14 February 1858
15. RA, Z 70/39, Lady Churchill to Queen Victoria, 24 February 1858
16. *Dearest Child*, pp. 50-2, 20 February 1858
17. *Queen Victoria's Journal*, 4 March 1858
18. *Dearest Child*, pp. 64-5, 27 February 1858
19. RA, Z 1/8, the Princess Royal to the Prince Consort, 20 February 1858
20. RA, Z 261/74-6
21. *The Greville Memoirs*, V, p. 201
22. *Dearest Child*, p. 138, *note*
23. RA, Z 261/69
24. The Prince Consort to the Princess Royal, 1 December 1858, Kronberg Archive
25. The Prince Consort to the Princess Royal, 22 December 1858, Kronberg Archive
26. *Dearest Child*, p. 141, 27 October 1858
27. RA, Z 63/117, Sir James Clark to Queen Victoria, 31 January 1859
28. RA, Z 261/94

29. RA, Z 261/91-2
30. RA, Z 7/91, Lady Bloomfield to Queen Victoria, 5 March 1859
31. RA, Z 7/113, the Princess Royal to Queen Victoria, 16 April 1859

CHAPTER THREE: DIVIDED LOYALTY

1. Queen Victoria to the Princess Royal, 5 February 1859, Kronberg Archive
2. Queen Victoria to the Princess Royal, 9 April 1859, Kronberg Archive
3. RA, Z 7/113, the Princess Royal to Queen Victoria, 16 April 1859
4. RA, Z 7/120, the Princess Royal to Queen Victoria, 30 April 1859
5. RA, Z 8/6, the Princess Royal to Queen Victoria, 16 June 1859
6. Queen Victoria to the Princess Royal, 18 June 1859, Kronberg Archive
7. RA, Z 2/23, the Princess Royal to the Prince Consort, 18 June 1859
8. RA, Z 2/25, the Princess Royal to the Prince Consort, 25 June and 2 July 1859
9. RA, Z 2/26, the Princess Royal to the Prince Consort, 9 July 1859
10. RA, Z 8/17, the Princess Royal to the Prince Consort, 16 July 1859
11. RA, Z 2/29, the Princess Royal to the Prince Consort, 18 February 1860
12. RA, I 31/85, the Prince Consort to Lord John Russell, 18 March 1860
13. RA, I 30/2, Sir A. Malet to Lord Clarendon, 24 June 1857
14. RA, I 30/77, Sir A. Malet to Lord Malmesbury, 30 June 1858
15. Queen Victoria to the Princess Royal, 2 April 1860, Kronberg Archive
16. Quoted by Sir Theodore Martin in *The Life of the Prince Consort*, V, p. 196. The meeting took place on 25 September 1860
17. See William II, Emperor of Germany, *My Early Life* (London 1926), pp. 9-13
18. RA, I 33/78
19. RA, I 37/63, Lord Clarendon to Lord John Russell, 2 November 1861
20. RA, Z 4/2, the Princess Royal to the Prince Consort, 19 January 1861
21. RA, I 34/20, the Princess Royal to Queen Victoria, 2 January 1861
22. RA, I 34/21, the Princess Royal to Queen Victoria, 4 January 1861
23. RA, I 34/29, Colonel Ponsonby to Sir Charles Phipps, 7 January 1861
24. RA, Z 4/1, the Crown Princess of Prussia (the Princess Royal) to the Prince Consort, 11 January 1861
25. RA, Z 10/63, the Crown Princess to Queen Victoria, 4 March 1861
26. RA, I 35/24, the Crown Princess to the Prince Consort, 15 March 1861
27. RA, Z 4/10, the Crown Princess to the Prince Consort, 8 March 1861
28. Queen Victoria to the Crown Princess, 16 March 1861, Kronberg Archive
29. *Further Letters*, p. 117
30. RA, Z 12/15-16, the Crown Princess to Queen Victoria and the Prince Consort, 25 and 26 September 1861
31. RA, Z 12/23, the Crown Princess to Queen Victoria, 19 October 1861
32. RA, Z 4/36, the Crown Princess to the Prince Consort, 16 November 1861
33. Queen Victoria to Benjamin Disraeli, memorandum, 1862, Hughenden Papers
34. Queen Victoria to the Crown Princess, 18 December 1861, Kronberg Archive
35. RA, Z 12/4, 50, the Crown Princess to Queen Victoria, 20 August and 15 December 1861

SOURCE NOTES

CHAPTER FOUR: BESIEGED BY BISMARCK

1. Theodore Juste, *Le Baron Stockmar* (Brussels 1873), p. 59
2. *Letters*, 2, 1, p. 11, King of the Belgians to Queen Victoria, 16 January 1862
3. RA, I 38/96, Lord Palmerston to Lord John Russell, 9 March 1862
4. RA, I 38/114, Lord Augustus Loftus to Lord John Russell, 13 March 1862
5. RA, Z 13/16, Lord Augustus Loftus to Lord John Russell, 17 May 1862
6. Major-General F. W. Hamilton to Lord John Russell, 22 February 1862. Queen Victoria had obviously asked for the information about the Prussian Army. The Major-General referred to his figures and wrote, 'I trust they are drawn up in conformity with the wishes of Her Majesty'
7. *Further Letters*, pp. 123-6, Queen Victoria to the King of Prussia, 26 March and 23 April 1862
8. Queen Victoria to the Crown Princess, 27 May and 2 July 1862, Kronberg Archive
9. Quoted in Corti, *English Empress* (London 1957) and p. 94. The letter was sent on 19 September 1862; the original is in the Kronberg Archive
10. Prince Otto von Bismarck, *Reflections and Reminiscences*, 2 vols. (London 1898), I, pp. 291-3
11. RA, Z 14/8, the Crown Princess to Queen Victoria, 1 November 1862
12. RA, Z 14/11, 15, the Crown Princess to Queen Victoria, 8 and 23 November 1862
13. *The Correspondence of John Lothrop Motley*, ed. G. Curtis, 2 vols. (London 1889), II, p. 105
14. RA, Z 14/22, the Crown Princess to Queen Victoria, 17 December 1862
15. *Die Gesammelten Werke Bismarcks*, ed. H. von Petersdorff *et al.*, 18 vols. (Berlin 1924-35), XV, pp. 194-5
16. RA, Z 14/27, the Crown Princess to Queen Victoria, 3 January 1863
17. *Aus dem Leben Theodor von Bernhardis*, 6 vols. (Leipzig 1895), V, p. 128
18. *Letters*, 2, 1, pp. 68-9, Queen Victoria to King of the Belgians, 24 February 1863
19. Queen Victoria to the Crown Princess, 14 February 1863, Kronberg Archive
20. *Journals and Letters of Reginald Viscount Esher*, ed. M. Brett, 2 vols. (London 1934), I, pp. 160-1
21. *Letters*, 2, 1, pp. 66-9, Queen Victoria to Lord Granville, 23 February 1863
22. RA, Z 15/15, the Crown Princess to Queen Victoria, 28 April 1863
23. Emperor William II, *My Early Life*, p. 5
24. *Europäischer Geschichtskalender, 1863*, ed. H. Schulthess, (Nördlingen 1864), pp. 130-1
25. RA, Z 15/18, 20, the Crown Princess to Queen Victoria, 11 and 16 May 1863
26. RA, I 40/56, Lord Palmerston to Queen Victoria, 29 May 1863
27. RA, Z 15/19, the Crown Princess to Queen Victoria, 7 April 1863
28. RA, I 40/57, the Crown Princess to Queen Victoria, 1 June 1863
29. There is a full account of the exchange of letters between the Crown Prince and the King of Prussia in Corti, *English Empress*, pp. 103-6
30. RA, I 40/62, the Crown Princess to Queen Victoria, 8 June 1863
31. Queen Victoria to the Crown Princess, 24 May and 8 June 1863, Kronberg Archive
32. RA, I 40/80, the Crown Princess to Queen Victoria, 11 June 1863 (misdated 21 June 1863)

33. RA, I 40/80, the Crown Princess to Queen Victoria, 11 June 1863 (misdated 21 June 1863)
34. Queen Victoria to the Crown Princess, 13 June 1863, Kronberg Archive
35. Corti, *English Empress*, p. 105
36. RA, I 40/68, Sir A. Buchanan to Lord John Russell, 13 June 1863
37. RA, Z 15/35, the Crown Princess to Queen Victoria, 29 June 1863
38. M. Busch, *Bismarck: Some Secret Pages of His History* (London 1899), p. 460
39. RA, Z 15/36, the Crown Princess to Queen Victoria, 3 July 1863
40. See Fritz Stern's important *Gold and Iron: Bismarck, Bleichröder, and the Building of the German Empire* (New York 1977), pp. 30-1
41. *Letters of the Empress Frederick*, ed. Sir F. Ponsonby (London 1928), pp. 46-7
42. RA, I 41/1, the Crown Princess to Queen Victoria, 1 August 1863
43. RA, I 42/2, Queen Victoria to the Crown Princess, 5 August 1863
44. *Memoirs and Letters of the Rt Hon. Sir Robert Morier*, ed. Mrs R. Wemyss, 2 vols. (London 1911), I, p. 343
45. *Letters*, 2, 1, p. 310, King of the Belgians to Queen Victoria, 21 September 1863
46. RA, I 41/32, Lord Clarendon on the Congress of Sovereigns at Frankfurt, 27 August 1863
47. RA, I 41/43, minute by Lord Granville of a conversation with Bismarck at the Rosenau, 21 August 1863
48. RA, I 41/45, Queen Victoria's memorandum on her meeting with the King of Prussia, 31 August 1863
49. Queen Victoria to the Crown Princess, 5 September 1863, Kronberg Archive
50. RA, Z 15/50, the Crown Princess to Queen Victoria, 8 September 1863
51. Quoted in A. J. P. Taylor's brilliant biography *Bismarck: The Man and the Statesman* (London 1955), p. 59
52. Corti, *English Empress*, p. 112
53. Corti, *English Empress*, p. 113
54. *Letters*, 2, 1, p. 117, Queen Victoria to King Leopold of the Belgians, 19 November 1863

CHAPTER FIVE: TO US GERMANS

1. RA, Z 16/16, the Crown Princess to Queen Victoria, 8 February 1864
2. *Letters*, 2, 1, p. 145, Lord Palmerston to Queen Victoria, 8 January 1864
3. Queen Victoria to the Crown Princess, 3 February 1864, Kronberg Archive
4. Queen Victoria to the Crown Princess, 13 February 1864, Kronberg Archive
5. RA, Z 16/37, the Crown Princess to Queen Victoria, 13 April 1864
6. RA, Z 16/41, the Crown Princess to Queen Victoria, 11 May 1864
7. *Letters*, 2, 1, pp. 282-3, Queen Victoria to King Leopold, 30 June 1864
8. RA Z 16/50, the Crown Princess to Queen Victoria, 26 May 1864
9. See Corti, *English Empress*, p. 125
10. Queen Victoria to the Crown Princess, 2 March 1864, Kronberg Archive
11. RA, Z 16/61, the Crown Princess to Queen Victoria, 16 July 1864
12. *Further Letters*, pp. 152-3, Queen Victoria to the Queen of Prussia, 13 July 1864
13. RA, Z 16/65, the Crown Princess to Queen Victoria, 16 August 1864

14. Queen Victoria to the Crown Princess, 27 January 1865, Kronberg Archive
15. Elisabeth zu Putlitz, *Gustav zu Putlitz*, 2 vols. (Berlin 1894), II, pp. 40–50
16. RA, I 42/8, R. B. Morier to Lord John Russell, 12 November 1864
17. RA, Z 17/29, the Crown Princess to Queen Victoria, 21 January 1865
18. *Alice, Grand Duchess of Hesse: Biographical Sketch and Letters*, ed. Princess Helena of Schleswig-Holstein (London 1884), p. 112, Princess Alice to Queen Victoria, 11 December 1865
19. *Letters*, 2, 1, p. 271, Queen Victoria to King of the Belgians, 3 August 1865
20. RA, Z 17/82, the Crown Princess to Queen Victoria, 1 August 1865
21. See Corti, *English Empress*, p. 145. Bismarck's sneers were recorded by the Crown Prince in his diaries, selections from which were published in Leipzig in 1929
22. *Die Gesammelten Werke*, XIV, p. 707, Bismarck to Thile, 23 October 1865
23. RA, I 42/10, Lord Napier to Lord John Russell, 18 November 1865
24. Queen Victoria to the Crown Princess, 5 April 1865, Kronberg Archive
25. *Letters*, 2, 1, pp. 449–50, Queen Victoria to Lord Charles Fitzroy, 20 July 1867

CHAPTER SIX: TO WIN, TO LOSE

1. Bismarck, *Reflections and Reminiscences*, I, pp. 164–5
2. RA, I 43/75, Lord Cowley to Lord Clarendon, 10 March 1866
3. RA, I 43/30, Consul-General Crowe to Lord Clarendon, 21 February 1866
4. *Diaries of Frederick III*, 19 and 23 February 1866, Kronberg Archive
5. RA, Z 18/26, the Crown Princess to Queen Victoria, 20 February 1866
6. RA, I 43/47, Lord Augustus Loftus to Lord Clarendon, 3 March 1866
7. RA, I 43/98, 100, Lord Augustus Loftus to Lord Clarendon, 17 March 1866
8. RA, Z 18/34, the Crown Princess to Queen Victoria, 16 March 1866
9. RA, I 43/101, Lord Clarendon to Queen Victoria, 18 March 1866
10. RA, I 43/105, the Crown Princess to Queen Victoria, 20 March 1866
11. RA, Z 18/39, the Crown Princess to Queen Victoria, 4 April 1866
12. RA, I 43/105, the Crown Princess to Queen Victoria, 20 March 1866
13. Queen Victoria to the Crown Princess, 24 March 1866, Kronberg Archive
14. RA, I 43/118, Lord Augustus Loftus to Lord Clarendon, 24 March 1866
15. RA, I 43/124, General Grey to Earl Russell, 26 March 1866. General Grey was the Queen's personal adviser on domestic and foreign affairs
16. RA, I 43/130, Earl Russell to Queen Victoria, 27 March 1866
17. RA, I 43/142, Queen Victoria to the Crown Prince of Prussia, 28 March 1866
18. RA, Z 18/38, the Crown Princess to Queen Victoria, 31 March 1866
19. RA, I 43/143, the Duchess of Coburg to Queen Victoria, 28 March 1866
20. RA, I 43/187, Lord Augustus Loftus to Lord Clarendon, 7 April 1866
21. For an excellent summary of Bismarck's manœuvring before the war against Austria see Alan Palmer's *Bismarck* (London 1976), p. 114; see also Bismarck, *Reflections and Reminiscences*, II, 64
22. RA, I 44/5, Queen Victoria to the King of Prussia, 10 April 1866
23. RA, I 44/24, Lord Augustus Loftus to Lord Clarendon, 14 April 1866
24. Full details of this temporary success of the 'Coburg intrigue' can be found in RA, I 44/51, Consul-General Crowe to Lord Clarendon, 19 April 1866. Another version

of the intrigue from the Austrian point of view is in Chester W. Clark, *Franz Joseph and Bismarck: The Diplomacy of Austria Before the War of 1866* (Cambridge, Mass. 1934), pp. 375–9

25. RA, I 44/72, Lord Clarendon to Queen Victoria, 25 April 1866
26. RA, I 44/95, Lord Augustus Loftus to Lord Clarendon, 28 April 1866
27. RA, I 44/171, Lord Augustus Loftus to Lord Clarendon, 12 May 1866
28. RA, Z 18/46, 48 the Crown Princess to Queen Victoria, 9 and 16 May 1866
29. Queen Victoria to the Crown Princess, 12 May 1866, Kronberg Archive
30. RA, I 44/132, 156, Lord Augustus Loftus to Lord Clarendon, 4 and 5 May 1866
31. RA, I 44/144, memorandum of Queen Victoria on her meeting with Lord Clarendon, 6 May 1866
32. RA, Z 18/47, the Crown Princess to Queen Victoria, 12 May 1866
33. Queen Victoria to the Crown Princess, 9 May 1866, Kronberg Archive
34. RA, I 44/155, Lord Clarendon to Queen Victoria, 7 May 1866
35. Queen Victoria to the Crown Princess, 19 May 1866, Kronberg Archive
36. The Crown Princess to the Crown Prince, 11 June 1866, Kronberg Archive
37. RA, Z 18/60, the Crown Princess to Queen Victoria, 19 June 1866
38. Emperor William II, *My Early Life*, p. 5
39. RA, Z 18/66, the Crown Princess to Queen Victoria, 9 July 1866
40. RA, Z 18/63, the Crown Princess to Queen Victoria, 30 June 1866
41. Busch, *Bismarck*, p. 196
42. RA, I 45/141, Colonel Walker to Sir Henry Stanley, 4 July 1866
43. Cardinal Antonelli actually said, 'Casca il mondo'. The quotation comes from Stern, *Gold and Iron*, p. 88
44. RA, I 46/21, Lord Augustus Loftus to Sir Henry Stanley, 14 July 1866
45. The Crown Prince to the Crown Princess, 20 July 1866, Kronberg Archive
46. Quoted in Corti, *English Empress*, p. 155. His account of these negotiations from the Crown Prince's point of view is important
47. The Crown Prince to the Crown Princess, 25 July 1866, Kronberg Archive
48. Bismarck, *Reflections and Reminiscences*, II, p. 52
49. RA, I 46/139, Princess Alice of Hesse to Queen Victoria, 31 July 1866 •
50. RA, I 46/124, Robert Morier to General Grey, 29 July 1866
51. RA, I 46/156, Princess Alice of Hesse to Queen Victoria, 6 August 1866
52. RA, I 45/147, the King of Saxony to Queen Victoria, 6 July 1866
53. RA, I 46/110, Queen Victoria to the King of Saxony, 28 July 1866
54. *Letters*, 2, 1, p. 356, George Duke of Cambridge to Queen Victoria, 7 July 1866
55. RA, Z 18/65, 72, the Crown Princess to Queen Victoria, 16 and 27 July 1866
56. RA, Z 18/76, the Crown Princess to Queen Victoria, 10 August 1866
57. Queen Victoria to the Crown Princess, 12 August 1866, Kronberg Archive
58. RA, I 46/124, Robert Morier to General Grey, 29 July 1866
59. RA, I 47/16, the Crown Princess to Queen Victoria, 19 August 1866

CHAPTER SEVEN: WAITING ON CEREMONY

1. Quoted in Rudolf Olden, *History of Liberty in Germany* (London 1946), p. 106
2. RA, I 48/96, Lord Augustus Loftus to Lord Clarendon, memorandum on a meeting with the King of Prussia, 12 December 1868

3. RA, I 48/115, Lord Augustus Loftus to Lord Clarendon, memorandum on a meeting with Bismarck, 17 April 1869
4. RA, Z 19/85, the Crown Princess to Queen Victoria, 20 April 1867
5. Queen Victoria to the Crown Princess, 24 April 1867, Kronberg Archive
6. *Further Letters*, pp. 163-4, Queen Victoria to the King of Prussia, 22 April 1867
7. RA, Z 20/1, the Crown Princess to Queen Victoria, 27 April 1867
8. RA, Z 20/13, the Crown Princess to Queen Victoria, 10 June 1867
9. Queen Victoria to the Crown Princess, 6 and 10 July 1867, Kronberg Archive
10. *Letters*, 2, 1, p. 369, Queen Victoria to the Prince of Wales, 16 October 1866
11. The Crown Princess to the Crown Prince, 9 November 1866, Kronberg Archive
12. RA, Z 19/67, the Crown Princess to Queen Victoria, 2 March 1867
13. RA, Z 23/23, the Crown Princess to Queen Victoria, 2 March 1869
14. RA, Z 24/42, the Crown Princess to Queen Victoria, 25 May 1870
15. RA, Z 20/74, the Crown Princess to Queen Victoria, 10 December 1867
16. RA, Z 23/16, the Crown Princess to Queen Victoria, 6 February 1869
17. RA, Z 24/5, the Crown Princess to Queen Victoria, 7 October 1869
18. RA, Z 19/21, the Crown Princess to Queen Victoria, 17 November 1866
19. RA, I 48/47, the Crown Princess to Queen Victoria, 27 August 1867
20. RA, I 48/59, Sir Henry Stanley to Lord Derby, 3 October 1867
21. RA, Z 19/20, the Crown Princess to Queen Victoria, 16 November 1866
22. Queen Victoria to the Crown Princess, 2 March 1870, Kronberg Archive
23. RA, Z 24/10, the Crown Princess to Queen Victoria, 31 October 1869
24. RA, Z 24/25, the Crown Princess to Queen Victoria, 14 January 1870
25. Queen Victoria to the Crown Princess, 13 February 1867 and 5 March 1870, Kronberg Archive
26. RA, Z 20/34, the Crown Princess to Queen Victoria, 17 August 1867
27. Emperor William II, *My Early Life*, p. 18
28. RA, Z 23/8, the Crown Princess to Queen Victoria, 16 January 1869
29. RA, Z 23/11, the Crown Princess to Queen Victoria, 26 January 1869
30. RA, Z 21/42, Prince William of Prussia to Queen Victoria, 20 May 1868
31. William II, *My Early Life*, pp. 36-7
32. RA, I 48/142, Lord Clarendon to Queen Victoria, 26 January 1870. When the Disraeli ministry lost an election and Gladstone became prime minister, Queen Victoria tried to stop Lord Clarendon's appointment as Foreign Secretary by what Gladstone called a 'Court manœuvre'
33. RA, I 48/148, Lord Augustus Loftus to Lord Clarendon, 8 February 1870
34. RA, I 48/174, Lord Augustus Loftus to Lord Clarendon, 18 March 1870

CHAPTER EIGHT: EMPIRE

1. Busch, *Bismarck*, p. 6
2. Busch, *Bismarck*, p. 16
3. RA, I 63/1, the Crown Princess to Queen Victoria, 12 March 1870
4. RA, I 63/94, Lord Augustus Loftus to Lord Granville, 16 July 1870
5. RA, I 63/73, Lord Lyons to Lord Granville, 12 July 1870
6. Busch, *Bismarck*, p. 20

7. *French Ministerial Statement* as reported by Reuter's and printed in *The Pall Mall Gazette*, 14 July 1870
8. Bismarck, *Reflections and Reminiscences*, II, pp. 95–100
9. RA, I 63/70, Lord Augustus Loftus to Lord Granville, 14 July 1870
10. RA, Z 24/70 and I 63/89, the Crown Princess to Queen Victoria, 13 and 16 July 1870
11. *The War Diary of the Emperor Frederick III*, ed. A. Allison (London 1927), pp. 4–7, 12–15 July 1870
12. RA, I 63/79, Lord Granville to Queen Victoria, 15 July 1870
13. RA, I 63/116, the Crown Princess to Queen Victoria, 18 July 1870
14. RA, I 63/129, Queen Victoria to Lord Granville, 20 July 1870
15. RA, I 63/128, Queen Victoria to the Crown Princess, 20 July 1870
16. RA, Z 24/74, the Crown Princess to Queen Victoria, 26 July 1870
17. RA, I 63/170, Sir Robert Morier to Queen Victoria, 25 July 1870
18. RA, I 63/176, the King of Prussia to Queen Victoria, 26 July 1870
19. RA, I 64/20, Sir Robert Morier to Lord Granville, 31 July 1870
20. RA, I 64/94, the Crown Princess to Queen Victoria, 9 August 1870
21. Quoted in Stern, *Gold and Iron*, p. 263. Chapter Eleven, 'The Fourth Estate', is a brilliant examination of Bismarck's manipulation and corruption of the press
22. RA, I 64/16, General Walker to Lord Augustus Loftus, 30 July 1870
23. RA, I 64/34, Sir Robert Morier to Lord Granville, 1 August 1870
24. *War Diary*, p. 19, 1 August 1870
25. RA, I 64/84, General Walker to Lord Augustus Loftus, 8 August 1870
26. *War Diary*, p. 63, 19 August 1870
27. RA, Z 25/2, the Crown Princess to Queen Victoria, 4 August 1870
28. Busch, *Bismarck*, p. 40
29. Busch, *Bismarck*, p. 43
30. *War Diary*, p. 88, 1 September 1870
31. Busch, *Bismarck*, p. 66
32. *War Diary*, p. 91, 1 September 1870
33. Busch, *Bismarck*, pp. 60–1
34. RA, I 65/42, the Crown Princess to Queen Victoria, 6 September 1870
35. RA, I 65/33, Lord Lyons to Lord Granville, 6 September 1870
36. RA, I 65/150, Lord Lyons to Lord Granville, 19 September 1870
37. *War Diary*, p. 75, 28 August 1870
38. RA, I 67/9, the Crown Princess to Queen Victoria, 6 November 1870
39. *War Diary*, p. 222, 14 December 1870
40. Bismarck, *Reflections and Reminiscences*, II, p. 123
41. *War Diary*, p. 241, 31 December 1870
42. Queen Victoria to the Crown Princess, 20 July 1870, Kronberg Archive
43. Quoted in Palmer, *Bismarck*, p. 157
44. RA, Z 25/44, the Crown Princess to Queen Victoria, 17 January 1871
45. RA, I 68/68, Princess Alice of Hesse to Queen Victoria, 25 January 1871
46. Bismarck, *Die Gesammelten Werke*, XIV, 2, p. 810
47. RA, I 67/104, Mr Odo Russell to Lord Granville, 18 December 1870
48. RA, I 68/142, the Crown Princess to Queen Victoria, 4 March 1871
49. RA, I 67/89, Mr Odo Russell to Lord Granville, 14 December 1870

CHAPTER NINE: HOW LONG, O LORD, HOW LONG?

1. Busch, *Bismarck*, p. 213
2. RA, I 49/39, Mr Crowe to Lord Granville, 15 November 1871
3. Felix Philippi, quoted in Gordon A. Craig, *Germany, 1866–1945* (New York 1978), p. 81
4. RA, I 50/30, Lord Odo Russell to Lord Derby, 16 October 1874; see also Russell's letter to Lord Granville, 18 October 1872, in *Letters from the Berlin Embassy, 1871–4*, ed. P. Knaplund (Washington, D.C. 1944), p. 71
5. RA, Z 25/63, the Crown Princess to Queen Victoria, 24 March 1871
6. RA, I 50/31, Colonel Ponsonby to Lord Derby, 19 November 1974
7. RA, I 49/140, the remark was made by Lord Odo Russell to Lord Otto Fitzgerald who, as her representative at the Queen Dowager's funeral, wrote to Queen Victoria on 20 December 1873
8. RA, Z 67/52, Queen Victoria to Prince William of Prussia, 28 August 1874
9. RA, Z 28/55, the Crown Princess to Queen Victoria, 29 August 1874
10. RA, Z 26/12, the Crown Princess to Queen Victoria, 9 September 1871
11. Busch, *Bismarck*, pp. 306–7
12. RA, I 49/98, Lady Emily Russell to Queen Victoria, 15 March 1873
13. Quoted in Taylor, *Bismarck*, p. 147
14. RA, I 50/11, Sir Robert Morier to Lord Granville, 27 March 1874
15. RA, I 49/93, Lord Odo Russell to Lord Granville, 2 March 1873
16. *Letters*, 2, 2, p. 155
17. RA, Z 64/78, 82, the Crown Princess to Queen Victoria, 19 and 26 December 1876
18. Queen Victoria to the Crown Princess, 30 October 1877, Kronberg Archive
19. *The Times*, 20 February 1878
20. RA, Z 65/31, Colonel A. Ellis to Queen Victoria, 19 February 1878
21. See Corti, *English Empress*, p. 127
22. See Lothar Gall's important re-evaluation, *Bismarck: Der Weisse Revolutionär* (Frankfurt/Berlin, 1980), pp 508–14
23. RA, I 50/108, Queen Victoria to Emperor Alexander II, 10 May 1875
24. RA, I 50/105, Lord Derby to General Ponsonby, 10 May 1875
25. RA, I 50/116, Lord Odo Russell to Lord Derby, 11 May 1875
26. RA, I 50/132, Queen Victoria to the Crown Princess, 8 June 1875
27. RA, Z 29/35, the Crown Princess to Queen Victoria, 12 and 19 June 1875
28. RA, I 50/128, Emperor William I to Queen Victoria, 3 June 1875
29. RA, I 50/136, Lord Derby to General Ponsonby, 14 June 1875
30. RA, Z 64/156, Lady Emily Russell to Queen Victoria, 10 February 1877
31. RA, Z 64/108, the Crown Princess to Queen Victoria, 10 February 1877.
32. RA, Z 28/10, the Crown Princess to Queen Victoria, 28 February 1874
33. See Gall, *Bismarck*, pp 516–20 for an analysis of the Kissinger Dictate and of Bismarck's policy after 1875
34. *Letters of the Empress Frederick*, p. 156, the Crown Princess to Queen Victoria, 19 December 1877
35. RA, I 51/122, Louise Grand Duchess of Baden to Queen Victoria, 11 May 1878
36. RA, Z 30/4, the Crown Princess to Queen Victoria, 4 June 1878

37. RA, I 51/159, the Crown Princess to Queen Victoria, 7 June 1878
38. *The Times*, 16 August 1878
39. Busch, *Bismarck*, p. 343
40. RA, I 53/13, Louise Grand Duchess of Baden to Queen Victoria, 14 August 1878
41. Busch, *Bismarck*, p. 356

CHAPTER TEN: ANGUISH AND OMENS

1. RA, Z 32/1, the Crown Princess to Queen Victoria, 15 December 1878
2. RA, Z 65/85, the Crown Princess to Queen Victoria, 27 March 1879
3. RA, Z 33/16, the Crown Princess to Queen Victoria, 18 June 1879
4. RA, Z 32/6, the Crown Princess to Queen Victoria, 1 January 1879
5. RA, Z 31/94, 95, the Crown Princess to Queen Victoria, 18 and 26 September 1878
6. RA, Z 33/34 and 34/26, the Crown Princess to Queen Victoria, 11 September 1879 and 24 May 1880
7. William II, *My Early Life*, p. 67
8. William II, *My Early Life*, p. 61
9. RA, Z 64/86, Lord Beaconsfield to Queen Victoria, 21 January 1877
10. Salisbury Mss, Vol. A 61/153-5, Colonel L. V. Swaine's memoranda to Lord Salisbury, 20 November 1887
11. RA, U 34/8, Prince William to the Crown Princess, 17 July 1879
12. RA, Z 34/6, the Crown Princess to Queen Victoria, 26 January 1880
13. RA, Z 34/9, the Crown Princess to Queen Victoria, 13 February 1880
14. RA, Z 34/40, the Crown Princess to Queen Victoria, 5 August 1880
15. RA, I 53/26, 28, 31, Lord Torrington to Queen Victoria, 26, 27 and 28 February 1881
16. RA, Z 35/6, the Crown Princess to Queen Victoria, 28 February 1881
17. RA, Z 35/53, the Crown Princess to Queen Victoria, 5 November 1887
18. *The Morning Post*, 9 January 1882
19. RA, Z 36/5, the Crown Princess to Queen Victoria, 18 January 1882
20. *Letters of the Empress Frederick*, pp. 192-3
21. RA, Z 35/12, the Crown Princess to Queen Victoria, 28 March 1881
22. Corti, *English Empress*, p. 212; Karl Marx was interviewed by Sir M. E. Grant Duff, MP. The full report is in the Kronberg Archive.
23. RA, I 53/20, the Crown Princess to Queen Victoria, 25 January 1881
24. See Palmer, *Bismarck*, p. 226
25. *Letters of the Empress Frederick*, p. 195
26. Corti, *English Empress*, pp. 222-3
27. RA, Z 30/14, the Crown Princess to Queen Victoria, 1 December 1883
28. J. Rennell Rodd, *Social and Diplomatic Memories, 1884-1893* (London 1922), p. 50
29. Busch, *Bismarck*, p. 481
30. RA, Z 37/1, the Crown Princess to Queen Victoria, 15 September 1883
31. Busch, *Bismarck*, p. 479
32. Busch, *Bismarck*, p. 481
33. Corti, *English Empress*, p. 219
34. Corti, *English Empress*, p. 227
35. RA, Z 30/26, the Crown Princess to Queen Victoria, 30 October 1885
36. RA, Z 38/38, the Crown Princess to Queen Victoria, 5 October 1886

37. See *Mitregenten und fremde Hände in Deutschland* (Switzerland 1887); also Busch, *Bismarck*, pp. 483–4
38. RA, I 55/19, Sir Garnet Wolseley to Queen Victoria, 3 January 1886

CHAPTER ELEVEN: AT THE THROAT

1. Corti, *English Empress*, p. 237
2. RA, Z 39/9, the Crown Princess to Queen Victoria, 15 March 1887
3. RA, Z 39/23, the Crown Princess to Queen Victoria, 17 May 1887
4. See the diary of General von Waldersee, 22 May 1887; also Corti, *English Empress*, p. 241
5. Corti, *English Empress*, pp. 307–8
6. RA, Z 39/23, the Crown Princess to Queen Victoria, 17 May 1887
7. RA, Z 39/25, the Crown Princess to Queen Victoria, 25 May 1887
8. Queen Victoria to the Crown Princess, 20 May 1887, Kronberg Archive
9. RA, Z 39/29, the Crown Princess to Queen Victoria, 27 May 1887
10. Queen Victoria to the Crown Princess, 26 May 1887, Kronberg Archive
11. RA, Z 39/33, the Crown Princess to Queen Victoria, 2 June 1887
12. RA, Z 39/36, the Crown Princess to Queen Victoria, 4 June 1887
13. RA, Z 39/34, the Crown Princess to Queen Victoria, 3 June 1887
14. RA, Z 39/25, the Crown Princess to Queen Victoria, 20 May 1887
15. RA, Z 66/64, Sir Morell Mackenzie to the Crown Princess, 8 August 1887
16. Malet Mss, FO 343/8/85–6, Sir Edward Malet to Lord Salisbury, 15 October 1887
17. Sir Morell Mackenzie, *The Fatal Illness of Frederick the Noble* (London 1888), pp. 65–6. This is a self-serving work, and of the many rejoinders to it in Germany and elsewhere, the best remains R. Scott Stevenson's biography, *Morell Mackenzie* (London 1946)
18. RA, Z 66/109, Prince William of Germany to Queen Victoria, 11 November 1887
19. RA, Z 38/88, the Crown Princess to Queen Victoria, 16 November 1887
20. Stevenson, *Morell Mackenzie*, p. 94
21. RA, Z 38/97, the Crown Princess to Queen Victoria, 29 November 1887
22. Malet Mss, FO 343/2/250–2, Lord Salisbury to Sir E. Malet, 16 November 1887
23. RA, Z 66/130, Lady Ponsonby to Queen Victoria, 3 December 1887
24. RA, Z 40/4, the Crown Princess to Queen Victoria, 11 January 1888
25. RA, Z 66/142, Lady Ponsonby to Queen Victoria, 13 January 1888
26. RA, Z 38/105, the Crown Princess to Queen Victoria, 15 December 1887
27. RA, Z 66/136, Lady Ponsonby to Queen Victoria, 25 December 1887
28. Corti, *English Empress*, p. 254
29. Corti, *English Empress*, p. 255
30. Corti, *English Empress*, p. 256
31. Corti, *English Empress*, p. 262
32. RA, Z 41/23, 24, the Crown Princess to Queen Victoria, 26 and 28 February 1888
33. Radziwill, *The Empress Frederick*, p. 185
34. RA, Z 68/11, Sir E. Malet to Queen Victoria, 9 March 1888

CHAPTER TWELVE: THE SHORT REIGN

1. RA, Z 68/34, Arthur Ellis to Sir Henry Ponsonby, 16 March 1888
2. *The Times*, 16 March 1888
3. RA, Z 41/27, the Empress Frederick to Queen Victoria, 16 March 1888. The Princess Royal chose the title Empress Frederick of Germany in preference to Empress Victoria in order to preserve her husband's name and to distinguish herself from her mother, Queen Victoria, Empress of India
4. PRO, Lord Salisbury to Sir E. Malet, 14 March 1888
5. The Empress Frederick's Diary, quoted in Corti, *English Empress*, pp. 285-6
6. Ludwig Bamberger, *Bismarcks grosses Spiel*, ed. E. Feder (Frankfurt 1932), p. 351
7. Ludwig Bamberger, *Bismarcks grosses Spiel*, ed. E. Feder (Frankfurt 1932), pp. 357-9
8. PRO, Sir E. Malet to Lord Salisbury, cipher telegram, 5 April 1888
9. *Letters of the Empress Frederick*, p. 296, Queen Victoria to Sir Henry Ponsonby, 9 April 1888
10. Mackenzie, *The Fatal Illness*, pp. 148-9
11. Stevenson, *Morell Mackenzie*, p. 123
12. PRO, Lord Salisbury to Sir E. Malet, 2 May 1888
13. Corti, *English Empress*, p. 76
14. *Queen Victoria's Journal*, 24 and 25 April 1888
15. Busch, *Bismarck*, pp. 490-1
16. Malet Mss, FO 343/9/64-5, Sir E. Malet to Lord Salisbury, 28 April 1888
17. *Queen Victoria's Journal*, 25 April 1888
18. *Queen Victoria's Journal*, 26 April 1888
19. RA, Z 68/63, Sir E. Malet to Queen Victoria, 17 May 1888
20. RA, I 56/45, Sir E. Malet to Lord Salisbury, 28 April 1888
21. Corti, *English Empress*, p. 291
22. RA, Z 41/40, 42, the Empress Frederick to Queen Victoria, 28 April and 2 May 1888
23. RA, Z 41/46, the Empress Frederick to Queen Victoria, 9 May 1888
24. The Empress Frederick's Diary, 24 May 1888, quoted in Corti, *English Empress*, p. 292
25. See Radziwill, *The Empress Frederick*, p. 215
26. The Empress Frederick's Diary, quoted in Corti, *English Empress*, pp. 295-6
27. RA, Z 42/64, the Empress Frederick to Queen Victoria, 15 June 1888
28. The Empress Frederick's Diary, quoted in Corti, *English Empress*, pp. 302-3
29. RA, Z 68/106, Sir E. Malet to Queen Victoria, 16 June 1888
30. Malet Mss, FO 343/9/75-7, Lord Salisbury to Sir E. Malet, 22 June 1888
31. Busch, *Bismarck*, p. 491
32. RA, Z 68/131, Sir E. Malet to Lord Salisbury, 24 June 1888
33. The Empress Frederick's Diary, quoted in Corti, *English Empress*, p. 304

CHAPTER THIRTEEN: OLD SCORES, NEW PLACES

1. RA, Z 43/1, the Empress Frederick to Queen Victoria, 13 September 1888
2. RA, Z 41/66, the Empress Frederick to Queen Victoria, 20 June 1888

3. RA, I 56/77, Queen Victoria to Sir Henry Ponsonby, 27 June 1888
4. RA, Z 68/154, Lord Salisbury to Queen Victoria, 15 July 1888
5. RA, Z 42/18, the Empress Frederick to Queen Victoria, 20 July 1888
6. See Professor Ernst von Bergmann *et al.*, *Die Krankheit Kaiser Friedrich des Dritten* (Berlin 1888)
7. RA, Z 43/25, the Empress Frederick to Queen Victoria, 18 October 1888
8. RA, Z 44/33, the Empress Frederick to Queen Victoria, 27 April 1889
9. The Empress Frederick's Diary, quoted in Corti, *English Empress*, p. 316
10. RA, Z 280/55, 57, 58, the Empress Frederick to Queen Victoria, 24, 26 and 27 September 1888
11. RA, Z 280/60, 61, the Empress Frederick to Queen Victoria, 6 and 8 October 1888
12. F. Greenwood in *The Times*, 5 January 1889. For Morier's part, see Agatha Ramm, *Sir Robert Morier: Envoy and Ambassador in the Age of Imperialism, 1876-1893* (Oxford 1973), pp. 270-304
13. Malet Mss, FO 343/10/36-40, Sir E. Malet to Lord Salisbury, 17 and 19 January 1889
14. See *The Times*, 9 January 1889
15. RA, Z 43/27, 29, 30, 31, the Empress Frederick to Queen Victoria, 20, 23, 27 and 30 October 1888
16. Ponsonby Mss, FO 800/3/182-3, Colonel L. Swaine to Sir H. Ponsonby, 4 July 1888
17. RA, Z I 56/84, the Emperor William II of Germany to Queen Victoria, 6 July 1888
18. RA, Z I 56/95, Queen Victoria to Lord Salisbury, 24 October 1888
19. RA, I 57/20, Sir E. Malet to Lord Salisbury, 30 March 1889
20. RA, Z 280/71, Lord Salisbury to Queen Victoria, 1 November 1888
21. Malet Mss, FO 343/3/20-5, Lord Salisbury to Sir E. Malet, 20 February 1889
22. RA, Z 43/32, the Empress Frederick to Queen Victoria, 2 November 1888
23. RA, Add. A 4/4, the Prince of Wales to the Empress Frederick, 10 April 1889
24. RA, Add. A 4/16, the Prince of Wales to the Empress Frederick, 4 July 1889
25. RA, I 57/33, the Emperor William II to Sir E. Malet, 14 June 1889
26. Ponsonby Mss, FO 800/3/192-3, Colonel L. Swaine to Sir H. Ponsonby, 8 March 1889
27. RA, Z 45/26, 41, the Empress Frederick to Queen Victoria, 13 July and 17 August 1889
28. See Prince William to the Emperor William I, 14 November 1880, reprinted in *My Early Life*, appendix 6, pp. 308-13
29. RA, Z 46/2, the Emperor William II to Queen Victoria, 24 August 1889
30. RA, I 57/53, the Emperor William II to Queen Victoria, 17 August 1889
31. RA, I 57/70, Mr E. Monson to Lord Salisbury, 31 October 1889
32. RA, I 57/75, the Emperor William II to Queen Victoria, 22 December 1889
33. RA, I 58/21, the Emperor William II to Queen Victoria, 24 February 1890
34. RA, Z 69/112, the Empress Frederick to Queen Victoria, 11 January 1890
35. RA, I 58/16, Sir E. Malet to Lord Salisbury, 12 February 1890
36. RA, I 58/34, memorandum of a conversation by the Emperor William II to Sir E. Malet, 27 March 1890
37. RA, I 58/32, the Emperor William II to Queen Victoria, 27 March 1890
38. RA, I 59/2, Colonel F. S. Russell to Lord Salisbury, 13 February 1891

39. RA, I 58/39, Lord Salisbury to Queen Victoria, 7 April 1890
40. RA, Z 69/123, the Empress Frederick to Queen Victoria, 25 March 1890
41. *Queen Victoria's Journal*, 26 April 1890
42. RA, Z 49/49, the Empress Frederick to Queen Victoria, 21 December 1890
43. Corti, *English Empress*, p. 337
44. RA, Add. A 4/25, the Prince of Wales to the Empress Frederick, 27 February 1891
45. RA, Z 50/45, the Empress Frederick to Queen Victoria, 12 June 1891

CHAPTER FOURTEEN: RETIREMENT AND REQUIEM

1. Paul Kennedy's important work, *The Rise of Anglo-German Antagonism 1860-1914*, (London 1981) makes clear how fundamental the differences were between the two nations, and how personal relationships and royal diplomacy were less and less able to bring them together
2. RA, Z 56/20, the Empress Frederick to Queen Victoria, 21 June 1894
3. Salisbury Mss, A/83/123, Queen Victoria to Lord Salisbury, cipher telegram, 24 October 1898
4. Salisbury Mss, A/114/51-2, Lord Dufferin to Lord Salisbury, 10 January 1896
5. RA, I 60/4, Queen Victoria to Sir H. Ponsonby, 15 January 1894
6. RA, I 60/64, the Emperor William II to Queen Victoria, 24 April 1894
7. RA, I 59/80, 98 the Emperor William II to Queen Victoria, 22 May 1892 and 28 January 1893
8. Salisbury Mss, A/120/67-70, Sir F. Lascelles to Lord Salisbury, 4 January 1896
9. Quoted by Corti in *English Empress*, p. 358
10. RA, I 61/27 and 60/149, Colonel L. Swaine to Sir A. Bigge, 16 November 1897, and a memorandum of January 1896
11. Salisbury Mss, A/122/38-9, Lord Salisbury to Sir F. Lascelles, 10 May 1899
12. RA, I 62/9, Sir F. Lascelles to Lord Salisbury, 31 March 1899
13. Salisbury Mss, A/121/68-71, Sir F. Lascelles to Lord Salisbury, 11 March 1899
14. RA, Add. A 4/104, the Prince of Wales to the Empress Frederick, 25 April 1899
15. RA, I 62/14, the Emperor William II to Queen Victoria, 27 May 1899
16. RA, I 62/18, Queen Victoria to the Emperor William II, 12 June 1899
17. Lascelles Mss, FO 800/9/297-9, Mr Sanderson to Sir F. Lascelles, 2 August 1899
18. RA, I 62/83, Sir F. Lascelles to Lord Salisbury, 9 March 1900
19. RA, I 62/90, the Emperor William II to Queen Victoria, 31 March 1900
20. RA, I 62/113, Colonel L. Swaine to Sir A. Bigge, 28 December 1900
21. Lansdowne Mss, FO 800/128/61, the Emperor William II to Sir F. Lascelles, 19 January 1901
22. George W. Smalley, *Anglo-American Memories* (New York 1911), pp. 402-8
23. RA, Add. A 4/217, King Edward VII to the Empress Frederick, 5 June 1901
24. RA, Add. A 4/71, King Edward VII to the Empress Frederick, 10 August 1898
25. Lansdowne Mss, FO 800/128/120-1, Sir F. Lascelles to King Edward VII, 13 April 1901

Select Bibliography

All the archives, papers and books that I have used are listed in the Source Notes. It would be tedious to repeat their titles or catalogue those which I have read, but not used. Of particular importance to the understanding of the background of this work, I would recommend the following:

Bonnin, Georges, *Bismarck and the Hohenzollern Candidature to the Throne of Spain* (London 1957)

Briggs, Asa, *Victorian People* (London 1954)

Craig, Gordon A., *The Politics of the Prussian Army, 1640–1945* (Oxford 1955); *Germany, 1866–1945* (Oxford 1978)

Eyck, Erich, *Bismarck and the German Empire* (London 1950)

Freund, Michael, *Das Drama der 99 Tage: Krankheit und Tod Friedrichs III* (Cologne/ Berlin 1966)

Gall, Lothar, *Bismarck: Der Weisse Revolutionär* (Frankfurt/Berlin, 1980)

Hardie, Frank, *The Political Influence of Queen Victoria* (London 1963)

Holburn, Hajo, *A History of Modern Germany, 1840–1945* (New York 1969); *Germany and Europe: Historical Essays* (New York 1970)

Howard, Michael, *The Franco-Prussian War: The German Invasion of France, 1870– 1871* (New York 1961)

Kennedy, Paul, *The Rise of Anglo-German Antagonism, 1860–1914* (London 1981)

Langer, William L., *European Alliances and Alignments, 1871–1890* 2nd ed. (New York 1956)

Mattingly, Garrett, *Renaissance Diplomacy* (London 1955)

Masur, Gerhard, *Imperial Berlin* (London 1971)

Pflanze, Otto, *Bismarck and the Development of Germany: the Period of Unification, 1815–1871* (Princeton 1963)

Stern, Fritz, *Gold and Iron: Bismarck, Bleichröder, and the Building of the German Empire* (New York 1977)

Taylor, A. J. P., *The Struggle for Mastery in Europe, 1848–1948* (Oxford 1954)

Wehler, Hans-Ulrich, *Bismarck und der Imperialismus* (Cologne/Berlin 1969)

SELECT BIBLIOGRAPHY

For particular biographical material, the following books are recommended:

Anon, *The Empress Frederick, a Memoir* (London 1912)

Auchinloss, Louis, *Persons of Consequence: Queen Victoria and Her Circle* (London 1979)

Barkeley, Richard, *The Empress Frederick, Daughter of Queen Victoria* (London 1956)

Bennett, Daphne, *King Without A Crown* (London 1977);
  Vicky, Princess Royal of England and German Empress (New York 1971)

Benson, E. F., *Queen Victoria's Daughters* (New York 1938)

Bismarck, Prince Otto von, *Reflections and Reminiscences*, 2 vols. (London 1898)

Blake, Robert, *Disraeli* (London 1966)

Bunsen, Chevalier Charles de, *Memoirs*, 2 vols. (London 1868)

Bunsen, Marie von, *The World I Used To Know, 1860–1912* (London 1930)

Busch, Moritz, *Bismarck, Some Secret Passages of his History*, 3 vols. (London 1898)

Duff, David, *Albert and Victoria* (London 1972);
  Hessian Tapestry (London 1967)

Empress Frederick, *The Empress Frederick Writes to Sophie*, ed. A. G. Lee, (London 1955)

Eyck, Erich, *Bismarck: Leben und Werk*, 3 vols. (Erlenbach/Zürich 1941–44)

Fulford, Roger, *The Prince Consort* (London 1949)

Lee, Sir Sidney, *King Edward VII*, 2 vols. (London 1925)

Longford, Elizabeth, *Queen Victoria: Born to Succeed* (New York 1964)

Magnus, Sir Philip, *King Edward the Seventh* (London 1964)

Martin, Sir Theodore, *Life of His Royal Highness the Prince Consort*, 5 vols. (London 1875–80)

Paget, Walburga Lady, *Scenes and Memories* (London 1912)

Palmer, Alan, *Bismarck* (London 1976);
  The Kaiser: Warlord of the Second Reich (London 1978)

Philippson, Martin, *Das Leben Kaiser Friedrichs III* (Weisbaden 1908)

Ponsonby, Sir Frederick, *The Letters of the Empress Frederick* (London 1929);
  Recollections of Three Reigns (New York 1952)

Radziwill, Princess Catherine, *The Empress Frederick* (London 1934)

Ramm, Agatha, *Sir Robert Morier: Envoy and Ambassador in the Age of Imperialism, 1876–1893* (Oxford 1973)

Reischach, Baron Hugo von, *Under Three Emperors* (London 1927)

Richter, Werner, *Bismarck* (London 1964)

Rodd, Sir Rennell, *Social and Diplomatic Memories*, 3 vols. (London 1922)

St Aubyn, Giles, *Edward VII, Prince and King* (London 1979)

Saxe-Coburg-Gotha, Duke Ernest II of, *Memoirs*, 4 vols. (London 1888)

Stockmar, Baron Ernest von, *The Memoirs of Baron Stockmar*, 2 vols. (London 1872)

Taylor, A. J. P., *Bismarck: the Man and the Statesman* (London 1955)

Tisdall, E. F. P., *She Made World Chaos: the Intimate Story of the Empress Frederick* (London 1940)

Waldersee, Count Alfred von, *Denkwürdigkeiten des Generalfeldmarschalls Alfred Grafen von Waldersee*, 3 vols. (Berlin 1922)

William II, Emperor, *My Early Life* (London 1926);
   My Memoirs, 1878–1918 (London 1922)
Woodham-Smith, Cecil, *Queen Victoria, Her Life and Times*, vol. I, 1819–1861 (London
   1972)

Index